The Deacon

The Deacon

Biblical Foundations for Today's
Ministry of Mercy

Cornelis Van Dam

Reformation Heritage Books
Grand Rapids, Michigan

The Deacon
© 2016 by Cornelis Van Dam

Reformation Heritage Books
2965 Leonard St. NE
Grand Rapids, MI 49525
616-977-0889 / Fax 616-285-3246
orders@heritagebooks.org
www.heritagebooks.org

Printed in the United States of America
17 18 19 20 21/10 9 8 7 6 5 4 3 2

Library of Congress Cataloging-in-Publication Data

Names: Van Dam, Cornelis, 1946- author.
Title: The deacon : biblical foundations for today's ministry of mercy / Cornelis Van Dam.
Description: Grand Rapids : Reformation Heritage Books, 2016. | Includes bibliographical references and index.
Identifiers: LCCN 2016041760 (print) | LCCN 2016042598 (ebook) | ISBN 9781601785114 (pbk. : alk. paper) | ISBN 9781601785121 (epub)
Subjects: LCSH: Deacons.
Classification: LCC BV680 .V25 2016 (print) | LCC BV680 (ebook) | DDC 270.092—dc23
LC record available at https://lccn.loc.gov/2016041760

In memory of
Rev. Gilbert Van Dooren (1911–1995)

Contents

Preface

It is a tremendous privilege to mature as a Christian within a godly home and under the tutelage of an inspiring pastor. In God's providence, I have been blessed with being raised in a Reformed church that was shepherded by the late Rev. Gilbert Van Dooren. He also taught me the diaconiological subjects in seminary. Van Dooren understood what it meant to take care of the needy in the fullest sense of the term and gave leadership in showing the riches of the diaconal office. He embodied the meaning of *diakonia*, as the service of love to God's people in Christ's name. It is therefore in his memory that this book is dedicated.

My ten years in the pastoral ministry (1971–1981) have been of great benefit in understanding some of the important dynamics and issues facing the deacons as they seek to provide for the needs of the congregation in their care. While this book is not designed as a practical diaconal manual, the material it covers has many practical implications and consequences for both deacons and members of the congregation. I am thankful for all the feedback I have received from deacons while serving Reformed congregations. More recently the following experienced deacons from the Ebenezer Canadian Reformed Church in Burlington, Ontario, participated in composing the Questions for Study and Reflection found in the back of this book: Brian Kalte, the late Bruce Hartman, Peter Sikkema, and Peter John Vandyk, as well as Rev. Gijsbertus Nederveen. These questions are intended to facilitate and encourage discussion on all aspects of the office of deacon.

Many people stimulated my thinking on the office of deacon, and I am grateful to all of them. It would be hazardous for me to list them by name, lest some be overlooked. Those who have made specific contributions are noted in the appropriate places in this study.

An unpayable debt of gratitude is owed to my dear wife, Joanne, who is a constant encouragement during the long process of research and writing and contributed materially with her aptitude for proofreading.

I am grateful for the interest of Joel R. Beeke and Reformation Heritage Books in this project. It has been a pleasure to work with its director of publications, Jay Collier, as well as Annette Gysen, manuscript editor. Above all, I am grateful to the Lord God who has enabled me to complete this project. *Soli Deo gloria!*

Introduction

God's gift of the office of deacon and the blessings associated with it may not always be fully appreciated, especially in congregations that are financially prosperous and do not have many materially poor in their midst. However, as this book hopes to demonstrate, the importance of the diaconate goes far beyond simply providing for material needs. In order to get a proper understanding of the significance of this office, we must consider it within the context of the entire Bible.

While the term "deacon" has different meanings in various Christian faith communities, this book deals with the diaconal office as Reformed and Presbyterian churches have historically understood it in the light of Scripture. Stated briefly, deacons are those charged with the ministry of mercy to show the love of Christ by providing for the poor and afflicted.

Once we get beyond this bare-bones description, however, questions arise: What is the biblical basis for this office? Why is the diaconal office conceived of so differently, for example, in the Roman Catholic Church? What are deacons supposed to do, and how do they go about exercising their responsibilities? How should the poor in less developed parts of the world benefit from Western deacons? Is the diaconal office open to women? A larger question is whether government, welfare agencies, and insurance plans have made the office redundant in the Western world. Is this office absolutely necessary for the well-being of the church? Those familiar with the life of Christ's church know that these and related issues affect the most practical aspects of experiencing the communion of saints.

This study seeks answers to these and similar questions from the fullness of Scripture. It soon becomes evident that in Old Testament times there were no deacons—a situation that requires some explanation. The New Testament does speak of deacons. It is, however, striking that the Greek term for deacons, *diakonos*, means "servant," and the related verb simply means "to serve." In other words, the term, as such, does not necessarily indicate a special office. In order to determine what the specific office of deacon entailed, we need to move beyond the general meaning of the terms and investigate the New Testament context.

Since the early Christian church had the Old Testament as their Scripture, we do well to begin there and to examine how that part of God's Word informs us of the principles of helping the poor and needy. Indeed, these divine principles are still authoritative for us today, are consequently relevant for ministering to the poor, and thus reward careful study.

Chapters 1 and 2 therefore consider the Old Testament background that is relevant for the diaconal office and seek answers to questions such as, Who exactly were the poor, and how were they to be provided for? What set God's people apart from the pagan nations that surrounded them with respect to caring for the poor? Only when we have a clear understanding of the Old Testament heritage can we begin to appreciate New Testament developments.

Chapter 3 examines Christ's life of service, including to the poor and downtrodden, and His teaching about helping the needy. Chapter 4 shows how the Savior's principles were put into practice after the Holy Spirit was poured out on the believers at Pentecost and seven men were ordained to care for the needy widows. Chapter 5 deals with the requirements for the office of deacon and the relationship the deacon has to the elder. What Scripture says about female deacons is covered in chapter 6.

Only after having first consulted authoritative Scripture are we in a position to judge how this office has fared in the history of the church. Chapters 7 and 8 record the good and bad developments of this office in the light of God's Word. It is a remarkable testimony to God's grace how He enabled the Reformation of the sixteenth century to recover the blessing of this office from the deformation it had undergone in the previous centuries.

On the basis of this legacy, chapter 9 explores ordination into the diaconal office, the length of service, and the deacon's relationship to the consistory or session of the church, taking into account the relevant highlights from Reformed and Presbyterian history. Chapters 10 and 11 cover the practical issues of how deacons are enabled to do their work and according to what principles and practices their work should be done in order to be most effective.

Chapter 12 deals with the issue of helping the poor who are outside the congregation, both locally and globally. The challenges are enormous, and this chapter endeavors to uncover the relevant biblical principles and apply them to today. Although we wish that the problem of poverty could be solved once and for all, the poor will always be with us in the present age (Matt. 26:11). We need the coming renewal of all things for poverty and hardship to be eradicated. Yet there are God-given blessings in having the poor to minister to. The final chapter shows how these blessings impact all involved.

The back of the book contains questions for group study and reflection. They are meant primarily for deacons, but also those who are not office-bearers will profit from them. They will help members of the congregation realize their responsibilities with respect to the poor, as well as some of the challenges and implications of the office, and enable them to pray more meaningfully for the deacons who labor in their midst.

Although the office of deacon is often undervalued and perceived to be of little importance, Scripture shows that this is far from the truth. It is a tremendous gift of God, and a church neglects this office to its detriment. May this book be a contribution to realizing that reality, and may it be an encouragement for all deacons who wrestle with what God requires of them in this high and privileged calling.

PART ONE

The Old Testament Background

CHAPTER 1

The Poor in Israel

Ancient Israel is in some respects close to us, and in other ways distant. The people of God today live in completely different political and economic circumstances from their counterparts of old. However, in one important area there is similarity and continuity: as the Lord Jesus indicated, the poor will always be with us (Matt. 26:11). And they are, both in the free West and especially in the developing world.

The Old Testament gives valuable insights into the hard reality of poverty and its accompanying miseries. We must attempt to place ourselves in the sandals of those who suffered much so that we have a greater appreciation for those suffering today, as well as for the solutions the Lord prescribed. Understanding the Lord's concern for the poor and His expectation that His people Israel take care of them is of great help in grasping the basic biblical principles that should apply today. Such an understanding should also impact any discussion about the office of deacon. In order to come to this understanding, this chapter discusses the poor whom God singled out and specific legislation affecting them, as well as God's law and its purpose within the ancient Near Eastern context.

Identifying the Poor

The Old Testament has an extensive vocabulary for describing the poor. For our purposes, three major categories of Hebrew terms are

important. These all come down to us in English with the translation "poor" or something similar.

The first and most obvious category is the materially poor
('*ebyon*). They lacked the basic necessities to exist. They were destitute, vulnerable, and without any hope unless they received help from
others. The Lord promised that these poor would not be in Israel if
God's people would only keep His commands (Deut. 15:4–5).

A second category of the poor is the powerless (*dal*) who have
experienced a sharp reduction or loss of their prosperity and social
status (Ex. 23:3). As such, they were the opposite of the rich (Ex.
30:15; Prov. 10:15) and therefore were allowed to present less
costly sacrifices (Lev. 14:21–22). For these people, poverty and help-
lessness may have resulted because they had become physically or
psychologically impaired (Ps. 82:3; Isa. 10:2).

A third type of poor is the afflicted and oppressed ('*anaw* and
'*ani*), who were intimidated and exploited by the rich (Prov. 31:9;
Isa. 3:14). Also, they could be the pious who were unfairly treated
by the wicked (Ps. 10:2; Isa. 14:32). In short, they were the vic-
timized who were bowed down and lowly, with people taking
advantage of their humble circumstances (Job 24:4; Ps. 37:14; Isa.
32:7). God had commanded that these disadvantaged people not
be afflicted (Ex. 22:22–23), so such situations were contrary to His
will. The original Hebrew term used for "afflicting" covers all manner of oppressing and humiliating people, including every kind of
cold or contemptuous treatment.[1] These people were therefore not
to be mistreated judicially (Deut. 24:17; Jer. 7:5–7). The Lord was
their protector (Pss. 68:5; 146:9).

Thus there were the materially poor, the powerless, and the
afflicted. But we must not imagine that these were three completely
separate categories of Israelites. These words are often used as
synonyms and can refer to the same people viewed from different

---

1. The word used is '*anah*. See, e.g., Paul Wegner, "6700 '*nh* II," in *New International
Dictionary of Old Testament Theology and Exegesis*, ed. Willem VanGemeren (Grand
Rapids: Zondervan, 1997), 3:449–52.

perspectives. The specific nuances of the different Hebrew terms for "poor" are difficult to articulate in English. It is important to appreciate this diversity. When the Lord expressed concern for the needy and commanded His people to take care of them, He did not have in view only their material needs, although these were certainly included (e.g., Deut. 14:29; 24:19–21). God's care for the poor, however, went beyond the purely physical aspects of poverty. He included the disadvantaged, the downtrodden, and the helpless.

This broad understanding of who is poor has implications for us today. It indicates that we should not conceive of the poor in our midst too narrowly. To appreciate as fully as possible what being poor, powerless, and afflicted entailed in ancient Israel, we need to picture the primary manifestations of poverty within Israelite society.

Manifestations of Poverty in Israel

The Lord safeguarded the interests of the poor in different ways and gave detailed directions on how an Israelite was to respond to their varied needs.

The Peasant Farmer and the Landless Poor

These people were not totally destitute. Although they suffered economically, they were expected to offer sacrifices, but they were permitted to offer less valuable animals (Lev. 5:7, 11; 12:8; 14:21). They were required, however, to give the same amount of atonement money as the rich, since all were of equal value to the Lord (Ex. 30:15). When the rich tried to take advantage of the poor, the Lord severely condemned them (Amos 5:11). Especially in the days of Jeroboam II (782–753 BC), small landowners were often reduced to poverty by the wealthy. God warned Israel of His wrath through Amos (2:6–7; cf. 8:4–6) and Isaiah (26:5–6) and promised restoration of the poor (Isa. 29:19–20).

The landless poor (Ex. 23:11; Lev. 19:10; 23:22; cf. Jer. 39:10), who were day laborers, were especially vulnerable because they were completely dependent on others for their livelihood. They could

easily be exploited and taken advantage of (Ps. 37:14; Isa. 32:7).
God therefore protected these people in the short term by requiring
such measures as the prompt daily payment of their wages, interest-
free loans, and returning by sundown a poor person's cloak that had
been submitted for a pledge so that he could sleep under it (Ex.
22:25–27; Deut. 24:10–15). Also, the needy could gather what
grew of itself when the fields were left fallow every seventh year;
they could harvest leftover grapes; and they could glean from har-
vested fields (Ex. 23:11; Lev. 19:9–10; 23:22). For the long term,
God provided the law of the remission of debt every seven years
for a creditor's fellow impoverished Israelite (Deut. 15:1–11)[2] and a
Year of Jubilee every fiftieth year so that the land could be returned
to the original owner (Leviticus 25).

The Widows and Orphans
A widow was without her husband's physical and economic protection and thus became vulnerable to being mistreated and exploited.
This state of affairs is reflected in the frequent mention of widows with other vulnerable segments of Israelite society—namely,
orphans, strangers, and Levites (e.g., Deut. 14:29; 16:11, 14; 26:12–
13). A widow with no sons or grown-up children had basically two
options.[3] First, if she had no sons, an unmarried brother-in-law
could marry her (the so-called levirate marriage). The first son to be
born would be reckoned as heir of the deceased's property, and he
would continue the line of the deceased. However, such a brother-
in-law could refuse to cooperate (Deut. 25:5–10; cf. Gen. 38:8–9),

2. Whether the remission of debt in the seventh year meant canceling the debt
altogether or simply deferring payment for a year is a contested point. See, e.g., for the
former and probably most likely position, David L. Baker, *Tight Fists or Open Hands?
Wealth and Poverty in Old Testament Law* (Grand Rapids: Eerdmans, 2009), 280; and,
for the latter, Christopher J. H. Wright, *God's People in God's Land: Family, Land, and
Property in the Old Testament* (Grand Rapids: Eerdmans, 1990), 147–48, 167–73.
3. A widow could move in with an older child's family. See Ruth 1:3–5; 2 Sam.
14:5–7; and Hans Eberhard von Waldow, "Social Responsibility and Social Structure
in Early Israel," *Catholic Biblical Quarterly* 32 (1970): 187.

and the option of more distant relatives fulfilling this duty was possible (Ruth 4:5–6). Second, she could return to her father's house, where she might wait for a levirate marriage to a brother of her late husband who was too young at that point (Lev. 22:13; cf. Gen. 38:11 and Ruth 1:8, 11).[4]

In exceptional cases, a widow could be wealthy and support her fatherless children, now considered orphans, on her own.[5] It was much more likely that the weak position of the widow was reflected in the dire plight of the orphans (see 2 Sam. 14:5–7; 2 Kings 4:1–7; Lam. 5:3). As long as family ties were strong, it could be expected that widows and orphans would be cared for through a levirate marriage or by the widow's returning to her father's house. However, with the coming of more centralized government and the development of great economic prosperity, the widow was apparently often left out in the cold. The loud protests of the prophets about the mistreatment of the widows and orphans show that their position was vulnerable (Isa. 1:17, 23; 10:2; Jer. 7:6–7; 22:3–5; Ezek. 22:7; Zech. 7:8–14; Mal. 3:5).[6]

The Lord, however, provided for the needs of the widows and the orphans in His law. God warned Israel not to afflict them, and, if they did, His wrath would burn against them, and He would make their wives widows and their children fatherless (Ex. 22:21–24). Orphans were to be treated justly, and the widow's garment was not to be taken in pledge (Deut. 24:17). Widows and orphans were to share in the festivities of the tithe of the produce every third year, along with the Levite and the sojourner (Deut.

---

4. It is even possible that if she did not remarry (and had no children) that she would eventually lose her husband's property to his family. See E. Neufeld, *Ancient Hebrew Marriage Laws: With Special References to General Semitic Laws and Customs* (London: Longmans, Green and Co., 1944), 241–42.

5. It is virtually impossible to isolate a case in the Old Testament where a child has lost both parents. An orphan is one without a father.

6. The issue of a widow's right to the land of her husband (see Ruth 4:3; 2 Kings 8:1–6) is debated. See, e.g., the discussions in Frederic W. Bush, *Ruth, Esther*, Word Biblical Commentary (Dallas: Word, 1998), 202–15; and Neufeld, *Ancient Hebrew Marriage Laws*, 241–42.

14:28–29; 26:12–13). They were likewise entitled to share in the celebrations of the Feast of Weeks (Deut. 16:11) and the Feast of Booths (Deut. 16:14). In all likelihood they were included with the poor when it came to the privilege of gleaning the edges and corners of the field (Lev. 19:9–10; 23:22) and receiving the produce of the Sabbath year (Ex. 23:10–11). The Lord reminded His people that He was the protector and sustainer of widows and orphans (Pss. 68:5; 146:9).

The Sojourners

When Israel left Egypt, "a mixed multitude went up with them also" (Ex. 12:38; cf. Num. 11:4). This multitude would have been non-Israelites who took advantage of the confusion to leave plague-ravaged Egypt in hope of a better life with Israel. Because these people were of a different origin, they would have been known as sojourners and strangers. They formed an important part of the mosaic of Israelite society. Later in Canaan more people of diverse backgrounds would become residents within the Israelite nation such as Doeg the Edomite (1 Sam. 21:7), Uriah the Hittite (2 Samuel 11) and Zelek the Ammonite (2 Sam. 23:37). These too would be reckoned as sojourners. A sojourner (*ger*) was therefore someone who had settled and established himself in Israel but who did not really belong there because he had no blood ties. In this sense, Abraham in Canaan (Gen. 23:4), Israel in Egypt (Ex. 22:21), and Elimelech with his family in Moab (Ruth 1:1) were strangers and sojourners because they too lived among a people with whom they had no kinship.

Using modern terminology, one could say that most of the sojourners were like immigrants or refugees. They had left their original social setting and entered into a new, dependent relationship in a new social setting.[7] Because they were non-Israelites, they

---

7. See Frank Antony Spina, "Israelites as *gērîm*, 'Sojourners' in Social and Historical Context," in *The Word of the Lord Shall Go Forth: Essays in Honor of David Noel Freedman in Celebration of His Sixtieth Birthday*, ed. Carol L. Meyers and M.

were not necessarily worshipers of the God of Israel.[8] But the Lord was gracious to the sojourner. Because a sojourner had established himself for a period of time in the land among the Israelites, he was not called a foreigner, and he had certain rights and privileges. God wanted the sojourner to be treated fairly and like a native-born Israelite (Lev. 19:33–34). Such a person was often vulnerable and poor since he was usually someone's servant (Deut. 10:18; 14:29; 24:14, 17–21; Ezek. 22:29), although there were exceptions (Lev. 25:47). God decreed that the strangers who were economically disadvantaged were to be helped, just like the widow and orphan. They were to have the right to glean (Lev. 19:10; 23:22; Deut. 24:19–21), to receive food from the triennial tithe (Deut. 14:29; 26:12–13), and, as sojourners, they were allowed to eat a dead animal that had not been killed properly with the blood drained out of it (Deut. 14:21; cf. 12:16). Also, they could participate in the Sabbath rest (Ex. 20:10) and the joyous harvest feasts of Weeks and Booths (Deut. 16:11, 14). God strictly forbade the oppression of the sojourner (Ex. 22:21; 23:9; Lev. 19:33–34). Israelites had to pay them their wages on the same day and not pervert justice due to them (Deut. 24:14–15, 17–18; 27:19). Also, sojourners could save their lives by fleeing to a city of refuge in case of an accidental homicide (Num. 35:15). Besides these material benefits, God extended to the sojourner the privilege to become part of His chosen nation by receiving the sign and seal of the covenant—namely, circumcision—and, having done so, he was able to partake of the Passover (Ex. 12:48). Apparently, whether he was circumcised or not, the sojourner could sacrifice

---

O'Connor (Winona Lake, Ind.: Eisenbrauns for the American Schools of Oriental Research, 1983), 323–25; and Richard H. Hiers, *Justice and Compassion in Biblical Law* (New York: Continuum, 2009), 180n26. The 1984 New International Version (NIV) usually rendered *ger* as "alien" while the updated 2011 NIV translated it as "foreigner."

8. "The *ger* must observe the prohibitive commandment not to worship other gods (Lev. 17:8–9), but he is not compelled to observe the performative commandment to worship Israel's God." Jacob Milgrom, *Numbers: The Traditional Hebrew Text with the New JPS Translation*, The JPS Torah Commentary (Philadelphia: Jewish Publication Society, 1989), 399.

to the Lord (Lev. 17:8; Num. 15:14) but was not allowed to sacrifice to any other god (Ex. 22:20; Lev. 20:2) or revile the Lord
(Num. 15:30).

It should be noted that since a sojourner or stranger can be
defined as someone who had left his ancestral family setting and
become a dependent in a new environment, an Israelite who moved
or was forced to move from his original home to elsewhere in
Canaan was, in essence, an immigrant. He could therefore be called
a sojourner in his new dwelling place. Due to geographical distance,
he had lost the support of his family. In Judges 17, for example, we
read of a young Levite who had, at one point, left a Levitical city
and had been sojourning as a stranger within the tribe of Judah in
the non-Levitical town of Bethlehem. He left this place in search of
another home, traveling north to Ephraim (Judg. 17:7–13). Another
example is found in Judges 19:16, which tells of an old man from
Ephraim who was sojourning in Gibeah in Benjamin, far from his
family. Although the people in these examples were Israelites, they
were strangers in a place outside their original social setting and
family support network and were thus dependent on their new
social setting for help, should it be needed. There is a similar example in the time of King Asa when people from Ephraim, Manasseh,
and Simeon, desirous to worship God according to His ordinances,
sojourned in Judah (2 Chron. 15:9).

God's people were apparently not sensitive to the needs of the
sojourner. The prophets warned against their mistreatment. Indeed,
the oppression of the sojourner, along with the fatherless and
widow, was one of the reasons for the exile (Jer. 7:6; 22:3–5; Ezek.
22:7, 29–31), but even after the return to the Promised Land, the
warnings against the oppression of the sojourner, the fatherless, and
the poor had to be sounded again (Zech. 7:10).

The Strangers

The term for a stranger (*toshab*) is often used synonymously with
that of the sojourner (*ger*; e.g., Lev. 25:6, 23; 1 Chron. 29:15; Ps.
39:12). What may have distinguished strangers is that they were

less integrated or assimilated into the social and religious life of Israel than were sojourners. The stranger was forbidden to eat of the Passover (Ex. 12:45). He was sometimes associated with the hired servant and slaves (Ex. 12:45; Lev. 22:10). Such an association would indicate that he was economically dependent. However, a stranger could become wealthy (Lev. 25:47).

The Foreigner

The foreigner (*zar* and *nokri*) was attached to his homeland and planned to return to it. He was not a permanent resident in Israel as were the sojourner and stranger. He had no close association with God's people. This meant that there was a certain detachment between the foreigner and the native Israelite, which is reflected in the legislation. Such a foreigner likely retained his own pagan faith and was forbidden to participate in the Passover (Ex. 12:43; cf. Ezek. 44:7–9). The status of the foreigner was reflected in his being economically at a disadvantage. If he (*nokri*) owed debts to an Israelite, he got no relief from making payments in the Sabbath year (Deut. 15:3). Also, he was charged interest on money owed to an Israelite (Deut. 23:20).

The Levite

Finally, members of the tribe of Levi were scattered throughout Israel as teachers of the law (see Deut. 33:10; 2 Chron. 17:7–9). The Levites had been set aside in the place of the firstborn for special service to God (Num. 3:40–51). Because the Lord was their inheritance (Deut. 10:9; 18:2), they had no landed property for their exclusive use like the other tribes, and they were to be supported by the tithes of Israel. Such tithes involved all the produce of the field (Num. 18:21–32).

In spite of their privileged status, Levites were, however, counted with the poor and needy who needed the special support of the community to survive. They were clearly vulnerable to the neglect and abuse of their rights. The Lord enjoined His people not to forget the Levites, but to have them share in their festivities and offerings and chief festivals, along with the other poor in Israel (Deut. 12:12, 18, 19; 14:28–29; 16:11–14; 26:11–13).

God's Law in its Ancient Near Eastern Context

While it is beyond the scope of this book to go into much detail, it is instructive to note briefly the context of God's law in the ancient world, for it highlights two important motifs in the Lord's giving Israel the law He did. First, God's law showed much more legislative concern for the poor and needy than the laws of any of the nations around Israel. This is not to say that there was no consideration or sympathy for the needy elsewhere, but only in the Old Testament do we find systematic legal protection of the vulnerable, such as the resident foreigners, widows, and orphans. In the ancient world around Israel, the legal rights of such people, insofar as they existed, were limited.[9] In other words, if God's law was obeyed, the vulnerable were far better off in Israel than anywhere else in the Middle East. This reality brings us to a second important motif.

By obeying God's law, Israel would be a light to the nations (Isa. 49:6). Prior to their entry into the Promised Land, the Lord had exhorted Israel through Moses to keep God's statutes and laws and do them: "For this is your wisdom and your understanding in the sight of the peoples who will hear all these statutes, and say, 'Surely this great nation is a wise and understanding people.' For what great nation is there that has God so near to it, as the LORD our God is to us, for whatever reason we may call upon Him? And what great nation is there that has such statutes and righteous judgments as are in all this law which I set before you this day?" (Deut. 4:6–8). God's law was to be an example to the world of, among other things, how to take care of the poor and needy, the strangers and sojourners. But for that to happen, Israel had to obey God and so fulfill their calling, which included being a blessing to

9. See, e.g., Baker, *Tight Fists or Open Hands?*, 175–95, 311–13; Norbert Lohfink, "Poverty in the Laws of the Ancient Near East and of the Bible," *Theological Studies* 52 (1991): 34–38.

the nations (Gen. 18:18). So care for the poor and needy had an important missionary aspect. Israel's obedience in providing for the poor and needy would be a vital factor in attracting the nations to the living God. Their obedience would make visible the mercy and love of God to the vulnerable and underprivileged.[10]

Summary and Conclusions

When the Lord instructed His people to take care of the poor, He was generous in indicating who the recipients of such help were to be. Support was to be given to a wide variety of needy. He did not identify just the materially poor as those requiring assistance; those who suffered from a loss of status in society or had a sudden calamity that impaired them physically or psychologically were to be aided also. Furthermore, those intimidated, exploited, and oppressed had a right to aid as well. Even sojourners, strangers, and foreigners were not to be neglected. If they needed assistance, God's people were duty bound to respond positively.

The principles embedded in God's generous provision in the past are normative for God's people today. We can never conceive of helping the needy too narrowly. However, to appreciate adequately what this truth implies, we need to ask why the Lord was so magnanimous in His provisions. Answering this question will enable us to better understand God's generosity and our obligations.

---

10. See on this missiological point, Christopher J. H. Wright, *The Mission of God: Unlocking the Bible's Grand Narrative* (Downers Grove, Ill.: IVP Academic, 2006), 378–80.

CHAPTER 2

Providing for the Poor

To help the poor in the most meaningful way, Israel had to understand why the Lord demanded that so much attention be paid to the needy in their midst. Furthermore, God's people had to know how the Lord wanted them to go about taking care of the indigent. Having a clear grasp of the why and how of caring for the needy allows us to see what abiding principles were at stake. This chapter therefore deals with the rationale God gave for helping the poor, and how the different structures of society were to be involved.

Why Israel Needed to Help the Poor

Why did the Lord repeatedly express such great concern for the plight of the needy in Israel and warn His people of His wrath and vengeance toward those who afflicted the needy and did not help them (e.g., Ex. 22:22–24)? At the base of the Lord's special interest in the needy and oppressed was that He loved His people, and He wanted Israel to reflect this divine love to their neighbor. They must love not only God but also their neighbor (Lev. 19:18; Deut. 6:5).

The way God had shown His love to Israel was instructive and paradigmatic for the manner in which He wanted His people to express their affection to their neighbor. Because the Lord loved His people, He had led them out of the bondage and oppression of Egypt and had claimed them as His own covenant nation (Deut. 7:7–8). And now, just as He had shown love to His afflicted people in that foreign land, so they must display their love for any neighbor who was under duress by executing justice for the orphans and widows and giving food and clothing to the sojourner (Deut. 10:18–19). To put it differently, as the Lord had set His people free from the oppression and bondage of cruel Pharaoh, in whose land they had lived as slaves and sojourners, so Israel must set the needy free from the want, poverty, and afflictions that oppressed them.

God therefore gave Israel the motivation for His laws regarding the poor and needy: "You shall remember that you were a slave in the land of Egypt, and the LORD your God redeemed you; therefore I command you this thing today" (Deut. 15:15).[1] God had set Israel free, and they must remain liberated from all oppression, including the oppression and bondage of poverty, fear, and loneliness. His people were His treasured possession, a kingdom of priests and a holy nation (Ex. 19:5–6). Thus, they must not suffer any kind of want. He, the Lord, would provide for them (Lev. 26:1–13). But God's provision presupposed that His people would remember their past deliverance by obeying His law in joy and thankfulness for the freedom they had not deserved but had been given to them by grace alone (Lev. 26:1–13; Deut. 24:19–22; 28:1–14). So if an Israelite, for instance, sold himself to pay debts, he was not to be treated harshly as a slave, but as a hired servant who would be set free in the year of release (Deut. 15:12–18) or the Year of Jubilee (Lev. 25:39–43). Furthermore, a servant was not to leave empty-handed (Deut. 15:13). Because God did not want any of His people to suffer want and be in bondage to privation, everything, including the material things of life, must serve their freedom and joy.

It is remarkable that God's law highlights the aspect of joy when the orphan, widow, Levite, and stranger share in God's gifts (Deut. 16:11, 14–15; 26:11). Indeed, God exhorts His people to be joyful because of His goodness to them. After all, a liberated people exults in God's salvation and celebrates their redemption by praising Him (e.g., Pss. 32:11; 33:1–5; 40:16–17; 146:1–2, 7–10). Joy

---

1. Similarly, see Ex. 22:21; 23:9; Deut. 16:12; 24:18, 22. Also see Lev. 25:38, 42, 55.

and gladness are important aspects of being God's people, and helping the poor and needy is a vital part of ensuring that all can share in the liberating joy of redemption.

Deliverance from affliction and oppression, whether from the bondage of Egypt or from poverty, was not an end in itself. People were not granted freedom so that they could simply rejoice. Liberation from bondage had the overriding purpose of setting the people free to serve the Lord their God according to His will. That was what motivated God to lead His people out of Egypt (Ex. 4:22–23; 5:1; 7:16; 8:1, 20; 9:1, 13; 10:3) and was the ultimate motive for ensuring that no one in God's holy nation was unnecessarily burdened by affliction, poverty, and want. A person could function best in God's service when unencumbered by affliction and material needs. Then he could truly do his calling joyfully and to the full, as God intended for His people.[2]

We will gain a deeper appreciation for this freedom of God's people and the proper use of possessions if we consider the main implications of the eighth word, or commandment, of the covenant. It is important that we understand this commandment in order to deal with the care of the poor and maintain ourselves in the freedom of God's salvation.

The Eighth Commandment

"I am the LORD your God, who brought you out of the land of Egypt, out of the house of bondage.... You shall not steal" (Ex. 20:2, 15). In this basic covenant word, the Lord laid down important principles for the freedom of His people and the use of their possessions.

In order to understand some of the implications of this word of the covenant, we must consider what the worst sin imaginable against this commandment was. The most grievous offense was an

---

2. The rationale of praying to be delivered from affliction and need included being able to praise God with joy and to savor His redemption (Pss. 30:8–12; 40:16–17). Note, in comparison, that the chief and highest end of man in question 1 of the Westminster Larger Catechism is "to glorify God, and fully to enjoy him forever."

Israelite stealing or kidnapping a fellow Israelite for gain—that is, for sale abroad as a slave. This crime was not unknown in Israel, as is clear from passages that refer to this outrage. For example, Exodus 21:16 states, "He who kidnaps a man and sells him, or if he is found in his hand, shall surely be put to death" (similarly Deut. 24:7; cf. 1 Tim. 1:10).

What made this sin so horrific was that a kidnapper was stealing from the Lord God a most precious possession of His (Deut. 7:6; 32:6). A kidnapped person would almost always be sold abroad and separated from the covenant community, and this meant that he would be effectively separated from the Lord and His people. So the Lord would be deprived of someone who was most dear to Him. The kidnapped Israelite would lose his place and freedom within God's covenant community. But God's people must not be bound in any way! Each Israelite's place and freedom must be guaranteed within the covenant nation. Therefore, the clear message of the eighth commandment is do not steal any of God's people.

However, for the purpose of the present topic, we must consider something else. We can paraphrase the eighth word of the covenant this way: do not rob *yourself* from the Lord and from the freedom in which God has placed you by binding yourself to your possessions and being enslaved to them. When a person seeks by whatever means possible to increase his possessions, then he is in bondage to them. Such bondage is terrible, for it will ultimately bring hardship to the widows and the poor. They will be oppressed because those who have the means to help the indigent will prioritize keeping the wealth entrusted to them for themselves. We see the abuse and suffering of the widows and the poor occurring, for example, in the days of Isaiah and Amos (Isa. 3:14–15; 10:1–3; 58:6–7; Amos 2:7; 4:1; 5:11).

The eighth commandment is a reminder that we are merely stewards of our material possessions. We own nothing in any absolute sense. All we have belongs to God, and He has given it to His people by grace alone, without their earning it. How clearly the Lord taught this truth to His people by leading them into the land of Canaan! They would take possession of great and good cities they had not built, houses full of good things they had not filled, cisterns they had not dug, and vineyards and olive trees they had not planted (Deut. 6:10–11; Josh. 24:13). Human nature being what it is, the danger was great that God's people would forget that they had earned nothing but had received all their material things by grace alone and that they were only stewards (Lev. 25:23). But as stewards of what God had entrusted to them, their aim in working was not to gather riches and simply ensure their food and drink. Their purpose in life was to be seeking God's kingdom and laboring for the Lord and His precious possession—namely, His people—so that they might remain in the joy of their Lord, free from all bondage (cf. Lev. 25:39–46).[3]

Having looked at key reasons why God commanded that the poor be provided for and some implications of the eighth commandment, we will consider how, practically speaking, the needs of the poor were to be met. In the first chapter we saw how the Lord provided for the poor by various laws that were designed to alleviate their needs. Our goal now is to consider God's will for caring for the poor from the perspective of who has responsibility for what. What were the structures in place for caring for the needy? Answering these types of questions will help us derive principles that we can trace through the New Testament or apply directly to today.

How to Help the Poor

A general basic principle for how to help the poor is equality in meeting all the needs of the indigent. No one should be overlooked or receive more than he needs. At the same time, meeting all needs equally did not necessarily mean that each poor individual would

---

3. See also Matt. 6:31–33. The Heidelberg Catechism is to the point when it says concerning the eighth commandment in Q. 111: "What does God require of you in this commandment? I must promote my neighbor's good wherever I can and may, deal with him as I would like others to deal with me, and work faithfully so that I may be able to give to those in need."

receive exactly the same in terms of relief, whether food, money, or material possessions. This principle is evident in the way the Lord provided food for His people in the wilderness en route to the Promised Land. He gave them manna, bread from heaven (Ps. 78:24–25), which the people had to gather from the ground. Some gathered more, some less: "So when they measured it by omers, he who gathered much had nothing left over, and he who gathered little had no lack. Every man had gathered according to each one's need" (Ex. 16:18). God had told the people to gather an omer per person. Some, however, had gathered more than that, and some less. On measuring the amount precisely, though, it turned out that everyone had exactly enough to satisfy his needs. God intervened, and miraculously no one lacked anything in spite of the disparity in the amounts that different Israelites had gathered. The apostle Paul used this account to establish the necessity of equality in caring for poor believers. No one should suffer want (2 Cor. 8:13–15).[4]

To meet the needs of the indigent, the Lord God engaged key societal structures: the family, society at large, and the state. What were their respective responsibilities, and how did they relate to each other? Was there some kind of diaconal office that oversaw the care of the indigent?

The Family

It is difficult to imagine a society without the family unit. For our purposes, it is important to note that in Israel, the extended family, or clan, was an economic unit and power within society. The extended family worked as a protective association of families or households (each of which was called a "father's house") to preserve the minimal conditions for the economic integrity of each of the

---

4. For this understanding, see, e.g., Eugene Carpenter, *Exodus*, Evangelical Exegetical Commentary (Bellingham, Wash.: Logos Bible Software, 2012), on Ex. 16:17–18; Victor P. Hamilton, *Exodus: An Exegetical Commentary* (Grand Rapids: Baker Academic, 2011), 255; and Murray J. Harris, *The Second Epistle to the Corinthians: A Commentary on the Greek Text*, New International Greek Testament Commentary (Grand Rapids: Eerdmans, 2005), 592–93.

member families by giving help as needed. God's laws were designed for Israel's agriculturally based and labor-intensive society. These precepts prevented the accumulation of vast wealth by only a few so that the family unit could survive intact.[5] The economic viability of a family was maintained in various ways.

In a worst-case scenario, if a person's land was lost through poverty and debt, then his next of kin was to redeem what had been sold to keep it within the family or clan (Lev. 25:23–28; Jeremiah 32). The order of responsibility went from brother to uncle to cousin and from there to any blood relative (Lev. 25:49). The one who redeemed was the kinsman-redeemer. The redemption of the land made it possible for each family to keep its inheritance intact so it could be economically self-sufficient. The Year of Jubilee, which occurred every fiftieth year, assured that land lost would eventually revert to the family that had originally owned it.

Should a person become indebted, the kinsman-redeemer was to care for him and his dependents (Lev. 25:35–55). The kinsman-redeemer was expected to provide interest-free loans (Lev. 25:35–37), and, if the needy one had lost his land (until it was returned in the Year of Jubilee), he was to take him on as a servant, not a slave, and feed him and his family (Lev. 25:39–43). If the family member had been forced to sell himself outside the clan, then the kinsman-redeemer was expected to redeem him from bondage (Lev. 25:47–52). If a woman became widowed and was without a male heir to take over the land, her brother-in-law, acting as the kinsman-redeemer, was expected, but not forced, to marry her so

---

5. The "father's house" was the kinship structure with which one felt the strongest sense of inclusion. It was the most important small unit in the nation and for the individual Israelite and the basic unit for Israel's land tenure system. The father's house "included the head of the house and his wife (or wives), his sons and their wives, his grandsons and their wives, plus any unmarried sons or daughters in the generations below him, along with all the nonrelated dependents." This could have included some fifty to one hundred persons residing in a cluster of dwelling places. C. J. H. Wright, "Family," in *Anchor Bible Dictionary*, ed. D. N. Freedman (New York: Doubleday, 1992), 2:762–63.

that he could raise up an heir for her and keep the patrimonial land within the family (Deut. 25:5–10).[6]

So the household and its economic viability were protected in a number of ways. There was also a general duty to support the poor, especially the widows and orphans. The immediate family were expected to be the first to give help. The obligation to help went from the most immediate to the more distant family members, just as in the process of redemption. Such needy people could be incorporated into the household that helped them (see Est. 2:7, 15; Job 31:18).

Being needy and afflicted could, however, entail more than a dismal financial situation. Indeed, often coupled with the difficulties of material poverty were the problems of being oppressed by others in society or by circumstances beyond one's control. Here, too, according to the principles just considered, the family would be first to help its members in need. The immediate family's obligation to be first to give assistance is an important principle. The family's assistance made it possible for the widow, orphan, or poor and afflicted to function as God intended in the place He had given that unfortunate person.

As any office-bearer today knows, things do not always work out the way they are supposed to. This was also the case in Israel. It might be that, for one reason or another, a family's land was lost, either through economics or through unresolved, ruinous family conflict. The result would be the dispersal or destruction of that family as a viable unit. It could also be that not all members of such a dysfunctional family would be able to join related households as family members. So what happened to those left out? The remaining options were to become marginal members of other unrelated households as debt servants or day laborers. Alternatively, a per-

---

6. There is no biblical support for the notion that the levirate institution prescribed or encouraged polygamy. A levirate marriage was monogamous. See Ron du Preez, "Does Levirate Law Promote Polygamy?," in *To Understand the Scriptures: Essays in Honor of William H. Shea*, ed. David Merling (Berrien Springs, Mich.: Institute of Archaeology / Siegfied H. Horn Archaeological Museum Andrews University, 1997), 273–90.

son could join the underclass of the poor who basically lived off the goodwill of society.[7]

Another possible devastating scenario could occur if a husband died with debt that his widow was unable to repay because she and her children could not be provided for in any way by the extended family. It then could happen that the creditor would take the widow's children as his slaves (2 Kings 4:1; cf. 1 Kings 17:8–15). Another possible source of distress was if a family member voluntarily moved elsewhere, away from the social and economic security of his household and home clan. Such a person would become a sojourner, like the Levite in Judges 17, and be dependent on others for his economic security, especially if he came into difficulties. All this leads to our next point—how society outside the family took care of the poor and disadvantaged in Israel.

Society

In the event that a person was deprived of the support of his family, God gave laws to His people so that society as a whole would step in and provide. We must bear in mind that Israel was God's chosen people, the church of those days, so to speak. These people were to be a communion of faith that showed the love of God to each other (Lev. 19:18; Deut. 6:5).

God's laws addressed two basic concerns. First, justice must be done to the poor, and their rights had to be upheld (Ex. 23:3; Deut. 16:19; Ps. 82:3). Second, charity was to be exercised toward the poor. They were to be given assistance. An Israelite must not be tightfisted but should be generous to the needy (Deut. 15:7–11). An underlying principle was that all the needs in the community should be met. Not everyone would require the same amount, but

---

7. Ex. 21:2–11; Lev. 25:35–55; 2 Kings 4:1; and Neh. 5:1–5. See further, Leo G. Perdue, "The Israelite and Early Jewish Family," in *Families in Ancient Israel*, by Leo G. Perdue et al., Family, Religion, and Culture Series (Louisville, Ky.: Westminster John Knox Press, 1997), 169, 193–98; and, for greater detail, see Shunya Bendor, *The Social Structure of Israel: The Institution of the Family* (Beit'Ab) *from the Settlement to the End of the Monarchy*, Jerusalem Biblical Studies, vol. 7 (Jerusalem: Simor Ltd., 1996), 230–44.

everyone's needs were to be equally satisfied (see Ex. 16:17–18; 2 Cor. 8:15).

God's law provided in various ways for the poor, widows, orphans, and Levites when there was no household to care for them. God helped preserve their dignity by not allowing the lender to enter their homes to collect the collateral. The poor borrower was to provide a pledge, and if it was a cloak that he needed to keep warm at night, it had to be returned to him before evening (Deut. 24:10–13). Furthermore, the poor were allowed to borrow utensils or implements without leaving their garment as pledge (Deut. 24:17; Job 24:3; cf. Ex. 22:22–26; Amos 2:8), and households were enjoined to include them in the festivals that followed the harvests (Deut. 16:9–15). Prior to the harvest, the needy could eat grain or fruit from the fields and vineyards of their neighbors (Deut. 23:24–25). During the harvest they could gather the leftovers (Lev. 19:9–10; 23:22; Deut. 24:19–21; Ruth 2–3). Also, they could live off the land every seventh year during the Sabbath years (Ex. 23:11; Lev. 25:6). Annually, the poor were to be included in the festivities and meals associated with the Feast of Weeks, the Feast of Tabernacles, and the presentation of the tithes (Deut. 16:11, 14; 14:26–29). Note that this requirement to share meals not only helped fill the stomachs of the disadvantaged but also gave them fellowship and a sense of belonging. They could share in the joy of God's people and be encouraged. In chapter 1 we considered the laws that dealt directly with matters of financial import, making it illegal to charge the poor interest and establishing that every seventh year there would no repayment of loans and that during every fiftieth year (the Year of Jubilee) property would be returned to the original owner.[8]

---

8. On the remission of debt, see note 2 in chapter 1. Other passages dealing with God's care for the poor and needy include Deut. 10:18; 24:17–21; 26:12–13; 27:19; cf. Job 29:13; Isa. 1:23; Jer. 7:6; 22:3. Deut. 27:19 issues a curse against those who subvert the justice due to widows.

To appreciate the legislation that in some way obligated society as a whole to ameliorate the plight of the poor, we must not forget that all these laws were essentially elaborations on God's demand to love our neighbor as ourselves (Lev. 19:18; cf. 19:33–34; Matt. 22:36–40).[9] Loving the neighbor involved moving outside the circle of the immediate family and including those who were separated from their family structure and were vulnerable and on their own.

There are several implications of the command to love being the ultimate foundation of all the detailed legislation regarding the poor. God's law was not in the first place a legal code with a comprehensive system of penalties for disobedience, but it was covenant law, teaching Israel the right way to go. Israel was to obey it not out of fear, but out of gratitude for God's deliverance (Ex. 19:4–6; 20:2; Deut. 5:6) and out of love to God for His choosing them as His holy nation (Deuteronomy 6; 7:6; 11; 14:2; 26:18). We can also characterize this legislation as preached law, with its warnings, motivations, and goals all directed toward a person's relationship with God.[10]

This feature of the law, including the injunctions regarding the poor, means that the legislation was not followed up by detailed penalties for disobedience. The Lord was not interested in fostering legalism, but rather a love for Him and the neighbor. This meant that it could be difficult to enforce the laws regarding the poor if the people were unwilling and no longer took seriously the injunctions of God's law. Israel's history and God's concern for the poor communicated through His prophets bear out this point. A related matter is that since the law was not a detailed legal code of what was and was not allowed, it mainly enunciated principles. It was not

---

9. For the primary commandment being to love, see Walther Eichrodt, *Theology of the Old Testament*, trans. J. A. Baker, Old Testament Library (1964; repr., Philadelphia: Westminster, 1961), 1:93.

10. See N. D. Kloosterman, "Casuistry as Ministerial Ethics," in *Nuchtere noodzaak: ethiek tussen navolging en compromis. Opstellen aangeboden aan Prof. Dr. J. Douma*, ed. J. H. F. Schaeffer, J. H. Smit, and Th. Tromp (Kampen: Kok, 1997), 113.

an exhaustive catalog of how the poor could be helped. It was up to God's people to make further application.[11]

God encouraged His people to help the indigent by reminding them that He is the defender of the poor and needy, and He avenges those who do not heed their cry (Ps. 68:5; Prov. 22:22–23; 28:27). Indeed, so closely does God associate Himself with the down-and-out that lending to the poor is like lending to God (Prov. 19:17). God Himself takes on the debt of the needy and repays those who helped them (Ps. 41:1–3; Prov. 11:24–25; 22:9). Assisting the poor is a safe and rewarding investment.

Finally, it should be noted that loving the neighbor shows itself in two basic ways. Love helps by providing handouts, but it also shows responsibility. It is of no small importance that the Lord expected the poor to work for their food and drink. Think of the law of gleaning and taking the leftover grapes (Lev. 19:10; 23:22; Deut. 24:19) and the law of living off the land's Sabbath year yield (Ex. 23:11; Lev. 25:6). Both required hard labor to gather sufficient amounts of food. Ruth, for example, labored from early morning to late at night (Ruth 2:7, 17).

The corollary to this is that the lazy poor were not to be assisted, because such relief would only encourage their indolent, ungodly behavior. Giving assistance to such people would not help them, so it would not be showing love to them. After all, God warned that laziness results in poverty (Prov. 6:10–11; 14:23; 19:15; 20:13; 21:5; 24:33–34). A slothful poor person is associated with the wicked (Prov. 15:19). Indeed, laziness can even lead to death (Prov. 21:25). We must learn from the diligent and be wise (Prov. 6:6). Likewise, those who live beyond their means invite poverty (Prov. 21:17), and they should correct their priorities before we give them assistance.

---

11. Kloosterman, "Casuistry as Ministerial Ethics," 113–14.

The State

We have seen that the family and society as a whole—all Israelites—had obligations to help the poor. What about civil government in Israel? Did it have obligations? When we ask a question like that, we must be careful not to impose our problems on Scripture, for ancient Israel did not have the government-sponsored security nets that are increasingly in vogue in our world today. God's Word makes clear that responsibility for the poor was given to the people as a whole, and not in the first place to the king or state as the mediator between rich and poor.[12]

The king, as God's earthly representative, however, did have obligations to the poor. We see this in Solomon's prayer for his kingship, which includes these petitions:

Give the king Your judgments, O God,
And Your righteousness to the king's Son.
He will judge Your people with righteousness,
And Your poor with justice.
The mountains will bring peace to the people,
And the little hills, by righteousness.
He will bring justice to the poor of the people;
He will save the children of the needy,
And will break in pieces the oppressor....

For He will deliver the needy when he cries,
The poor also, and him who has no helper.
He will spare the poor and needy,
And will save the souls of the needy.
He will redeem their life from oppression and violence;
And precious shall be their blood in His sight. (Ps. 72:1–4, 12–14)

As God's representative, Israel's king had to show something of the glory of *the* King, the Lord God Himself.[13] This applied to his relationship with the poor. The king had to see to it that the poor shared in the redemption and salvation of God's people,

---

12. Jon D. Levenson, "Poverty and the State in Biblical Thought," *Judaism* 25 (1976): 235.

13. See, e.g., Deut. 17:18–19; 1 Chron. 29:23; 2 Chron. 9:8; Ps. 2:6.

typified in the material prosperity that God had given in the land flowing with milk and honey. He had responsibilities to ensure that the oppressed were helped and that the downtrodden received justice. Indeed, King Josiah did "justice and righteousness.... He judged the cause of the poor and needy" (Jer. 22:15–16). Of the great messianic King who was to come it was predicted that "with righteousness He shall judge the poor, and decide with equity for the meek of the earth" (Isa. 11:4).

Which responsibilities were included in the king's office in terms of defending the poor and needy we do not know. Certainly, the king's duty as court of appeal was an important aspect (e.g., 1 Kings 3:16–28; Prov. 31:1, 8–9; cf. 2 Sam. 8:15). As God's vice-gerent, representative, and servant, the king would have had to make sure that God's law was upheld in the land. Whether the king defended the cause of the poor and upheld their rights had tremendous impact on the well-being of his throne and country (Prov. 29:14; cf. Ezek. 16:49). After all, it was God's law that the king had to uphold (Deut. 17:18–20). Indeed, if Israel obeyed the Lord, then the land would be blessed economically as well (see Deut. 28:1–14).

It is important to note in summary that all these laws involving those in need had three important results. First, the family unit, the immediate household in difficulty, was protected and retained its economic viability due to the laws of borrowing and the Year of Jubilee, when their land, forfeited because of debt, was returned. Second, the poor were able to retain their personal dignity. They were able to work and not live on handouts. They could take out loans rather than rely on grants, and the lender could not simply enter their homes to collect collateral. Third, the provisions of the Jubilee legislation meant especially that households were prevented from becoming permanently destitute and financially dependent on the larger community.[14]

---

14. For more on these three points, see Michael Schluter, "Welfare," in *Jubilee Manifesto: A Framework, Agenda, and Strategy for Christian Social Reform*, ed. Michael Schluter and John Ashcroft (Leicester, U.K.: Inter-Varsity, 2005), 176–81.

Having considered the place of the family, the larger community, and the king in providing for the needs of the poor, the question arises whether ancient Israel had an office similar or analogous to that of a New Testament deacon.

An Old Testament Deacon?

There is no evidence in the Old Testament for a special diaconal office charged with caring for the poor. Although the early Christian church sometimes considered deacons analogous to Levites, an analogy that became common in Jerome's day,[15] the offices had different responsibilities. There is no direct line from the task of the Levites to that of the deacons. Some have sought to connect the office of deacon to an official of the Jewish synagogue, the *hazzan*, an assistant who could be responsible for a myriad of different tasks, including choir director, janitor, and teacher. The differences in the two offices are too numerous to make the one a model for the other.[16]

The emphasis in the Old Testament was on the family unit taking care of its needy; if the family failed, the larger community, and ultimately the monarch, had responsibilities to see to the needs of the indigent. The Lord God did not institute a special diaconal office at that time. He had made the necessary provisions for the

15. E.g., *Apostolic Constitutions* 2:25, in "Constitutions of the Holy Apostles," trans. James Donaldson, in *Ante-Nicene Fathers, Vol. VII: Fathers of the Third and Fourth Centuries*, ed. Alexander Roberts et al. (Buffalo, N.Y.: Christian Literature Company, 1886), 410; and Jerome, "Letter 146," in *The Letters of St. Jerome*, trans. W. H. Fremantle, G. Lewis, and W. G. Martley, in *A Select Library of the Nicene and Post-Nicene Fathers of the Christian Church, Second Series, Volume VI: St. Jerome: Letters and Select Works*, ed. Philip Schaff and Henry Wace (New York: Christian Literature Company, 1893), 289. See further the listing under *leuitēs* in G. W. H. Lampe, *A Patristic Greek Lexicon* (Oxford: Oxford University Press, 2003), 798.

16. See James Tunstead Burtchaell, *From Synagogue to Church: Public Services and Offices in the Earliest Christian Communities* (Cambridge: Cambridge University Press, 1992), 246–49; and Emil Schürer, *The History of the Jewish People in the Age of Jesus Christ (175 B.C.—A.D. 135)*, ed. and rev. Geza Vermes et al. (Edinburgh: T&T Clark, 1979), 2:438. Also see chapter 3 of this book, note 5.

poor in His law, and it was up to the individuals who comprised
the nation to look to the needs of the indigent and to take action.[17]

As we saw in the preceding chapter, the poor and needy were
often neglected in spite of prophets' admonitions. Indeed, the
neglect of the vulnerable in Israel was an important reason for
God's judgment in the Babylonian exile (Zech. 7:8–13; cf. Deut.
4:27). The failure of the old covenant to provide adequately for
the needy was obvious. For this reason also the new covenant was
needed (see Heb. 8:7–9). The coming of salvation in Christ and the
outpouring of the Holy Spirit at Pentecost would have enormous
consequences for taking care of the poor. Caring for the poor as
stipulated by Mosaic law would be exchanged for a Spirit-filled joyous life of gratitude that could not tolerate any grief or sadness due
to poverty or want.

Summary and Conclusions

There are a number of interrelated reasons why the Israelites needed
to help the poor. The Israelites were to reflect God's love by loving
their neighbor. As the Lord had heeded Israel's afflictions while in
Egyptian bondage and had compassion on them, so the people were
to have compassion on each other and, specifically, they had the obligation to take care of the poor and needy (see Deut. 15:15). God
had set His people free, so none of God's people should be burdened
by any kind of oppression. To that end God gave laws that targeted
those in society who were most at risk to being bound by troubles
and want, such as the widows, orphans, and strangers.

Liberation from affliction and oppression brings the joy of
deliverance. God wanted everyone to share in the joy of redemption, and for that reason no one was to be in bondage to affliction
and poverty. Destitution or grief of whatever sort was not to form
a lasting impediment to that joy. However, the happiness of release

---

17. For the emphasis on private persons needing to respond to the laws for the
poor and needy, see Hiers, *Justice and Compassion in Biblical Law*, 185–211.

from bondage was not the ultimate goal of God's laws for the poor and afflicted.

When God led His people out of the slavery of Pharaoh's dominion, He had set them free so that they could be His precious possession, who would serve Him in liberty (Ex. 4:22–23; 19:5–6). No affliction or want was to bind or hinder them in any way in their service to God in the fullness of life. And as we saw in chapter 1, the needs that could cause unnecessary burdens were not only material and financial. There were many more things that could weigh people down and make them less effective in God's service. Basically, the needy were those who were unable to share in the joy of deliverance and were therefore hindered in their service to the Lord.

In this context, the worst sin possible is that a person would steal (kidnap) from God one of His precious possessions, a fellow Israelite. The eighth commandment underlined that the place and freedom of every Israelite in the covenant nation had to be jealously safeguarded. It was necessary, then, for members of the community to watch so that they did not also enslave themselves to the possessions of this world and rob themselves from God, who had a claim on their lives.

This commandment was also a reminder of the need to recognize that God's people are only stewards of their possessions, which ultimately belong to God. Only God has absolute ownership. He entrusted material goods and prosperity to His people so that they could serve Him with them. By His miraculous intervention in the distribution of manna, the Lord showed that a basic principle in helping the poor is that there is to be equality. No one should lack anything.

In helping the poor, the family was first in line to provide assistance, as God's law made clear. Those who fell through the cracks were to be helped by society as a whole—that is, by individuals in society who were not family responding to the needs of the indigent by following the stipulations of God's law. When the people obeyed God's law, they avoided extreme needs and hardships. When hardships did occur, it was due to disobedience. The king, as God's vicegerent and representative, had to defend the right of the afflicted and ensure that God's law with respect to the poor was upheld in the land. When obeyed, God's laws regarding the poor had the effect of protecting the family unit, safeguarding personal dignity, and preventing long-term destitution.

The history of Israel shows that the poor were often neglected, and prophets would preach against this. The people would need to repent, for the Lord expected His people to obey His laws concerning the poor out of love for Him and for the neighbor and in gratitude for His salvation. There were no detailed penalties for disobedience, because God appealed to His people's hearts and did not want to foster a rigid legalism. Love and thankfulness were to be the motivators for compliance to God's will. It is therefore not surprising that God did not try to cover every possible scenario in His law, but taught the necessary principles, entrusting His people to apply these laws to their circumstances.

There was no special diaconal office in ancient Israel. The family and the people as a whole had the responsibility to see that the needs of those impoverished or afflicted were met. Because this arrangement did not always function as it should, the promised new covenant was needed.

PART TWO

New Testament Times

CHAPTER 3

Christ's Teaching on the Poor and Needy

When we consider the subject of helping the poor, it is important to stress the continuity between the Old and New Testaments. After all, God's command that His people love their neighbors as themselves forms the basis for caring for the needy in the times both of ancient Israel and of Jesus and the apostles (Lev. 19:18; Matt. 22:39). Before considering the teachings of the Lord Jesus, we need to reflect briefly on how the needy were provided for prior to and during the time the Savior was on earth. This chapter therefore deals with the care of the poor in Judaism, and Christ's life and teaching regarding the poor.

The Historical Context of Christ's Teaching

In general, postexilic Judaism emphasized a concern for the poor that was consistent with the Old Testament injunctions. A "neighbor" was generously considered to be whomever a person had to deal with in life. Although Jews did not always practice their official teachings, Judaism did provide a context for Jewish Christians that helped them take care of the poor in accord with Old Testament principles.[1]

---

1. See the studies of Frank Crüsemann, "Das Alte Testament als Grundlage der Diakonie," in *Diakonie—biblische Grundlagen und Orientierungen*, ed. Gerhard K. Schäfer et al. (Heidelberg: Universitätsverlag, 1998), 67–93; and K. Berger, "'Diakonie' in Frühjudentum. Die Armenfürsorge in der jüdischen Diasporagemeinde zur Zeit Jesu," in *Diakonie—biblische Grundlagen und Orientierungen*, ed. Gerhard K. Schäfer

Those who practiced Judaism during Christ's time on earth were well aware of their obligations to the needy. The Jews knew the Old Testament laws, such as debt remission in the sabbatical year and tithes for the poor, but they did not always honor them, judging from complaints found in early Jewish literature. In Jerusalem the temple could be expected to meet its obligations to the poor, but much of the responsibility toward them was left to others.[2]

Wherever synagogues were found, the needy received organized care. This assistance was legally based on the tithe for the poor (Deut. 14:28–29; 26:12) and was funded by alms or donations that were received (see Matt. 6:1–4). According to traditions found in early Jewish writings, the local poor were supported once a week from the "poor basket" (*quppah*) and were given food and clothing, while any needy person from out of town could receive a daily portion of food from the "poor bowl" (*tamhuy*). At least two men were assigned to gather the alms and at least three to distribute them. Everyone in the community was required to make a donation. It is difficult to say whether this elaborate practice was actually the pattern in New Testament times, and scholarly opinion on the matter is divided. It is possible that this division into two streams of aid developed later. In any case, there is no doubt that the synagogue as an institution was active in helping the poor in New Testament times. Given the importance of this institution, the early Christian church, also referred to as a synagogue in its earliest period (as is the case in the original text of James 2:2), probably benefited from its example.[3]

---

et al. (Heidelberg: Universitätsverlag, 1998), 94–105. Also see Lútzen Miedema, "Vroeg Jodendom en *Diakonia*," in *Diaconie in Beweging: Handboek Diaconiewetenschap*, ed. Hub Crijns et al. (Kampen: Kok, 2011), 58–63.

2. Joachim Jeremias, *Jerusalem in the Time of Jesus: An Investigation into Economic and Social Conditions during the New Testament Period*, trans. F. H. Cave and C. H. Cave (1962; repr., London: SCM, 1969), 132, 134; and George Foot Moore, *Judaism in the First Centuries of the Christian Era: The Age of Tannaim* (1927; repr., Peabody, Mass.: Hendrickson, 1997), 2:164.

3. Jeremias, *Jerusalem in the Time of Jesus*, 130–31; Schürer, *History of the Jewish People*, 2:437; Martin Hengel, *Property and Riches in the Early Church: Aspects of a Social*

Private charity, which could take different forms depending on the situation, ranging from giving alms to beggars to allowing the poor to glean fields, was also important in alleviating poverty. Given the importance of charity, it is not surprising that the disciples at the Last Supper thought that Judas had left to "give something to the poor" (John 13:29). It was not by chance that beggars would sit in places frequented by many people, hoping for charity from passersby (Matt. 20:29–30; Acts 3:2).

An interesting example of charity is found in the Testament of Job, a noncanonical Greek writing dating from the first century BC to the first century AD. Among other things, it reflects Jewish piety of that period and features Job's generosity to the poor (T. Job, 9–12).[4] It is interesting to note that the Testament of Job uses the words *diakonia* and *diakoneō* (related to our word "deacon") for the work of caring for the poor, including the collecting and disbursing of funds (see in its context T. Job 11:1–4; 12:1). These terms are never used in the ancient Greek translation of the canonical Old Testament but are found in the New Testament for ministering to the saints (1 Cor. 16:15), and specifically for caring for the poor, as in the daily distribution (Acts 6:1–2). These terms are, therefore, a bridge from Judaism to New Testament usage.[5]

History of Early Christianity (Philadelphia: Fortress, 1974), 20; and Moore, *Judaism in the First Centuries*, 2:176–78. In James 2:2, the text has the Greek term for synagogue (*sunagōgē*), here translated as "assembly" in the New King James Version (NKJV).

4. R. P. Spittler, "Testament of Job," in *The Old Testament Pseudepigrapha*, ed. James H. Charlesworth (Garden City, N.Y.: Doubleday, 1983), 1:830–36.

5. See Miedema, "Vroeg Jodendom," esp. 40–43. Interestingly, in Judaism the *diakonos*, the Greek word for the office of deacon in the New Testament, is used of the minister or servant of the synagogue (*hazzan*). He was the one who had to bring out the holy scrolls for the services and later replace them. He also announced the beginning and end of the Sabbath by blowing a trumpet. Schürer, *History of the Jewish People*, 2:438. Also see Max Schloessinger, "Ḥazzan," in *The Jewish Encyclopedia.*, ed. Singer Isidore (New York: Funk & Wagnalls, 1901–1906), 6:284. This office does not appear to have anything to do with the church office of deacon as has been suggested, e.g., by James M. Willson in *The Deacon: An Inquiry into the Nature, Duties, and Exercise of the Office of the Deacon in the Christian Church* (Philadelphia: William S. Young, 1841), 30.

Unfortunately, almsgiving, as a significant part of Jewish piety, came to be considered a work of merit before God rather than a sacrificial service of love to others. The Hebrew term "righteousness" was translated into the Greek as "alms." Intertestamental literature even speaks of almsgiving as a means of atonement. It suggests that it is better to give alms than to hoard up gold, because giving alms saves from death and wipes out sin (Tobit 12:8b–9a; similarly Sir. 3:30).[6] Having surveyed the general thoughts and practices of Judaism regarding the poor, we turn to Christ's life and teaching on the subject.

Christ's Teaching in Deed and Word

Christ came as the promised, perfect messianic king (Isa. 11:4) who would judge the needy with justice, defend the cause of the poor, and deliver the needy and those who have no helper when they call. He would have pity on the weak and the needy and save their lives (Ps. 72:2, 4, 12–13). Though true God, the Son came in love and humility, as a servant, to give His life as the ultimate sacrifice (Phil. 2:2, 7–8; cf. Matt. 20:28; John 15:13). Christ's entire ministry, then, was an embodiment of the divine command to love our neighbors as ourselves; therefore, we must see Christ's instruction on providing for the poor within this context. Important to understanding this is Christ's declaration at the Last Supper: "I am among you as the One who serves [diakoneō]" (Luke 22:27). Indeed, waiting on tables has always been considered a basic root meaning of diakoneō. More recently it has been argued that the primary basic meaning of this verb is to function as an intermediary and to be at someone's

---

There is no prototype in Judaism for the deacon. James M. Barnett, *The Diaconate: A Full and Equal Order* (Minneapolis: Seabury, 1981), 37–38.

6. Also see Jeremias, *Jerusalem in the Time of Jesus*, 128–30; Abraham Cronbach, "The Social Ideals of the Apocrypha and the Pseudepigrapha," *Hebrew Union College Annual* 18 (1943–1944): 132–34, 140–41; Hermann W. Beyer, "diakoneō, diakonia, diakonos," in *Theological Dictionary of the New Testament*, ed. Gerhard Kittel, trans. Geoffrey W. Bromiley (Grand Rapids: Eerdmans, 1964), 2:83.

service. This sense fits well with Christ's ministry. After all, sent by the Father, He "did not come to be served, but to serve [*diakoneō*], and to give His life a ransom for many" (Matt. 20:28; cf. John 3:17; 20:21). As we shall see in a subsequent chapter, the deacon today also serves as an intermediary in someone else's service since he represents Christ and shows His love for His people. Positing the basic meaning of functioning as an intermediary does not, however, negate that the terms for serving (*diakoneō*) and servant (*diakonos*) are often associated with and carry nuances of humble service to others in a variety of circumstances. In other words, the meanings traditionally associated with this word group, such as serving, assisting, waiting tables, meeting immediate needs, encouraging, and caring for someone, are justified. The context determines how best to translate the terms in question.[7]

Christ characterized His life as one of serving (*diakoneō*), and He showed His disciples by deed and precept how they ought to minister to each other, particularly to those in need. We therefore must consider how Christ embodied and taught service to the poor and needy and, in the process, understand the implications for the office of deacon (*diakonos*).

Christ's Life as Service
Christ's ministry was distinguished by serving, and He is called a servant (*diakonos*; Rom. 15:8). This serving originated in the love

---

7. See, e.g., I. Howard Marshall and Philip H. Towner, *A Critical and Exegetical Commentary on the Pastoral Epistles*, The International Critical Commentary (Edinburgh: T&T Clark, 1999), 486–87. For the traditional meanings, see W. Bauer et al., *A Greek-English Lexicon of the New Testament and Other Early Christian Literature*, 2nd ed. (Chicago: University of Chicago Press, 1979), 184; for the newer meaning, see John N. Collins, Diakonia: *Re-Interpreting the Ancient Sources* (Oxford: Oxford University Press, 1990); and for this meaning being added to a standard lexicon, see F. W. Danker, rev. and ed., *A Greek-English Lexicon of the New Testament and Other Early Christian Literature*, 3rd ed. (Chicago: University of Chicago Press, 2000), 229–30. For a more recent study, see Clarence DeWitt "Jimmy" Agan III, "Deacons, Deaconesses, and Denominational Discussions: Romans 16:1 as a Test Case," *Presbyterion* 34, no. 2 (2008): 99–104.

of God (John 3:16–17). He came in great compassion to a world
lost in sin to bring the final solution to both spiritual and material
poverty. He could therefore make that momentous announcement
of the arrival of the great Year of Jubilee when he read from Isaiah
61 in the synagogue of Nazareth:

> The Spirit of the LORD is upon Me,
> Because He has anointed Me
> To preach the gospel to the poor;
> He has sent Me to heal the brokenhearted,
> To proclaim liberty to the captives
> And recovery of sight to the blind,
> To set at liberty those who are oppressed;
> To proclaim the acceptable year of the LORD. (Luke 4:18–19)

And then, having closed the scroll, He said, "Today this Scripture is
fulfilled in your hearing" (v. 21). As the servant of the Lord, He came
to bring the joy of salvation.

He gave a foretaste of the perfection to come, for the kingdom
of God had arrived, although not yet in the fullness of the final age
(Matt. 6:10). In performing His servant mission, Christ showed
the arrival of the kingdom by His works. He comforted those who
were poor, both in spirit and materially (Matt. 5:3; Luke 6:20;
cf. Luke 6:24). He healed the sick and blind and cast out evil spirits
(Luke 7:21). He reached out to the marginalized and the despised,
such as the tax collectors, prostitutes, and sinners (Matt. 21:31;
Mark 2:15–17). He called all the weary and burdened to come
to Him for rest (Matt. 11:28). His ultimate service was going the
way of the cross for the salvation of sinners. Even though Christ
recoiled at the thought of the suffering that lay ahead, He subjected
His will to the Father who sent Him: "O My Father, if it is possible,
let this cup pass from Me; nevertheless, not as I will, but as You
will" (Matt. 26:39).

Those who seek to follow Christ can never duplicate His unique
mission, yet to be His disciple means being willing to serve rather than
to be served—in short, to be a servant (*diakonos*; Matt. 20:26) in love
for God and neighbor. Christ taught and dramatically illustrated this

truth by washing the feet of His disciples prior to their partaking of the final Passover meal. He took off His outer garments and dressed like a slave in a loincloth (see Phil. 2:7), wrapped a towel around His waist, and washed their feet. Then He said: "If I then, your Lord and Teacher, have washed your feet, you also ought to wash one another's feet. For I have given you an example, that you should do as I have done to you. Most assuredly, I say to you, a servant is not greater than his master; nor is he who is sent greater than he who sent him. If you know these things, blessed are you if you do them" (John 13:14–17). By these words and actions Christ not only demonstrated His love for the disciples but also showed something of the love of God that brought Him to this world. The obligations of serving one another, and especially the needy, also rest on those who identify with Christ. Their attitude should be the same as that of Christ Jesus (Phil. 2:5). Christ's teaching further elaborated on what the service that His life embodied entails.

Christ's Teaching about Service to the Poor

Christ's teaching on all matters related to helping the poor, including such matters as principles of giving and wealth, took several forms. He made use of the incidents that occurred and so instructed His disciples, gave indirect indicators, or devoted an entire discourse or parable to the subject. All these sources enable us to distill some important principles that Christ has taught His people.

First, as already indicated, this service is an absolute necessity. To love God and neighbor sums up the law and the prophets (Matt. 22:36–40). This love is obligatory (1 John 4:21). Loving your neighbor as yourself means doing for others what you would have them do for you (Matt. 7:12). Christ taught that when the Son of Man comes in His glory (Matt. 25:31–46), those who fed the hungry, gave drink to the thirsty, welcomed the stranger, clothed the naked, visited the sick, and came to the imprisoned will enter eternal life. As they did it to one of the least of these, Christ's brothers, they ministered to Christ Himself (see Matt. 10:40, 42).[8] Those who did not do this service (*diakoneō*; Matt. 25:44) will go into eternal punishment. The parable of the rich man who neglected to help poor Lazarus and was in torment in Hades has a similar message (Luke 16:19–31).

In a somewhat subtle way, the Lord Jesus underscored the necessity of this service by teaching His disciples to pray, "Give us this day our daily bread" (Matt. 6:11). We do not just pray this prayer for ourselves but include others—"Give *us* this day"—which obligates us to help bring that petition to fruition. This prayer also teaches us moderation when we are tempted to place a premium on wealth and possessions. Christ teaches us to pray for bread, not luxury items, for only one day at a time.

This point brings us to a second truth that Christ taught. Possessions are ultimately God's, and He has entrusted them to us. One day He will ask for an accounting of how well we have managed them. The parable of the talents teaches these verities (Matt. 25:14–30). Because we are ultimately only stewards of what has been entrusted to us in this life, our possessions have only a relative value. We must therefore deal with possessions accordingly and not be covetous or enslaved to our property, making it the focus of life. A child of God must remain free from the idols of this world, such as materialism, to serve God. Christ illustrated this truth with the parable of the rich fool who laid up treasures for himself, which God, as absolute owner of all, prevented him from enjoying. This rich man was actually poor, for he was not rich toward God. Life does not consist in the abundance of one's possessions (Luke 12:13–21). Consistent with these truths, the Sermon on the Mount included the admonition not to lay up for yourself treasures on earth but in heaven, "for where your treasure is, there your heart will be also." You

---

8. There is disagreement about to whom "the least of these My brethren" (Matt. 25:40) refers. Some exegetes say they are all the needy among humankind. However, the text clearly refers to Christians. For a full discussion, see Donald A. Hagner, *Matthew 14–28*, Word Biblical Commentary (Dallas: Word, 1998), 744–45.

cannot serve both God and money (Matt. 6:21, 24). In this context, Christ reminded His hearers not to be anxious about life and what they would eat or wear. They were told to take one day at a time. Your heavenly Father knows what you need (Matt. 6:25–34).

Also, being stewards of what God has entrusted to them means that Christians use their resources for the needy as fully as possible so that all needs can be satisfied (see Ex. 16:18). That seems to be the basic message when Christ said to His disciples: "Sell what you have [*huparchonta*]" and give to the needy (Luke 12:33; cf. 14:33). Similarly, He told the rich young ruler who thought he had kept the law: "You still lack one thing. Sell all that you have and distribute to the poor, and you will have treasure in heaven" (Luke 18:22). What was Christ saying with these injunctions? We know that the Lord did not come to undo the law but to fulfill it (Matt. 5:17). In other words, Christ was not opposing the stipulation in the law that the family inheritance should never be sold (Lev. 25:23–28; Prov. 19:14) nor the idea that parents should save up for their children (2 Cor. 12:14). The meaning of the word for possessions (*huparchonta*) in Luke 12:33 is that which is presently at one's disposal. In other words, whatever is available for which there is no direct immediate need should be made available for the poor. No estate sale is in view, but an intensive use of what is available.[9]

A third principle is that it is important how you give. Do you give willingly from a generous heart, or grudgingly from a stingy disposition? A poor widow put the equivalent of a penny in the temple offering box for the poor. In spite of what seemed like a small amount, Christ says that she put in more than the wealthy donors who contributed large sums of money: "For they all put in out of their abundance, but she out of her poverty put in all that

---

9. Danker, *Greek-English Lexicon of the New Testament*, 1029. See Coert H. Lindijer, *De armen en de rijken bij Lucas* ('S-Gravenhage: Uitgeverij Boekencentrum, 1981), 110–11. Darrell L. Bock notes, "The stress is not on literally selling all, but on making use of one's resources in a way that benefits others," in *Luke 9:51–24:53*, Baker Exegetical Commentary on the New Testament (Grand Rapids: Baker Academic, 1996), 1167.

she had, her whole livelihood" (Mark 12:44). Also, we should not give in order to get praise from men: "But when you do a charitable deed, do not let your left hand know what your right hand is doing, that your charitable deed may be in secret; and your Father who sees in secret will Himself reward you openly" (Matt. 6:3–4).

Furthermore, we should give to the poor out of love and never with a view to performing a meritorious good deed. The Pharisees considered strict observance of the letter of the law as works of righteousness. Their self-righteousness was evident in their condescending attitude toward others whom they considered less righteous (Luke 18:9–14) and in their intent to do the minutest demands of the law by tithing even the herbs they owned. But Christ condemned them for neglecting justice and the love of God (Luke 11:42; Mic. 6:8) and warned that to enter the kingdom of heaven, one's righteousness had to exceed that of the Pharisees (Matt. 5:20).

Fourth, loving your neighbor means loving all whom the Lord puts on your path, including those outside your comfort zone and even those considered to be an enemy (Matt. 5:43–48). Christ illustrated this truth in the well-known parable of the good Samaritan (Luke 10:25–37). In answer to the question, "Who is my neighbor?" Christ told the story of a Samaritan who helped a robbed man left half dead on the road from Jerusalem to Jericho. A priest and a Levite had not bothered to help and had avoided the wounded man, passing by on the other side. But the Samaritan, whom the Jews would consider to be an outcast, had compassion and took care of him in every possible way. Christ then asked, "So which of these three do you think was neighbor to him who fell among the thieves?" The lawyer who had asked the original question said, "He who showed mercy on him." And Jesus said to him, "Go and do likewise" (Luke 10:36–37). The theoretical question "Who is my neighbor?" is not the right approach. Christ indicates that the real question is this: Whose neighbor am I? Do I show love and mercy to anyone put on my path? By using the Samaritan as an example of mercy and neighborliness to his fellow man, Christ teaches that there is no boundary that excludes anyone from being a neighbor. We are not neighbors to someone because of race, color, creed, or nationality but simply because God has placed someone on our life's path. This parable illustrates another principle.

A fifth principle is that helping the poor and needy should never be conceived of too narrowly, as if need and want are only quantifiable in the material sense of being financially poor. The good Samaritan attended to the man's physical need for medical attention. Christ's teaching about the coming judgment also showed that who the needy are must not be defined too narrowly. He indicated that we must show love by feeding the hungry, clothing the naked, and visiting the sick and imprisoned lest we be condemned on judgment day (Matt. 25:31–46).

When Christ declared that He was the fulfillment of the prophecy found in Isaiah 61—"the Spirit of the LORD is upon Me, because He has anointed Me to preach the gospel to the poor" (Luke 4:18, 21)—then it was obvious that more than the financially poor were in view. He continued quoting:

> He [the Spirit of the Lord] has sent Me to heal the brokenhearted,
> To proclaim liberty to the captives
> And recovery of sight to the blind,
> To set at liberty those who are oppressed;
> To proclaim the acceptable year of the LORD.
>   (Luke 4:18–19; cf. Lev. 25:10)

Christ ministered to the poor—that is, to all who were burdened with all sorts of trials and afflictions but who sought their help from God. The definition of who is poor is therefore broad (see Isa. 66:2; Matt. 5:3; Luke 6:20), and God's people and the deacons need to be sensitive to that. Spiritual needs are sometimes greater than material needs.

Summary and Conclusions

Christ's teaching took place within Judaism, which was aware of God's will with respect to providing for the poor. The Old Testament ordinances were well known, if not always followed. Synagogues provided organized care for the needy, but private charity was important for meeting the needs of the poor. Unfortunately, some Jews came to view giving to the poor as meritorious and as a means of atonement. Christ opposed that way of thinking. God demands obedience from the heart in true love for Him and our neighbor. Outward obedience to the letter of the law is not enough.

While the Pharisees flaunted their good deeds, Christ humbly and compassionately did His work. Sent by the Father and in His service, the Lord Jesus as servant brought good news to the poor, healed the sick, reached out to the marginalized, and called sinners to true peace with God. It is obvious that Christ's understanding of who the poor and needy are was comprehensive, just as in the Old Testament. He set free those oppressed by the consequences of sin in this life and gave them the joy of redemption. Rather than being served, He served, and so set an example for others.

Christ calls all those who believe in Him to emulate His example of service. Loving your neighbor is not an option but a necessity. Failing to do so means exclusion from eternal life. Christ calls His people to be moved with willing hearts grateful to God for His salvation and generous to their neighbors. In this way He sets them free from being enslaved to their possessions. We are only stewards of our possessions, which we have in trust from God to be used to His glory. Just as in ancient Israel, the children of God must not be in bondage to poverty or possessions but experience the freedom in which they have been set free for service to God and neighbor. Showing love to the least of those belonging to Christ, whatever the need or affliction, is showing love to Christ Himself. Love for our neighbor must extend beyond the boundaries of the church to all whom God puts on our life's path.

CHAPTER 4

Ministering to the Poor in Acts 6

With His ascension into glory, the Lord Jesus physically left this world, but He did not abandon those who believed in Him. As He promised, He poured out His Spirit on the church (Acts 1:7–8; 2:1–4). This gift of the Spirit meant, among other things, that the people of God were now equipped to serve each other as Christ had taught them by deed and word. This had profound implications for how the church ministered to the poor, who, as Christ had indicated, would always be with them (Matt. 26:11). To understand the current diaconal office, we need to carefully consider how the Spirit guided the church to take care of the needy, beginning with Acts 6. This chapter therefore deals with the basic problem that the church needed to address in Acts 6; the identity, ordination, and activities of the seven; and the blessing that followed.

The Joy of the Congregation Threatened

After the outpouring of the Holy Spirit, the church experienced the joy of fellowship and prayer, sharing the teaching of the apostles and food together (Acts 2:42–43). Deliverance had come in Christ, and they knew themselves as those who had been set free from the bondage of sin, Satan, and death in the great year of release and Jubilee (Luke 4:18–21). Christ had come in *the* covenant service of love for *the* freedom of the children of God!

There was therefore much happiness in Jerusalem, and the church saw to it that this joy would stay. They loved each other and, with the love of Christ, made sure that no one had material need (Acts 2:44–47). They shared food together with glad and generous hearts (Acts 2:46). So the church expressed joy and gratitude for salvation in Christ, and they were strengthened. In the tradition of the Old Testament, the believers held festive meals with the brothers and sisters, including the needy (cf. Deut. 14:26–29; 16:10–11, 14–15). They took care of each other in loving service for the joy and freedom of the children of God. No poverty or affliction must bind anyone and take that happiness away. They rejoiced in their fellowship.

But one day that joy was not there as it should have been. Complaints were heard in the rapidly growing church of the Lord. Some widows were being neglected in the daily distribution (Acts 6:1). The joy and therefore the freedom of God's children were threatened. It was then that the apostles took action. The matter of maintaining and providing for fellowship in the joy of the Lord was of great importance, so seven men were appointed to wait (*diakoneō*) on tables. In this way the joy of salvation could continue to be tasted and savored and the fellowship function properly.

When we consider ministry to the needy, we should never forget the motive of protecting communal joy so that murmuring should cease. The men in Acts 6 were appointed to make sure that no one was overlooked or neglected within the communion of saints. In the church, no members should be murmuring because of oppression or want so that they can no longer experience the joy of salvation and release from all bondage in Christ. Ministering to the poor is never just a matter of seeing to it that no one is without food. This ministry includes comforting and encouraging the oppressed and ensuring that joy in the Spirit for free children of God who have been liberated by Christ should be realized in the communion of saints. In this communion every member of the church has a place and should feel secure and free from bondage and affliction. Among the forms of poverty and want are sickness, mobility issues, loneliness, and feeling inadequate due to unemployment, which can lead to genuine needs and wants that must be dealt with. In the fellowship of the church, believers provide for each other and carry each other's burdens (Gal. 6:2) so that everyone is able to function according to the responsibilities they have been given without justified murmuring and complaining.

Clearly continuity exists between this key motivation for ministry to the needy and the Old Testament care for the needy as discussed in the first two chapters. Then, too, "need" was broadly defined as anything unjustifiably robbing God's people of the joy of salvation. Because God had set His people free from the oppression of Egypt, He wanted everyone to be provided for so that no one would be in bondage anymore. Similarly, now that the Passover Lamb, Jesus Christ, had truly set His people free from the bondage of the evil one, God wanted the freedom of His Pentecost people to be safeguarded so that all of them could celebrate and savor the joy of redemption (1 Cor. 5:7–8; cf. John 8:36; Gal. 5:1).

Besides the provision of food, there was another closely related issue that endangered the happiness of this large congregation. The neglect of widows was a serious matter. Once a widow became a Christian and was likely expelled from the synagogue (see John 9:22; 12:42), she gave up the material security the synagogue had provided and could no longer benefit from its aid to the indigent. A Christian widow, then, needed help immediately. To be left unattended was unconscionable. What made matters worse was that only Greek-speaking widows were neglected. The failure to provide occurred along cultural lines, threatening the unity of this church.

But God had composed the church so that there would be no division in the body, "but that the members should have the same care for one another" (1 Cor. 12:25). In Jerusalem the threat of unholy division endangering the joy of redemption was real. Greek-speaking Jews lodged serious complaints about the neglect of their widows against those believers who spoke Aramaic (or possibly Hebrew) and whose widows were apparently well taken care of. We can well imagine how this grievance concerning such a vulnerable part of the community could potentially mean big trouble, especially when language and cultural differences played a role. Many of the Hellenistic Jews had probably been born abroad (see Acts 6:9) but wanted to spend their last years in Jerusalem to be buried near the Holy City.[1] The indigenous Hebraic believers had always called Jerusalem home and could have regarded the Greek-speaking Jews as newcomers. When a dispute arises between such groups about an emotional issue such as caring for widows, tensions can easily escalate. Neglecting Greek-speaking widows could have raised the larger question of whether they were welcome and were truly being included in the congregation.

Such questions were relevant, for even though widows received relief from the synagogue, they were often still left disadvantaged, marginalized, and not taken seriously in society. Would the Christian church do likewise with certain widows? Christ's parable of the persistent widow who sought so strenuously for justice (Luke 18:1–8) probably reflected the reality widows faced. Even the religious teachers treated widows with disdain and without any sensitivity for their situation. Hypocritical scribes could make long pious prayers but at the same time "devour widows' houses" (Luke 20:47) with apparent impunity. Within such a social context, it was extremely important that widows felt at home in the church, for they truly belonged there. After all, it was precisely such vulnerable poor people whom Christ included and who will be at the great eschatological banquet (Luke 14:13, 21). If left unresolved, the crisis of the neglected widows therefore had enormous potential for damaging this young, vibrant, and large church of at least eight thousand members (Acts 2:41; 4:4). These widows must know and the entire congregation must realize that those who believe in Christ welcome and take care of all widows in their midst. If there was one place where widows should feel completely at home in the present world, it was in the church. To resolve this issue, the apostles needed to appoint men to work for the true joy and unity of the congregation.

---

1. Ernst Haenchen, *The Acts of the Apostles: A Commentary* (1965; repr., Oxford: Blackwell, 1971), 260–61, 266.

The Identity of the Seven

The apostles recognized the seriousness of the situation and acted decisively. Realizing that they were incapable of doing everything that needed to be done, they decided to delegate responsibilities to others. In this manner they followed the example of Moses, who also delegated when faced with a workload that became too heavy (Deut. 1:9–14). Seven men were to be selected and ordained with the laying on of hands in order to resolve the complaints and restore the joy of the congregation. Why seven men were to be chosen is not specified, but it may be because for Jews this was a number of completeness. It was also associated with the number serving in local Jewish community councils.[2] In any case, seven were chosen.

Who were these seven ordained men who were to serve tables? Were they deacons, or something else? An office is not specified, just as with the apostles, who here are referred to simply by a number, "the twelve." There has been much interesting academic discussion about the identity of the seven. When all factors have been considered, it seems best to understand the ordination in Acts 6 as to an office that would later be called deacon.[3] Although they are not called deacons here, the first readers of Acts may have seen the seven as deacons.[4] This identification of the seven as the first ordained deacons has been the mainline position of the Christian church since the second century.[5] In Acts 6 the young Christian church in

---

2. Haenchen, *Acts of the Apostles*, 263.

3. For those denying that the diaconal office is involved, differing positions have been put forward. For example: "Their office was unique and was not continued in the Church." Barnett, *Diaconate: A Full and Equal Order*, 30. "There is no official or 'deacon' office here. These men take on this assignment to make sure that it is dealt with and no longer remains a problem." Darrell L. Bock, *Acts*, Baker Exegetical Commentary on the New Testament (Grand Rapids: Baker Academic, 2007), 259. Among those who consider Acts 6 as the beginning of the office of deacon is J. B. Lightfoot, *The Christian Ministry*, ed. Philip Edgcumbe Hughes (Wilton, Conn.: Morehouse-Barlow, 1983), 33–35.

4. Haenchen, *Acts of the Apostles*, 262–63. Also see Marshall and Towner, *Commentary on the Pastoral Epistles*, 487.

5. E.g., Irenaeus of Lyons (about AD 135–200) identified Stephen as the first deacon in his *Against Heresies* 3.12.10; 4.15.1, in *The Ante-Nicene Fathers, Vol. 1: The Apostolic Fathers with Justin Martyr and Irenaeus*, ed. Alexander Roberts, James

Jerusalem received men ordained to an official task, or office, with
the responsibility to provide for the poor. As the first and oldest
church and under apostolic leadership, this congregation established
the pattern for others in caring for the poor. Not surprisingly, then,
considering its mandate, this office was later established in other
congregations under the name deacon.

Three main considerations point in the direction of a new office
being established in the Jerusalem church. First, a specific justification was given for this new position—namely, that the apostles
should not give up preaching the Word of God to serve tables (Acts
6:2). Second, an ordination took place. Third, when the apostle
Paul later gives the qualifications for the office of deacon, he obviously assumes its existence. But where did this office come from if
not from the events recorded in Acts 6? The ordination highlighted
in Acts 6 merits a closer look after which the activities of those
ordained will be dealt with.

The Ordination of the Seven

Luke describes the ordination in great detail. Such a careful relay-
ing of events becomes more understandable if a new office is being
inaugurated in the Christian church that was unknown in the Old
Testament. The procedures followed in this first Christian congregation therefore serve as an example for other churches should they
need special people to see to material needs existing among believers. That Luke pays no such attention to the office of elder in the
book of Acts underscores the significance of this event. Elders being
inducted into office are mentioned (Acts 14:23), but no detailed
description of their ordination is recorded in Acts. The elder office
was known in Judaism and, as such, was nothing new. The church
assumed the office as a natural matter of continuity with the one
God had provided His people in the past, and it continued to func-

Donaldson, and A. Cleveland Cox (Buffalo, N.Y.: Christian Literature Company,
1885), 434, 480. See further, Richard I. Pervo, *Acts: A Commentary on the Book of Acts*,
ed. Harold W. Attridge, Hermeneia (Minneapolis: Fortress, 2009), 161n86, 161n87.

tion moving forward. But now a new office was being given to the church, and Luke carefully recorded the event.

The extensive attention given to this ordination argues against the view that the seven are simply appointed as temporary workers to meet current needs.[6] The ordination does, however, support the idea that what became known as the office of deacon was here established. For that reason, when the office of deacon is later mentioned, it is referred to as an established office with no need for any explanation as to its origin or mandate (Phil. 1:1; 1 Tim. 3:8–13).

The twelve—that is the twelve apostles—called together the full number of the community of believers, here referred to as disciples for the first time (Acts 6:2, 7). It is striking that the full number is convened. Depending on how many actually came, that number could have been in the thousands. However, "as the place of meeting is not named, it is an over-hasty conclusion that the whole church could not have assembled all at once."[7] It is important to note that the entire congregation had to participate in finding a solution, even though the problem was with only a part of the congregation. The congregation of Christ is one, united by the Spirit.

The apostles said, "It is not desirable that we should leave the word of God and serve tables. Therefore, brethren, seek out from among you seven men of good reputation, full of the Holy Spirit and wisdom, whom we may appoint over this business; but we will give ourselves continually to prayer and to the ministry of the word" (Acts 6:2–4). The apostles gave leadership. They recognized that the current crisis needed a solution. In order that they would be able to continue to devote themselves to preaching, others must be ordained

---

6. See, e.g., Phillip W. Sell, "The Seven in Acts 6 as a Ministry Team," *Bibliotheca Sacra* 167 (2010): 58–67.

7. Heinrich August Wilhelm Meyer, *Critical and Exegetical Handbook to the Acts of the Apostles*, ed. William P. Dickson, trans. Paton J. Gloag, Critical and Exegetical Commentary on the New Testament (Edinburgh: T&T Clark, 1877), 1:167. Cf. Bradley Blue, "Acts and the House Church," in *The Book of Acts in Its Graeco-Roman Setting*, ed. David W. J. Gill and Conrad Gempf, The Book of Acts in Its First Century Setting (Grand Rapids: Eerdmans, 1994), 136.

to serve tables—that is, to provide food for the body while the
apostles concentrated on providing it for the soul. Also, the twelve
showed leadership by determining the necessary qualifications and
then involving the congregation. Indeed, although the apostles led,
the congregation had to participate and be completely involved.
Unlike with the choosing of Matthias to replace Judas when the lot
was cast between two men (Acts 1:23–26), the congregation now
needed to decide who was to be chosen. The gift of the Holy Spirit
given at Pentecost enabled them to discern the necessary gifts and
to choose the right people. The involvement of the congregation in
the choosing of office-bearers is a principle that is dear to churches
of the Reformation. This principle stands in sharp contrast to hierarchical church structures such as in the Roman Catholic Church,
where the laity is not involved in the election of clergy.

They "chose Stephen, a man full of faith and the Holy Spirit,
and Philip, Prochorus, Nicanor, Timon, Parmenas, and Nicolas, a
proselyte from Antioch" (Acts 6:5). We are not told how the process
of choosing took place. In their collective Spirit-guided wisdom,
the congregation picked seven men with Greek names. Although
some Jews had Greek names (for example, Philip and Andrew), it is
likely that most of those chosen would have been Hellenistic Jews,
thus dispelling any doubts the upset Greek-speaking Jews may have
had about their complaints being handled fairly. Their "own" people
were involved in the process. Picking such men was thus motivated
by an eager desire for "endeavoring to keep the unity of the Spirit in
the bond of peace" in the church (Eph. 4:3).

These men were "set before the apostles; and when they had
prayed, they laid hands on them" (Acts 6:6). From the procedure
followed, it is clear that here we see men being inducted into a special office. It is noteworthy that although the congregation chose the
seven, the apostles, and not the congregation, did the actual induct-
ing into office. Christ gave office-bearers to the church by means of
His apostles in this case, and today He does so by means of His
office-bearers (who form a session or consistory), who involve the
congregation. Those ordained are not responsible to the congre-

gation in the first place but to Christ, the head of the church, as
He acts through the ecclesiastical offices. In this case, the meaning
of the name deacon (*diakonos*), as one who serves as an intermediary or gets something done at the behest of a superior, is quite
appropriate.[8]

The ordination took place with the laying on of hands, just as
in the case of others ordained to special office (Acts 13:3; 1 Tim.
4:14; 2 Tim. 1:6). The apostles were the ones who laid hands on the
seven. The full number of disciples set these men before the apostles, who prayed and laid their hands on them (Acts 6:6). Herewith
they were consecrated for holy service with the acknowledgment by
prayer that God alone could enable them for their office.[9]

The Activities of the Seven

It is noteworthy that Acts 6 does not call these brothers deacons,
which is the main reason there have been questions about whether
they really were deacons. The description of their task is clearly diaconal. Furthermore, the absence of the specific title "deacon" need not
hinder us from recognizing the seven as the first deacons. After all,
in Acts 6 the apostles are not named as such but are simply mentioned as "the twelve," and the newly ordained are similarly referred
to as the seven later, in Acts 21:8.

There is, however, another reason for doubt about whether
the seven were the first deacons. Two of the seven, Stephen and
Philip, later preached (Acts 6:8–15; 8:5). Why would deacons be
preaching? What are we to make of this? We do not know whether
Stephen, full of grace and power, was already doing great wonders
and signs among the people (Acts 6:8) at the time of his election
for diaconal work. We need to bear in mind that there is a logical progression in Luke's account. With Stephen being the first
Christian martyr, it can be expected that his being a deacon and his

---

8. Danker, *Greek-English Lexicon of the New Testament*, 230.

9. On ordination and laying on of hands, see Cornelis Van Dam, *The Elder: Today's
Ministry Rooted in All of Scripture* (Phillipsburg, N.J.: P&R, 2009), 129–34.

subsequent death due to his testimony of Christ would be closely linked in the narration. The text has no clear chronological indicator that tells us how Stephen's defense of the gospel is connected to his work as deacon. At the same time, the setup of the narration may provide a hint that some time had passed. Acts 6:7 is a summary verse coming immediately after the election of the seven, and it concludes a major segment of Luke's narration. Verse 8 takes us to the next major block of Luke's account beginning with Stephen's testifying to the gospel and being brought before the Sanhedrin.[10]

It is clear that the seven were not ordained to preach. The apostles made it clear that there was a division of labor. They would take care of the ministry of the Word of God, and the seven would serve tables (Acts 6:2). At the same time, the congregation wisely chose men who were gifted and capable of proclaiming the gospel. Perhaps these men were already elders or recognized leaders in the church to whom this difficult diaconal task could be delegated. In any case it is clear that Stephen was theologically astute and thus able to serve not only the physical needs of the widows but also to address the spiritual distress they probably endured. With his understanding of the gospel, he would have been able to use his knowledge of Christ's loving concern for the widows (see Luke 4:25–26; 7:11–15) to reassure these vulnerable women of their full inclusion in the community of believers, especially as that was exemplified in the meals of fellowship. The same could be said of Philip, who later became an evangelist. In other words, the ministry of serving tables was more than just providing the physical necessities of life. It was also a means to include those who may have felt marginalized, giving the necessary reassurance that they truly belonged to the communion of saints. Giving such reassurance would have meant ministering

---

10. Philip E. Satterthwaite, "Acts against the Background of Classical Rhetoric," in *The Book of Acts in Its Ancient Literary Setting*, ed. Bruce W. Winter and Andrew D. Clarke, The Book of Acts in Its First Century Setting (Grand Rapids: Eerdmans, 1993), 354–55; D. G. Peterson, *The Acts of the Apostles*, Pillar New Testament Commentary (Grand Rapids: Eerdmans, 2009), 237.

the Word of God to them. Such ministration was not their main task but was subservient to their providing them with what was necessary at the table, and that included the fellowship that comes with eating with others.

Seen from this perspective, Luke's report of Stephen's powerful proclamation and defense of the good news (Acts 6:8–10) shortly after writing about his ordination to serve tables is not entirely surprising or out of place. There is no reason why he, as a gifted member of the church and as one especially endowed by the Spirit, could not hold a diaconal office, with all that was involved, and at the same time publicly defend the gospel against the calumny of the unbelieving Jews. After his arrest by the Jewish authorities, he became the first Christian martyr (Acts 6:10–15; 7:58–60). Also, his death brought an end to the work for which he had been ordained.

Philip also does not appear to have labored long in his diaconal office. After Stephen's death, a great persecution arose against the Jerusalem church, and the Christians were "scattered throughout the regions of Judea and Samaria" (Acts 8:1). But "those who were scattered went everywhere preaching the word" (Acts 8:4). Notice how all Christians are characterized as proclaiming Christ. So why could especially gifted diaconal workers not do the same? Philip evangelized with great effect in Samaria. Miraculous signs and healings accompanied his proclamation (Acts 8:5–13). An angel of the Lord and the Holy Spirit also directed him to the Ethiopian eunuch, and he explained Scripture to him and then baptized him. Philip subsequently preached the gospel in different towns (Acts 8:28–40). Later he is identified as "Philip the evangelist, who was one of the seven" (Acts 21:8).

With the scattering of the church, the diaconal office in Jerusalem as instituted by the apostles is not mentioned again. We later read that when offerings were made for the Jerusalem church, this relief (*diakonia*) was delivered to the elders of that church (Acts 11:29–30). Still, new ground was broken in Jerusalem with the appointment of seven men to serve tables. This reality seems to be reflected in the reference many years later to this group as "the seven"

(Acts 21:8), remembered as the first men specifically appointed for diaconal work.

The Blessing That Followed

The measures taken by the apostles were blessed. They could concentrate on proclaiming the Word of God, and the widows were provided for materially and spiritually. The murmuring stopped, and joy returned to the congregation. With the apostles free to preach and those ordained to serve tables providing for physical and accompanying spiritual needs, the result was that "the word of God spread" (Acts 6:7), which could be translated literally as "the word of God increased." This expression is remarkable. It does not say that the congregation increased but that the word of God did so. This characterization implies that the administration of the word of God played a part along with serving tables.[11] As the word of God spread and increased, the result was that "the number of the disciples multiplied greatly in Jerusalem, and a great many of the priests were obedient to the faith" (Acts 6:7). The word of God was powerful to salvation, sharper than any two-edged sword (Heb. 4:12), working faith in those hearing the gospel (Rom. 10:17).

Christ uses the congregation that experiences the joy of salvation and hears the Word preached to gather others into the flock. We can assume that it was not just the seven who were active. Just as before the appointment of the seven, the members of the congregation undoubtedly continued to show the love and support for each other that had characterized the Pentecost church from the beginning. It was the members of the congregation who broke bread in their homes with glad and generous hearts and had favor with all the people (Acts 2:46–47). It is noteworthy that Luke used the passive when he wrote about the proceeds of what was sold. The passage literally says that "it was distributed to each as any had

---

11. For a connection between waiting on tables and the proclamation of the Word of God, see David W. Pao, "Waiters or Preachers: Acts 6:1–7 and the Lukan Table Fellowship Motif," *Journal of Biblical Literature* 130 (2011): 139–41.

need" (Acts 4:35), implying that the congregation was mobilized in the distribution. We may therefore assume that the seven did not personally do the distributing but would have played a coordinating, helping, and overseeing role to ensure that none was bypassed. The participation of the congregation as a fellowship that shared their resources remained vital. Without it the seven would not have been able to function.[12]

Summary and Conclusions

When complaints arose in the young Jerusalem church because the Grecian widows were being overlooked in the daily distribution of food, the apostles realized that they could not properly devote themselves to prayer and the ministry of the Word as well as to caring for the needy. They proposed that the congregation choose seven godly, Spirit-filled, wise men to provide for the poor. The congregation did so, and the apostles ordained them for this task with prayer and laying on of hands. That hereby a new office was instituted in the church, which became known as deacon, underscores the importance of providing for the indigent in the church. The joy of salvation in Christ and of liberation from the dominion of the evil one must not be threatened in any way, certainly not because of material wants. At least two of the seven who were ordained were capable in administering the Word of God. This shows that the congregation considered such a gift of importance for those entrusted with caring for the needy. Indeed, they were then able not only to give necessary physical provisions but also to address the special spiritual needs of the poor with the comfort of the gospel. The Lord blessed their efforts, and the number of believers grew.

---

12. Herman van Well, *Diaken in de praktijk* (Kampen: Kok, 2009), 39.

CHAPTER 5

The Office of Deacon

The events in the Jerusalem church recorded in Acts 6 had lasting consequences for the Christian church. Although Luke never mentions the office of deacon by name, it is obvious that during the period he covers in Acts, the office was known among the churches. Writing to the Philippians in Greece about AD 62, the apostle Paul mentions the office as if it were a well-known and common reality. He simply addresses his letter "to all the saints in Christ Jesus who are in Philippi, with the bishops [or overseers] and deacons" (Phil. 1:1).[1] About three years later he wrote in some detail to Timothy in Ephesus in Asia Minor about the qualifications necessary to be ordained to the diaconal office (1 Tim. 3:8–13). Thus the diaconal office was found in widely separated geographical locations and over quite a time span.[2]

It is therefore remarkable that we read relatively little about this office as such in the New Testament. The apostle Paul mentions

---

1. In the phrase "overseers and deacons" in Phil. 1:1, the lack of a definite article indicates that these terms are official designations that did not require the article. Heinrich August Wilhelm Meyer, *Critical and Exegetical Handbook to the Epistles to the Philippians and Colossians*, ed. William P. Dickon, trans. John C. Moore (Edinburgh: T&T Clark, 1875), 13.

2. The evidence for the general term *diakonos* referring to a specific office in Phil. 1:1 and 1 Tim. 3:8, 12 is strong since it can be shown that the cognate Greek terms also had a specialized technical usage in the New Testament. See C. E. B. Cranfield, "Diakonia in the New Testament," in *Service in Christ: Essays Presented to Karl Barth on His 80th Birthday*, ed. James I. McCord and T. H. L Parker (Grand Rapids: Eerdmans, 1966), 37–39.

both elders and deacons when he writes Timothy, who is working in
Ephesus (1 Tim. 1:3), but mentions only elders when he addresses
Titus in Crete (Titus 1:5–9). Probably the church in Crete was
not yet fully organized. After all, Titus was left in Crete so that he
could put matters in order and see to the appointment of elders in
every town (Titus 1:5). At such an early stage in the life of a church,
it is possible that any needs arising from poverty or want would
have been addressed by the elders, just as the apostles had done in
Jerusalem until the work became too onerous. In his first missionary journey, the apostle Paul oversaw the appointment of elders but
not deacons (Acts 14:23).[3]

In discussing the office of deacon, we therefore have relatively
little information compared to the eldership. Using the available
information from Scripture, this chapter discusses the requirements
of the office of deacon, the task of the deacon, and the ministries of
the deacon and the Word.

The Requirements of the Office of Deacon

The requirements for the office are found in 1 Timothy 3. It is possible that the gift of helping (1 Cor. 12:28) also has reference to the
diaconal office. Furthermore, the gifts of serving and showing mercy
(Rom. 12:7–8) obviously are relevant for deacons. The qualifications for the offices of elder and deacon as listed in 1 Timothy 3
are similar. Indeed, after those for the elder have been mentioned,
the qualifications for the deacon are introduced with the words,
"Likewise deacons must be" (1 Tim. 3:8), after which the criteria for
deacon follow. One important difference is that deacons do not need
to have the gift of teaching.

The previous chapter defended the position that those
ordained in Acts 6 were essentially the first deacons. The necessary
qualifications for the office given in Acts 6 will therefore need to

---

3. See further, George W. Knight III, *The Pastoral Epistles*, The New International
Greek Testament Commentary (Grand Rapids: Eerdmans, 1992), 175.

be considered, along with the requirements for a deacon set forth in 1 Timothy 3. In a sense the apostle Paul's teaching in his letter to Timothy fills out the more general qualifications mentioned in Acts 6.

Acts 6 points out the following requirements: "of good reputation, full of the Holy Spirit and wisdom" (v. 3). First Timothy 3:8–12 reads: "Likewise deacons must be reverent, not double-tongued, not given to much wine, not greedy for money, holding the mystery of the faith with a pure conscience. But let these also first be tested; then let them serve as deacons, being found blameless. Likewise, their wives must be reverent, not slanderers, temperate, faithful in all things. Let deacons be the husbands of one wife, ruling their children and their own houses well." Let's take a closer look at these requirements.

Of Good Repute and Full of the Spirit and Wisdom

The apostles determined that those who were to be entrusted with serving tables had to be men of good reputation (Acts 6:3; cf. 16:2; 22:12). It was vital for the young Christian church that those with leading positions be well spoken of and also known outside the church as men of sound repute. A good name is of great value (Prov. 22:1), and the believers needed good names if the church of Christ and the gospel were to have credibility. It would not do if a deacon was well spoken of within the church but someone outside the community of believers could bring charges against him. It would hurt the reputation of the entire community of believers for having such a person as a leader. The devil would seize the opportunity to hurt the cause of Christ. Not surprisingly, therefore, the elder also had to have "a good testimony among those who are outside, lest he fall into reproach and the snare of the devil" (1 Tim. 3:7). The devil will do anything to bring an office-bearer and the church into disrepute. Leaders in the church must be of irrefutable good repute.

Such a sound reputation would include characteristics such as honesty, integrity, and holiness of life. Leaders in the church were to be individuals who could be counted on. Although they would manage the resources of the church for the benefit of the poor, they would not abuse their position for self-enrichment. They would be known as those with a high moral standing and would be respected on that account.

The good reputation of such men had to be accompanied with being full of the Holy Spirit and of wisdom (Acts 6:3). Being full of the Spirit meant that their whole life was controlled and guided by the Spirit within them (see Luke 4:1). The Spirit of wisdom occupied them entirely (Isa. 11:2; Eph. 1:17). So one result of the Spirit's indwelling and guidance would be the wisdom and insight that would enable the seven to act prudently with the complicated scenarios that could arise in meeting the needs of the poor without antagonizing those who might be thinking that they were being shortchanged.

The wisdom given by the Spirit is not, however, restricted to such practical issues. This wisdom would also enable them to minister to the spiritual needs of the indigent. Relieving want and poverty is never just a matter of supplying some physical necessities. Spiritual needs must be met also.

Worthy of Respect
After detailing the requirements for the office of elder, the apostle Paul tells Timothy which qualifications are necessary for the office of deacon. Like the elders, a deacon must be worthy of respect. The NKJV translates that deacons must be "reverent" (1 Tim. 3:8). The original term (*semnos*) denotes dignified and serious conduct that demands respect, so the word could also be rendered "worthy of respect" (NIV). Such respect is garnered in part by not being "double-tongued, not given to much wine, not greedy for money" (1 Tim. 3:8).

"Double-tongued" is "saying one thing and meaning another, or the habit of saying one thing to one person, another to another."[4]

---

4. Marshall and Towner, *Commentary on the Pastoral Epistles*, 489.

Being insincere and deceitful in this way would threaten the credibility and stability of the fellowship and is rightfully condemned elsewhere as well (see Prov. 11:3). The tongue is a powerful instrument that can easily disrupt a fellowship. Since a deacon can be intimately involved in people's lives, it is imperative that his speech be free from gossip and lies and be edifying and holy. He must in all circumstances control his tongue (see James 3).

Being addicted to much wine would show lack of self-control and hurt the reputation not only of the deacon but of the church as a whole. It would be conduct more in tune with the world of sin than with God's demands. It would be intolerable for a deacon to be addicted when he has to set an example and lead others away from having a compulsive need for alcohol. Deacons are to work so that people are free in the joy of redemption and not captivated by the things of this world, including liquor, money, and belongings. Diaconal leadership in this area is so important that this requirement for soberness and self-discipline is repeated for church leaders elsewhere (1 Tim. 3:3; Titus 1:7).

It therefore follows that deacons, as those entrusted with material resources to help the needy, must not be greedy for dishonest gain. Greed was a characteristic of false teachers (1 Tim. 6:3–10; Titus 1:11), but those holding office in the church must distance themselves from that (1 Tim. 3:3; Titus 1:7, 11; 1 Peter 5:2). The work of a deacon can expose him to temptation with respect to money, but he must be prepared to maintain his integrity at all costs. He must work for the well-being of the congregation and not for selfish ends. The way diaconal work is organized can minimize any temptation in this regard; for example, at least two deacons should always be present when offerings are counted and careful records need to be kept.

Of course everyone should avoid sins of greed and dishonest gain (Titus 2:3), but these sins are especially harmful when committed by church leaders, who have a high office to perform and must set an example for others to follow. When church leaders fall into the sins forbidden here, the church will lose the world's respect, and its mission will be severely compromised, if not made impossible.

Holding the Mystery of the Faith

The upright conduct of the deacon can be sustained only by remaining faithful to the faith—that is, the content of the faith. Deacons must be those "holding the mystery of the faith with a pure conscience" (1 Tim. 3:9). "The mystery of the faith" does not refer to some esoteric secret knowledge known only to the initiates who have been ushered into the inner sanctum of the Christian faith. Rather, this mystery refers to God's plan of salvation, which must be revealed and believed, for it is inaccessible to human reason, which considers it to be foolishness (1 Cor. 1:23–31). The content of this mystery is therefore the promised Christ (Col. 1:26–27; 2:2; 1 Tim. 3:16), who can now be proclaimed (Rom. 16:25; 1 Cor. 4:1).

When deacons are enjoined to hold the mystery of the faith with a clear conscience, they are thus expected to embrace the gospel and live wholeheartedly according to it. The gospel sets the standard for Christian living, and a deacon's life must reflect that. This is only possible if a person's conscience is fed and guided by the gospel through the working of the Spirit. Then there will be no discrepancy between his verbal profession of faith and his lifestyle. Any discord between words and actions is disastrous for the diaconal task, for it exposes the deacon as a hypocrite and undermines his credibility.

Although deacons do not need to be able to teach, they must be capable of encouraging with the gospel those to whom they minister and give sound counsel to the needy. For this reason as well they are required to hold to the mystery of the faith with a clear conscience. Their understanding of Scripture and God's will for godly living must be sound. To put it differently, a deacon must be spiritually mature.

Let Them Be Tested First

Paul instructs Timothy, "Let these also first be tested; then let them serve as deacons, being found blameless" (1 Tim. 3:10). Testing is necessary, and although the nature of the testing is not specified, the context indicates that a deacon's life and reputation must be examined so that he is proved to be blameless. This examination must occur before he is ordained. Testing does not mean that a deacon is at first put on probation.

Like the elders (1 Tim. 3:6), deacons must not be recent converts but must have a credible track record of blameless Christian living, and no one should be able to bring a justifiable charge against their life and conduct (1 Tim. 3:2). The congregation can test candidates by using the stated qualifications for the diaconal office. Indeed, the impersonal passive form of the verb for "testing" in the original may suggest that the whole community should be involved in evaluating prospective candidates.[5] This procedure would accord with the involvement of the congregation in the appointment of the seven in Acts 6:3.

Women Worthy of Respect

Suddenly we find qualifications for women in the context of the diaconal office. The first word in the Greek of 1 Timothy 3:11 is literally "women." There is disagreement whether these women are the wives of deacons (NKJV) or whether they are "women in this office" (Revised English Bible [REB]). Taking all factors into consideration, it seems best to understand these women as the wives of deacons. Contextually it seems to make the most sense since with this verse and the next we are entering the domestic sphere, an important area with respect to the necessary qualifications for a deacon. The next chapter will address the identity of the women in more detail.

The women—that is, the wives of the deacons—must be "reverent." This is the same term used in regard to the deacons in

---

5. Marshall and Towner, *Commentary on the Pastoral Epistles*, 492.

1 Timothy 3:8 and here also can be understood as worthy of respect. Indeed, all the qualifications for the wives of deacons virtually match the qualities desired in their husbands: "likewise"—that is, just like the deacons—they must be "reverent, not slanderers, temperate, faithful in all things" (1 Tim. 3:11). Being slanderous, a sin of the tongue, would be roughly analogous to being "double-tongued" (1 Tim. 3:8), with its deceit and lack of honesty. Being "temperate" or "sober-minded" (ESV) can literally recall "not given to much wine" (1 Tim. 3:8) or be an exact parallel (in the original language) with the being "temperate" or "sober-minded" expected of an overseer (1 Tim. 3:2). "Faithful in all things" indicates being loyal to Christ in every aspect of life and therefore echoes the requirement of "holding the mystery of the faith with a pure conscience" (1 Tim. 3:9).

When we consider these qualifications and the type of work that a deacon does, we can understand why these stipulations are included for the wife of the deacon and not for those of the elder.[6] Because deacons were entrusted with caring for the poor, who often included widows and women who were ill, it is likely that the wives of deacons would assist their husbands, under diaconal supervision, in meeting some of the needs that could best be met by a woman, especially if the congregation had no female deacons (which is discussed in the next chapter). By engaging in this work, a deacon's wife would undoubtedly become privy to much intimate knowledge of those who are being assisted. It was therefore imperative that she be dignified, not a gossip, sober-minded, and faithful in all things. With these qualifications, the wife of a deacon would be a great help for her husband and not be a hindrance or distraction from his work. Indeed, she would be an excellent support for his diaconal office.

---

6. For what follows, see Peter Y. De Jong, *The Ministry of Mercy for Today* (Grand Rapids: Baker, 1961), 97–98.

Husband of One Wife

In 1 Timothy 3:12, the apostle turns to the deacons again, mentioning the office by name: "Let deacons be the husbands of one wife, ruling their children and their own houses well." As office-bearers in Christ's service, deacons must set a good example for the congregation.

What does being "husbands of one wife" mean? The NKJV rendering "husbands of one wife" is literal, but there is some ambiguity. Does it mean that unmarried men are excluded from being a deacon? Other translations interpret the original literal text differently. The New American Standard Bible (NASB) has "husbands of only one wife," which suggests that the point is to forbid polygamy. On the other hand the New Revised Standard Version (NRSV) has the translation "married only once," a qualification that would forbid remarriage should one's spouse die. Today's New International Version (TNIV) has "faithful to his wife." In evaluating these interpretations, the following can be noted. Monogamy was the general rule, and a prohibition of polygamy would seem to have been unnecessary. To exclude unmarried men from the office would contradict the apostolic endorsement of celibacy under certain conditions (1 Cor. 7:32–40). Remarriage was not prohibited, and indeed, widows were encouraged to remarry (1 Cor. 7:8–9, 39–40; 1 Tim. 5:14). So the best interpretation is that marital faithfulness to one's wife is in view. To qualify for the office of deacon, a man had to be faithful to his wife and not break the marriage vow.[7]

Also, deacons must be "ruling their children and their own houses well" (1 Tim. 3:12). Like the overseers (1 Tim. 3:4), deacons are to give biblical spiritual leadership to their children and to their household. One result should be that their children are not open to an outsider's charge of being wild and disobedient (cf. Titus 1:6). Because "houses" or "households" are mentioned

---

7. For the above, see in more detail Philip H. Towner, *The Letters to Timothy and Titus*, New International Commentary on the New Testament (Grand Rapids: Eerdmans, 2006), 250–51.

along with children, the stipulation here "exceeds issues of parent-
ing and husbanding to include management of slaves, property,
business interests, and even maintenance of important relationships with benefactors/patrons or clients."[8] Clearly deacons must
show the necessary leadership qualities and the ability to take care
of all their financial affairs in an exemplary manner before being
entrusted with the care of the needy.

So as Christ's servant, a deacon must be someone who is faithful as a husband and thus reflects Christ and His love for the church
in his marriage (Eph. 5:22–32). Also, he must be experienced in
administering his family and household so that he can show the
love of Christ in the practical ways necessary when assisting the
indigent in managing their financial affairs and providing monetary
support. He must not be out for himself but should have a mind-
set of serving others.

As an encouragement, the apostle Paul notes two rewards for
faithful service: "Those who have served well as deacons obtain for
themselves a good standing and great boldness in the faith which
is in Christ Jesus" (1 Tim. 3:13). They will be highly regarded by
the congregation. Such high respect should not be the motivation
for becoming a deacon, but it can function as an encouragement to
dedicate oneself to the service of God's people. Furthermore, they
will have "great boldness in the faith which is in Christ Jesus." This
boldness, or confidence, can refer to the increasing assurance that
the deacon has of his faith in Christ,[9] but the vocabulary Paul uses
probably indicates that the first reference is to "a freedom to speak
that carries with it the nuances of confidence and boldness."[10] In
other words, the deacon will receive the ability to speak openly and
frankly in exhorting and comforting those to whom he ministers.

---

8. Towner, *Timothy and Titus*, 254. For more on "ruling their children and their
own houses well," including practical implications for today, see Van Dam, *The Elder*,
141–42.

9. Towner, *Timothy and Titus*, 268.

10. Knight, *Pastoral Epistles*, 174.

Those who are suffering need to experience the power of God's Word. This confident speaking does not come from the deacon himself but from his faith in Christ Jesus, who came to serve (Mark 10:45) and who equips His office-bearers (see Philem. 8).[11]

In conclusion, it is striking that Scripture highlights the spiritual qualifications needed for the diaconal office. In today's society, criteria such as education, innovation, and an energetic image are often at the top of what is considered a desirable professional profile. God's Word directs us to look for wisdom in the practical management of life at home, maturity in the faith, integrity in all dealings, a good public reputation, and a selfless commitment to service.[12] The reason for such qualifications becomes evident when we consider the task of the deacon in general.

The Task of the Deacon

In chapter 4 we noted that a key reason for appointing men to minister at the tables was to protect the joy of the fellowship of believers. When the legitimate needs of the saints were not being met, there were complaints, indicating that there was unhappiness. Fractures were developing in the community. To address this situation, the seven were chosen. Their task, in a nutshell, was to see to it that there were no needy so that everyone could rejoice and celebrate the salvation and freedom given by Christ. They could employ others to make sure that all needs were taken care of. These seven and the deacons that followed, like other office-bearers, were given to the church "for the equipping of the saints for the work of ministry [*diakonia*], for the edifying of the body of Christ" (Eph. 4:12). Deacons are to safeguard the communal joy of the fellowship of believers so that everyone in the church can function according to the God-given responsibilities each has been given. Several responsibilities

---

11. Herman Ridderbos, *De pastorale brieven*, Commentaar op het Nieuwe Testament (Kampen: Kok, 1967), 100. For more on this passage, see chapter 13 of this book under the heading "Blessings for the Deacon."

12. See Towner, *Timothy and Titus*, 271–72.

derive from this key duty. Deacons need to focus on the poor and needy, on the lonely and sick—indeed, on all those whose joy in the Lord is being challenged by their circumstances. Also, deacons need to direct their attention to those members of the congregation who have the necessary gifts that can help restore joy in those who are losing it. In other words, deacons are to see to it that the appropriate resources, talents, and attributes found in the congregation are put to use to alleviate suffering and want. Finally, deacons have the responsibility to mobilize the members of the church to diaconal service both within and outside the congregation. After all, believers were to do good to all people (Gal. 6:10). We will be returning to this matter in chapter 12.

At this point, though, we suggest that since the Jerusalem church had favor with all the people and many joined it (Acts 2:47; 6:7), possibly the believers were already considerate of needs outside their fellowship. Deacons can mobilize the gifts of the congregation by sensitizing the body of believers to present needs and acting as a resource, support, and coordination center for any service. Wisdom and tact are required to define needs, and knowledge and expertise are necessary to follow through on ministering to the needy.

In light of this, it may not be so surprising that apart from Acts 6, there is no specific list of duties for those who are entrusted with caring for the poor and needy. While we might expect such a list to accompany the qualifications for deacons in 1 Timothy 3, apparently it was not necessary, because those duties have already been sufficiently described for us in Acts 6.[13]

It is possible, however, to conclude from the qualifications listed in 1 Timothy 3 that the main duty of deacons is to provide for the needy. Deacons must be respected men of integrity, not greedy for dishonest gain (1 Tim. 3:8), and this indicates that they can be entrusted with gathering and distributing money in an honest and equitable manner. Because they must "[hold] the mystery

---

13. J. Kamphuis, *Altijd met goed accoord: opstellen uit de jaren 1959–1969* (Amsterdam: Ton Bolland, 1973), 127.

of the faith with a pure conscience" (1 Tim. 3:9), they need to have a mature faith, for the diaconal task can and often should be accompanied by the administration of the Word for the spiritual encouragement of the needy. Deacons' wives must "be reverent, not slanderers, temperate, faithful in all things" (1 Tim. 3:11); they should be sensitive as they help the indigent and take care to protect confidentiality. Since deacons must be good managers of the funds entrusted to them, they need to have proven the ability to manage their own households (1 Tim. 3:12). All the necessary qualifications for office reflect the deacon's primary task of helping the poor in an effective, confidential, and spiritual way. Having considered the basic task of deacons, we will consider how their office relates to that of the elders.

The Ministry of the Deacon and the Ministry of the Word

It is important to note that both the preaching of the Word of God and the serving of tables are characterized in Acts 6 as ministries of service. The literal sense of the vocabulary used makes that clear. The apostles devote themselves to "the ministry [*diakonia*] of the word" (v. 4), while the seven were to "serve [*diakoneō*] tables" (v. 2). This manner of referring to two different tasks, preaching and helping the needy, shows that they have the common identity of a service performed for God and His people; elders and deacons should, therefore, labor in concert with each other. Their ministries to the flock complement each other. Not surprisingly then, these two offices are mentioned together (Phil. 1:1; 1 Tim. 3:1–13).[14] There is a certain unity between these offices. After all, they both address the one need for the gospel to be administered by word and deed because of the reality of sin and its effect on human life (see 1 Peter 4:10–11).

---

14. "The deacons are linked with the bishops and mentioned after them. At the time of this epistle there are thus two co-ordinated offices." Beyer, "diakoneō, diakonia, diakonos," 2:89.

At the same time, these were two separate ministries. There is no evidence in Scripture that the seven were appointed to an office midway between elder and deacon. The seven in Acts 6 were specifically appointed to do diaconal work. Furthermore, both the ministry of the Word and the ministry to serve tables are ministries of the risen and ascended Christ. This reality has at least three important implications.

First, Jesus as ascended Lord raised up men full of the Spirit to carry on diaconal work. As those ordained to holy office, they are responsible to Christ, who taught by word and deed what it means to serve and minister to the poor and needy (Matt. 20:28; John 13:4–15; Rom. 15:8).[15] Christ in heaven continues His work on earth through the deacons, who represent Him in His care for the needy (see John 13:15). At the beginning of Acts, Luke set his account in the context of what Christ had done and what He will continue to do by the coming baptism of the Holy Spirit (Acts 1:1–5). The ordination to the office for diaconal ministry is not just a human affair. It is part of Christ's continuing work. He gives offices to the church (Eph. 4:11–12).Through those whose office it is to minister to the indigent, the risen Christ shows Himself to be the compassionate king described in Psalm 72 who defends the cause of the poor among the people and gives deliverance to the children of the needy:

> He will deliver the needy when he cries,
> The poor also, and him who has no helper.
> He will spare the poor and needy. (vv. 12–13)

Also through the deacons, Christ nourishes and cherishes His body, the church (Eph. 5:29). Deacons are therefore those who facilitate the distribution of the riches and gifts of Christ to those in need in the congregation.

---

15. In this connection it is also significant that the Greek root for the word translated "ministry" has the sense of serving as an intermediary or doing something at the behest of a superior, in this case Christ. Danker, *Greek-English Lexicon of the New Testament*, 230.

Second, the deacon should not be characterized as being a servant of the overseer, who labors in the ministry of the Word. Both the deacon and the overseer are in the service of Christ and are responsible to Him. Christ gave deacons the necessary gifts, not to serve an overseer but to serve Christ for the good of the congregation (see Rom. 12:4–8; 1 Corinthians 12).[16] It is noteworthy that when the apostle Paul and Timothy address the believers in Philippi, they stress that they are servants of Christ. They address the leaders as a unit ("the bishops [or overseers] and deacons")—not as those set over the congregation but as those who serve together with the church. The emphasis is that all are under Christ and in the service of the gospel (Phil. 1:1, 27).[17] It is unfortunate that soon after the apostolic age, deacons were made subject to the overseers. This was the beginning of what eventually became a Roman Catholic hierarchy of ecclesiastical offices.[18]

Third, the two ministries should labor in cooperation with each other. The diaconal office should underline the significance of the ministry of the Word by accompanying their giving of practical assistance with words of encouragement and comfort of the gospel of the risen Christ. In giving assistance to those in need, deacons should emphasize the importance of regularly attending public worship, where the living Word is proclaimed. "Man shall not live by bread alone, but by every word that proceeds from the mouth of God" (Matt. 4:4). In turn, the pulpit should support the work of the deacons by stimulating and encouraging the congregation to supply them with the necessary funds. The apostle Paul correctly

---

16. The subordination of the deacon to the overseer is often suggested. See, e.g., John N. Collins, *Deacons and the Church: Making Connections between the Old and the New* (Harrisburg, Pa.: Morehouse, 2002), 89–93; and Towner, *Timothy and Titus*, 261. But see, e.g., Herman Ridderbos, *Paul: An Outline of His Theology*, trans. John Richard de Witt (Grand Rapids: Eerdmans, 1975), 447; and Ridderbos, *De pastorale brieven*, 97. Also see Elsie Anne McKee, *John Calvin on the Diaconate and Liturgical Almsgiving*, Travaux d'Humanisme et Renaissance (Geneva: Librairie Droz, 1984), 180–82.

17. G. Walter Hansen, *The Letter to the Philippians*, The Pillar New Testament Commentary (Grand Rapids: Eerdmans, 2009), 42.

18. Burtchaell, *From Synagogue to Church*, 319. Also see chapter 7 of this book.

saw that it was within his duty as bearer of the Word of God to remind his hearers of the privilege of providing for the needy (1 Cor. 16:1–4; 2 Corinthians 8–9). He personally brought gifts for the poor from the churches to Jerusalem (Acts 24:17; Rom. 15:26). The preaching should make members of the congregation aware of what it means to show mercy and compassion to each other and so equip and encourage them to use their gifts in diaconal service to each other (Eph. 4:12).

Summary and Conclusions

One who qualifies for the office of deacon is of good repute, has a track record of a solid Christian life, and exhibits the fruit of the Spirit, as does his wife. His family is well managed, and his faith is integrated into his whole walk of life. Unlike the elder, he is not required to have the gift of teaching, but as one who has fully embraced the Christian faith, he will be able to encourage those to whom he ministers with the gospel.

These qualifications serve the deacon well in his task of ensuring that there are no unmet needs in the communion of saints. At the core of his duty is the responsibility to ensure that the joy of redemption is shared by all by making certain that the poor and needy are helped and that no one lives uncomforted in the communion of saints.

The diaconal ministry is separate from the elders' ministry of the Word, but both are ministries of the risen and ascended Christ. He continues His work on earth through the labors of the deacons. Since both elders and deacons are in Christ's service, the office of deacon is not lower than that of the elder. They should therefore cooperate in every possible way for the building up of the church.

CHAPTER 6

Are Female Deacons Biblical?

A topic frequently discussed in our time is whether the church should open the office of deacon to women. What does the New Testament tell us? Does it mandate ordaining females to the office? This chapter discusses these and related issues, taking into consideration all the relevant biblical evidence. Chapter 8 will look at the involvement of women in helping the needy in the history of the church and will also delve further into some of the issues raised in the light of current discussion. We will now consider the following passages in the chronological order in which they were written: Romans 16:1–2; 1 Timothy 3:11; and 1 Timothy 5:9–10. We will also look at office and authority and the service of women.

Romans 16:1–2

Near the end of his letter to the Christians in Rome, the apostle Paul writes: "I commend to you Phoebe our sister, who is a servant [*diakonos*] of the church in Cenchrea, that you may receive her in the Lord in a manner worthy of the saints, and assist her in whatever business she has need of you; for indeed she has been a helper [*prostatis*] of many and of myself also" (Rom. 16:1–2). This passage raises the question of whether *diakonos* should be translated as "deacon" as in the 2011 NIV (a change from the 1984 version, which translated it "servant"). There has been considerable debate about this issue since it could justify opening the office of deacon to the female members of the church. The intent here is to list the different factors for interpreting this passage and then see if we can come to a clear resolution.

First, it is necessary to take a closer look at the term "deacon" (*diakonos*). We have seen in chapter 5 that the word can refer to the one holding the office of deacon. This is clear from Philippians 1:1, where the mention of one office, overseer, is immediately followed by the mention of another office, deacon. In 1 Timothy 3:8–13 specific qualifications are given for someone who is a deacon, again clearly referring to the office, which has certain requirements. The question is whether it also refers to the office of deacon when used in conjunction with Phoebe. It is not easy to answer this question simply on the basis of the vocabulary used because the term *diakonos* is, as such, employed many times in the New Testament in the sense of identifying someone "who is busy with something in a manner that is of assistance to someone."[1] It can then be translated as "servant" or "helper." This general usage of the word therefore covers a multitude of possibilities, ranging from simply being the subordinate and being of a serving mind-set (Matt. 20:26) to being servants of a king (Matt. 22:13) or of Christ in a general sense (Rom. 15:8).

Phoebe's being designated as *diakonos* has therefore been interpreted in different ways. She was a servant of the church (ESV) or a deacon of the church (NRSV), or she held some other position of service, for example, as an unordained helper, a messenger, or even as an official pastor.[2] The context is decisive for determining which meaning of *diakonos* was intended. So what is the context of Romans 16? There are various interpretations of the passage, none of which, due to the lack of sufficient detail, presents an airtight case.

One interpretation suggests that Phoebe was "neither a 'servant' nor a 'deacon' of the church at Cenchrea, but its 'emissary,' 'envoy,'

---

1. Danker, *Greek-English Lexicon of the New Testament*, 231.
2. For a useful overview of opinions, see Agan, "Deacons, Deaconesses," 94–95.

or 'spokesman.'"[3] The immediate context gives no indication that Phoebe is coming in any diaconal capacity. The apostle commends her to the Roman Christians as "Phoebe our sister, who is a [*diakonos*] of the church in Cenchrea, that you may receive her in the Lord in a manner worthy of the saints, and assist her in whatever business she has need of you." Here was a lady coming from one of the ports of Corinth, Cenchrea, as a messenger from the church there. Because she probably would not be known in Rome, she would need a commendation with the request that she be given every necessary assistance. It is quite possible that she came with Paul's letter to the Romans[4] and that, whatever other business she may have had, she represented the Corinthian church with the request that the Roman church support Paul's mission to Spain (Rom. 15:17–24, 28).[5]

Other interpreters factor in more consciously that Phoebe "has been a helper [*prostatis*] of many and of myself [Paul] also" (Rom. 16:2). Such a helper, or patron, as the term can also be translated, was a person who provided material support to her beneficiaries.[6] In a harbor city like Cenchrea, a Christian patron such as Phoebe would have looked after many foreign visitors, including visiting Christians. Her being such a patron made her an obvious candidate for the position of deacon in the church. The two responsibilities would have fit together naturally. Furthermore, the Greek grammar seems to indicate a recognized position of responsibility within the congregation.[7] The position of *diakonos* "could be understood

3. Agan, "Deacons, Deaconesses," 106; and Collins, Diakonia: *Re-Interpreting the Ancient Sources*, 224–25.

4. As indicated by some of the ancient subscriptions to the letter. Thomas R. Schreiner, *Romans*, Baker Exegetical Commentary on the New Testament (Grand Rapids: Baker, 1998), 786.

5. Agan, "Deacons, Deaconesses," 106.

6. Gregory R. Perry, "Phoebe of Cenchreae and 'Women' of Ephesus: 'Deacons' in the Earliest Churches," *Presbyterion* 36, no. 1 (2010): 15.

7. James D. G. Dunn, *Romans 9–16*, Word Biblical Commentary (Dallas: Word, 1998), 286–87, 289.

simply in terms of a regular pattern of service undertaken by Phoebe on behalf of her local church."[8]

Others, however, see evidence of an established diaconal office with Phoebe as deacon. Reasons for this include the conviction that the women in 1 Timothy 3:11 are deacons. We will be coming to that passage shortly. Furthermore, the designation "deacon of the church in Cenchrea" suggests that Phoebe served officially as a deacon, for this is the only occasion in which the term *diakonos* is linked with a particular local church. And finally, the use of the masculine term *diakonos* suggests that the office is intended.[9] While it is possible that *diakonos* has reference to an office, the terminology and the grammar of the Greek in Romans 16:1 are such that it is impossible to dogmatically hold that the passage is referring to the office of deacon rather than an unordained activity in the service of the congregation. Furthermore, nowhere else does the New Testament speak of a woman serving in the office of deacon.[10]

In conclusion, there is not enough information in Romans 16:1–2 to insist on one specific understanding of this passage. However, we can draw a general conclusion. The passage does indicate that Phoebe held some kind of position of service that appears to have been recognized by the church to which she belonged. But the available evidence is not sufficient to conclude that Phoebe was an ordained deacon. The evidence could also suggest that she was a

---

8. Dunn, *Romans 9–16*, 286.

9. C. E. B. Cranfield, *A Critical and Exegetical Commentary on the Epistle to the Romans*, International Critical Commentary (London: T&T Clark, 1979), 2:781; and Schreiner, *Romans*, 787.

10. For this line of reasoning, see, e.g., Herman Ridderbos, *Aan de Romeinen*, Commentaar Op Het Nieuwe Testament (Kampen: Kok, 1959), 341–42; John Murray, *The Epistle to the Romans*, NICOT (1965; repr., Grand Rapids: Eerdmans, 1968), 2:226. J. van Bruggen, acknowledging that the Greek text indicates a position in the church, does not want to use the term "deacon" (considered to be an ordained position), but prefers the term "functionary." See J. van Bruggen, "Een vrouw waar geen woorden voor zijn (Romeinen 16,1–2)," in *Ambt en aktualiteit*, F. H. Folkerts, P. Houtman, and P. W. van de Kamp (Haarlem: Vijlbrief, 1992), 51–55; and Jacob van Bruggen, *Ambten in de apostolische kerk: een exegetisch mozaïek* (Kampen: Kok, 1984), 114–18.

messenger, or one appointed for special service in the congregation, or a well-respected volunteer who devoted much of her time and resources to help wherever help was needed.

1 Timothy 3:11

In his first letter to Timothy, the apostle Paul mentions the necessary qualifications for deacons. As he does so, he writes that "likewise, their wives [literally, women] must be reverent, not slanderers, temperate, faithful in all things" (1 Tim. 3:11). He then continues to list more qualifications, such as that deacons should also be the husband of one wife (v. 12). The question is how the word "women" in verse 11 should be understood. Are these female deacons, or are they the wives of the deacons whose qualifications are listed? It should be noted at the outset that the Greek term in question can mean either "women" or "wives."[11]

Those who favor interpreting "women" as female deacons point out that just as verse 8 moved the discussion from one distinct group (the overseers) to another (the deacons) by using the expression "likewise," so now with that same expression we can expect verse 11 to move the discussion to another task in the church—namely, that of female deacons. However, it is as plausible to say that just as the deacons are to be dignified and not double-tongued, so also their wives are to be dignified and not slanderous. We need not understand any further implied meaning with the term "likewise."[12] That this is probably the case is evident, because if one interprets the women as deacons, then the renewed reference to male deacons and their qualifications in verse 12 becomes an afterthought. But this can hardly be the case, for the qualifications in verse 12 are so

---

11. Danker, *Greek-English Lexicon of the New Testament*, 209. For the discussion that follows, I have benefited from the following. In favor of identifying the women as deacons: Marshall and Towner, *Commentary on the Pastoral Epistles*, 492–95; and Towner, *Timothy and Titus*, 265–67. In favor of identifying the women as wives of deacons: William D. Mounce, *Pastoral Epistles*, Word Biblical Commentary (Dallas: Word, 2000), 202–5; and Knight, *Pastoral Epistles*, 170–73.

12. E.g., the New English Bible (NEB) renders "their wives, equally, must be."

important that they are repeated elsewhere as well for the office of elder (1 Tim. 3:2, 4; Titus 1:6). Since the original text can literally mean "wives" and not "deacons," we could have expected the apostle to specifically mention that he had female deacons in mind. After all, if such had been the case, the sudden change of topic from the qualifications of a male deacon to a female one would have necessitated some explanation or at least a clear transition marker. Since it is somewhat unnatural to change topics twice in the short span of two verses (vv. 11–12) without obviously moving to a new subject, it seems best to maintain the unity of verses 11 and 12 by translating "women" as "wives."

Another argument in favor of seeing the "women" as deacons is that we could expect that the apostle would have written "their women" (rather than simply "the women") if the wives of deacons were meant. However, as noted, the term "women" in Greek can mean "wives," so the possessive pronoun is not necessary. The meaning "wife" for "woman" is found in the next verse (1 Tim. 3:12) and elsewhere in 1 Timothy (3:2; 5:9). We should not impose our modern preference for using a possessive pronoun on the style of an ancient writer.

The solution that best fits the context is that these women were the wives of the deacons with whom 2 Timothy 3:8–13 is concerned. After he mentions the women, the apostle continues with the qualifications necessary for the deacon. It would seem most natural, then, to assume that these women are closely connected to the deacons and are indeed their spouses. The mention of wives in verse 11 quite naturally leads the apostle to note in the next verse that deacons "be the husbands of one wife."

The qualifications of the deacon's wife are important. A deacon would be most effective in his work if he had a wife who would be supportive by exhibiting the type of characteristics that the apostle mentions: "reverent, not slanderers, temperate, faithful in all things" (1 Tim. 3:11). It is therefore not surprising that the apostle would mention such a wife as a qualification for being a deacon. As spouses of deacons, these women would be involved in some way with their husband's work of diaconal service by being their assistants, especially in helping other women. The character of the wives was not a factor in the qualifications for an overseer because the nature of his work was different and would not involve his wife. For that reason, their wives are not mentioned among the qualifications necessary for the office of overseer (1 Tim. 3:1–7).

The identity of the "women" as wives of deacons is further supported because their marital status and faithfulness are not mentioned, a consideration that plays an important part in the qualifications of both overseers and deacons (1 Tim. 3:2, 12; cf. 5:9). As wives of deacons, such mention was not necessary. This requirement is covered by their being the wife of a deacon.

A further indication that the women of verse 11 were not deacons is that there is no requirement for their being tested first, as is the case with the deacon (1 Tim. 3:10). They do need to be as committed and serious as their husbands in controlling their tongues and being faithful. But, since the reference is to the wife of the deacon and not to a female deacon, a period of testing is irrelevant.

In conclusion, the evidence points to the "women" in 1 Timothy 3:11 being the wives of the deacons. There is no convincing basis for considering them to be deacons and holding an official ordained office in the church. It is therefore not surprising that virtually all major English Bible translations prefer the translation of either "women" or "wives" rather than deacons or something similar.[13] It is possible that the apostle's somewhat ambiguous reference to women is meant to suggest that other women with qualities similar to the deacons' wives might be active in supporting the deacons' work.[14]

---

13. Translations that render "women" include the Revised Standard Version (RSV), the NASB, the NIV 2011 (the 1984 NIV had "their wives"); translations with "their wives" include the King James Version (KJV), the ESV, the Good News Bible, the NET, and the NEB, but the subsequent REB renders "women in this office." The 2001 edition of the TNIV had "women who are deacons," but the 2005 revision rendered "women." The interpretation "wives of deacons" has been dominant in the Western church, especially after the Reformation. See McKee, *John Calvin on the Diaconate*, 162–63.

14. Patrick Fairbairn, *The Pastoral Epistles* (Edinburgh: T&T Clark, 1874), 150–51.

1 Timothy 5:9–10

In 1 Timothy 5, the apostle Paul mentions the enrollment of widows. Who were these widows? What place did they have in the
church? To answer such questions, we must pay careful attention
to the context. The apostle begins by using the singular form of the
imperative and thus addressing Timothy: "Honor widows who are
really widows" (1 Tim. 5:3). In other words, the church has to provide for those widows who are really in need. They are those who
are "left alone" (v. 5)—that is, have no family to care for them. Those
with children or grandchildren are to be provided for by them. The
church is not to be burdened in such cases (vv. 4, 8, 16). In this way
the needs of all the widows are to be met by the family and by the
church for those without family to provide for them. And so the
long-standing duty of God's people to provide for needy widows is
met. After making this important point, the apostle mentions the
enrollment of widows (vv. 9–10). These widows are therefore to
be distinguished from the needy widows he just mentioned. Then,
after dealing with the enrolled widows, in order to emphasize a
point made earlier, he repeats that the family of a widow has the
duty to take care of its own (v. 16).[15]

The apostle broaches a new topic when he writes: "Do not let
a widow under sixty years old be taken into the number, and not
unless she has been the wife of one man, well reported for good
works: if she has brought up children, if she has lodged strangers,
if she has washed the saints' feet, if she has relieved the afflicted, if
she has diligently followed every good work" (vv. 9–10). This new
directive, which concerns being taken into the number, or being
enrolled, has nothing to do with explaining which widows should
be supported. That has already been done in the previous verses
(3–7). Now a specific group of widows is in view, and only those
with the specific qualifications that the apostle mentions are part of
this group. Such a widow had to be at least sixty years old. Younger

---

15. Ridderbos, *De pastorale brieven*, 127–31.

widows were not suitable for a number of reasons, such as wanting to marry again and, as a consequence, "having condemnation because they have cast off their first faith" (v. 12). The "first faith," or "previous pledge" (NASB), appears to refer to a commitment that enrolled widows had to make that could not be taken lightly.[16]

What was that commitment? As we just saw, it would have included their pledge not to remarry. But what, positively speaking, were the widows enrolled for? Judging from the criteria that determined whether a woman would be part of the enrolled-widow group, it would seem that these widows were expected to continue the service of love and good works in the congregation for which they justly had the reputation. Furthermore, to qualify as an enrolled widow, they would have had to have raised children. It is possible that this raising of children included taking care of orphans. As opportunity arose, they would therefore be expected, as enrolled widows and according to their circumstances, to care for children who had no parents. As experienced mothers and wives, they would be able to help young mothers with godly advice as well (see Titus 2:3–5). Also, in order to be part of the enrolled group, they would have had to have shown hospitality, especially to fellow believers, by washing their feet and taking care of the afflicted. Being enrolled as an elderly widow would require that they go on showing such hospitality. In summary, these widows would provide help in the service of love wherever possible.[17]

They were therefore enrolled for a special and dedicated service of love from which there was to be no distraction, such as a new marriage. What then was involved in their being enrolled? Did it mean that they had a special office in the church, or was it some-

---

16. Ridderbos, *De pastorale brieven*, 134. The Greek term in question (*pistis*) can also be rendered "faith," and then the point would be that these widows should not depart from the faith as younger widows might do (1 Tim. 5:12 ESV). See, e.g., Marshall and Towner, *Commentary on the Pastoral Epistles*, 599–600. This position is less persuasive.

17. Ridderbos, *De pastorale brieven*, 131–32; J. N. D. Kelly, *The Pastoral Epistles*, Black's New Testament Commentary (London: Continuum, 1963), 116–17.

thing less official, even though they were acknowledged as a special diaconal or serving group in the church? There is no immediate and obvious answer to this question, but the evidence can best be interpreted as pointing to a special unordained diaconal widow group in the church.

The arguments that have been used to conclude that an ordained office was in view include the following. The original verb translated "be taken into the number" can be understood as "selected for membership in a group" as, for example, recruiting soldiers. First Timothy 5:9 would then refer to being recruited for a special purpose or task with the meaning, "Let a widow be enrolled for a special task in the church." Such a special task is then understood as an ordained office. Also, the qualification for being an enrolled widow included "[having] been the wife of one man" (v. 9). This qualification is similar to what was required of the offices of elder and deacon (1 Tim. 3:2, 12; Titus 1:6), so the conclusion is drawn that a special office must be in view here also. Furthermore, it is adduced that since the apostle lists qualifications for an overseer in 1 Timothy 3:1–7, for deacons in verses 8 through 13, and discusses elders in 1 Timothy 5:17–19, it would appear likely that when enrolled widows are discussed in the midst of all this, they must likewise be church officials.[18] None of these arguments, however, are conclusive.

On the other hand, there are considerations that go against the notion of a special office of serving widows. The verb translated as "be taken into the number" or "enrolled" is not specific for being enrolled into an office. It simply indicates making a selection for membership in a group.[19] Furthermore, the text does not speak of election and appointment to office. It was not necessary for these widows to be ordained to an ecclesiastical office in order to do their

---

18. For the arguments, see Ridderbos, *De pastorale brieven*, 131–33; Bonnie Bowman Thurston, *The Widows: A Women's Ministry in the Early Church* (Minneapolis: Fortress, 1989), 44–55; also see van Bruggen, *Ambten in de apostolische kerk*, 129–40.

19. Danker, *Greek-English Lexicon of the New Testament*, 520.

diaconal work. Perhaps Dorcas and "all the widows" in Joppa (Acts 9:39) were such a group of serving widows.[20]

Since it is prudent not to draw conclusions that go further than the biblical data would justify, we must conclude that there is not sufficient evidence in 1 Timothy 5 that the enrolled widows had a special ordained diaconal office in the church. It is interesting to note that this conclusion is consistent with the lack of evidence for an ordained office of widows in the early Christian church.[21] Also, we can conclude that there was a group of unordained widows who were enrolled and thus had a certain public profile for the purpose of serving the church with acts of charity and love. It should, how-ever, be noted that there is no indication in Scripture that there is a unique office of widow that would oblige the church today to enroll such women for special diaconal service in the congregation.[22] Unlike with the office of deacon, there is no clear indication that a new office was being instituted (see Acts 6). But there is nothing to prevent the church from following the model of the ancient Ephe-sian church, where Timothy gave leadership and direction, of using widows for diaconal service.

Office and Authority

Other considerations suggest that women should not be ordained as deacons. It is striking that when the widows were neglected in the daily distribution in Jerusalem, the twelve asked the disciples to pick out seven men of good repute. These were duly ordained (Acts 6:1–6). Although those in need of help were women, the twelve asked for men to minister to them in an official capacity. If women qualified to be ordained in the office of ministering to the needy, this would have been the ideal place to introduce them

---

20. John R. W. Stott, *Guard the Truth: The Message of 1 Timothy and Titus*, The Bible Speaks Today (Downers Grove, Ill.: InterVarsity, 1996), 132.

21. Cf. Marshall and Towner, *Commentary on the Pastoral Epistles*, 575–78. For further discussion, see chapter 8.

22. As is the case with the office of elder: "Appoint elders in every city" (Titus 1:5).

since widows were involved. Restricting the office of deacon to men, therefore, appears to have been a matter of principle.

Furthermore, these men were to be appointed to this duty (Acts 6:3). The verb "to appoint" (*kathistēmi*) means "to assign someone a position of authority, put in charge."[23] The seven had authoritative oversight of caring for the poor. They oversaw the distribution and in that sense were overseers. Would women serving as deacons then—having oversight of caring for the poor—violate the rule of 1 Timothy 2:12, where Paul writes, "I do not permit a woman to teach or to have authority over a man"? As the context of this chapter makes clear, this injunction refers in the first place to a church assembled for public worship, because the apostle speaks of corporate prayer and issues related to that, such as how men and women should behave. In that context he prohibits women from teaching and exercising authority over men (cf. 1 Cor. 14:34–35). However, the matter of exercising authority over men is a principle that goes beyond the worship service (cf. 1 Tim. 2:13–15). The apostle Paul indicates the broader context of this prohibition in 1 Timothy 3:14–15: "These things I write to you, though I hope to come to you shortly; but if I am delayed, I write so that you may know how you ought to conduct yourself in the house of God, which is the church of the living God, the pillar and ground of the truth." So the question is whether the principle of forbidding women to have authority over men in the church would exclude them from the office of deacon. In other words, does the office of deacon involve the exercising of authority over fellow church members?[24]

---

23. Danker, *Greek-English Lexicon of the New Testament*, 492.

24. For the relevant context being broader than worship, see, e.g., Douglas Moo, "What Does It Mean Not to Teach or Have Authority over Men? 1 Timothy 2:11–12," in *Recovering Biblical Manhood and Womanhood: A Response to Evangelical Feminism*, ed. John Piper and Wayne Grudem (Wheaton, Ill.: Crossway, 1991), 180, 186–88. For what follows, I am indebted to Ian Davis et al., "Report of the Committee on Women in Church Office," in *Minutes of the Fifty-Fifth General Assembly of the Orthodox Presbyterian Church* (Philadelphia: The Orthodox Presbyterian Church, 1988), 333–34. This includes an appendix by Richard B. Gaffin Jr., one of the authors of the report.

We must note the following in answering that question. First, when the apostle Paul gives the criteria for the elders and deacons in 1 Timothy 3, he does so in a way that shows strong parallels between these offices. After he has dealt with the office of elder, he begins to describe the qualifications for the office of deacon in verse 8 by writing "likewise." This terminology indicates that there are similarities in the qualifications for both elder and deacon. There is a certain bond between them reflected in the fact that they are discussed together and elsewhere mentioned together (Phil. 1:1). So if women are excluded from the one office, they can be expected to be excluded from the other as well. Second, the qualifications of both elder and deacon assume that the holder of the office is a male. The requirements of both elder and deacon include their being the husband of one wife (1 Tim. 3:2, 12). Third, the deacon must, like the elder, exhibit leadership by managing his children and household well (1 Tim. 3:4–5, 12). The verb used (*proistēmi*) speaks of managing, leading, and ruling. Thus, the comment in verse 5 ("If a man does not know how to rule his own house, how will he take care of the church of God") also applies to the deacon (cf. v. 12). Leadership, and the exercise of authority that comes with it, is as important for the office of deacon as it is for that of elder. It is with a view to that authority that the apostle's admonition to respect holds true also for deacons: "recognize those who labor among you, and are over you (*proistēmi*) in the Lord" (1 Thess. 5:12). Fourth, it is clear from the first three points that the structure of authority in the home and in the household of God mirror each other. Not surprisingly, then, the apostle's directives in 1 Timothy 2 and 3 are framed in terms of "how you ought to conduct yourself in the house of God, which is the church" (1 Tim. 3:15). This is the topic sentence for 1 Timothy 2:1–3:16, as a 1988 Orthodox Presbyterian Church committee report on women in church office explains: "The location of this paragraph sentence, occurring immediately after the qualifications for deacons, confirms that the family-church analogy, as that analogy involves the exclusion of women from special office, still controls the argument to that point. The exercise of authority

over men prohibited to women in 2:11 [sic], apparently, includes
the office of deacon as well as that of overseer."[25]

Considering how closely authority is linked to ecclesiastical
office, it is not surprising that there is no evidence that women were
ordained to the office of deacon in New Testament times. This pattern held for the postapostolic period. As we will see in chapter 8,
there is no indication that women were ordained to the office of
deacon during that period.

The Service of Women

Even though women were not in an ordained office, they were still
active in ministering and providing for believers' needs. There is
plenty of evidence that this was indeed the case. We have already
seen that Phoebe held some kind of a recognized position of service in the church (Rom. 16:1–2). Deacons' wives were apparently
involved in an unofficial capacity in the diaconal work of their husbands and thus had to meet certain requirements (1 Tim. 3:11).
Furthermore, that certain widows were enrolled suggests that they
were committed to doing specific diaconal tasks of service within
the church. Elsewhere it is evident that women's contributions were
valued and appreciated.

Luke mentions that at one point in Christ's ministry, women
accompanied him. They were "certain women who had been healed
of evil spirits and infirmities—Mary called Magdalene, out of
whom had come seven demons, and Joanna the wife of Chuza,
Herod's steward, and Susanna, and many others who provided for
Him from their substance" (Luke 8:2–3). The verb *diakoneō* is used
to describe their provision, which is not further specified but probably involved financially supporting Jesus's itinerant ministry. The
description of the women suggests that they ministered to the Lord
out of love and gratitude for His work. We are not told how often
such women accompanied Jesus, but it is clear that He benefited

25. Davis et al., "Report of the Committee," 334; also see 353–55.

from their service on other occasions as well (Luke 10:40; John 12:2). Women witnessed His crucifixion, "among whom were Mary Magdalene, Mary the mother of James the Less and of Joses, and Salome, who also followed Him and ministered [*diakoneō*] to Him when He was in Galilee, and many other women who came up with Him to Jerusalem" (Mark 15:40–41). However, although women served the Lord and ministered to Him in different ways, He never appointed a woman to a leadership position. The twelve disciples who were to be the apostles and leaders of the church were all male (Matt. 10:1–4; Acts 2:14; 6:2), and they requested male candidates to take care of the needy in Jerusalem (Acts 6:3).

Along with these examples, there are other indications that women ministered and served the church, using their specific gifts. Every believer, male and female, has gifts given by the God of grace, not just those holding a special office. Dorcas was a woman who was "full of good works and charitable deeds" (Acts 9:36). She is an example of a woman who used her gift to minister to others in a practical way, but she was not the only one. The apostle exhorted the entire congregation at Rome, male and female: "having then gifts differing according to the grace that is given to us, let us use them: if...ministry, let us use it in our ministering [*diakonia*]...he who shows mercy, with cheerfulness" (Rom. 12:6–8). As the apostle reminds the Corinthian Christians, "The manifestation of the Spirit is given to each one for the profit of all" (1 Cor. 12:7). The church is a body with many members, and as with a human body, no part can be disregarded. All need to contribute to the common good and function in harmony (1 Cor. 12:12–30). There should be no division in the body of Christ, but the members should show the same care for each other. If one suffers, all suffer together; if one is honored, all rejoice together (1 Cor. 12:25–26).

Summary and Conclusions

A close look at the passages that have been used to defend the ordination of women to the office of deacon has shown that there is little basis for certainty that such ordination took place. The evidence adduced is too meager and so open to different interpretations that one simply cannot say with any justifiable conviction that women were ordained to diaconal office. Indeed, the contrary is true. The weight of the evidence points to their not being ordained.

In the case of Phoebe, servant (*diakonos*) of the church at Cenchrea (Rom. 16:1–2), different explanations as to her identity as *diakonos* are plausible, and it is impossible to insist that she was an ordained official. In 1 Timothy 3:11, the "women" and their necessary attributes included in a discussion on the qualifications for deacons leaves reasonable doubt that they could have been female deacons. Indeed, a most convincing case can be made that they are the wives of the deacons about whom this part of Scripture is dealing. As for widows sixty years old or more who were to be enrolled (1 Tim. 5:9–10), the evidence suggests they were being enlisted for special tasks in the church to help needy members, but there is no indication that they were ordained to the diaconal office. Another consideration that supports arguments against women as deacons is that holding the office would mean having authority in diaconal matters over the male members of the church. Such a position would be against the rule of 1 Timothy 2:12.

PART THREE

The Office of Deacon in the History of the Church

CHAPTER 7

The Testimony of the Early Church and the Heritage of the Reformation

In order to appreciate more adequately the current position of the deacon and the discussions surrounding the duties of this office, we need to step back and briefly note some of the highlights of how the diaconate has been understood and implemented in the history of the church. Also, this chapter will endeavor to evaluate key historical developments in the light of Scripture as understood in the preceding chapters.[1] We will now consider the testimony of the early and medieval church and the heritage of the Reformation.

The Early and Medieval Church

The events of Acts 6 formed an important starting point for understanding the office. As far as we can tell, the early Christian church regarded the appointment of the seven in Acts 6 as the beginning of the office of deacon. Irenaeus of Lyons (c. 130–200) wrote matter-of-factly that the apostles ordained these men to the diaconate and subsequently identified Stephen as a deacon.[2] This understanding of Acts 6 did not seem to be a controversial point that required

---

1. For more details on this period than can be given in this chapter, see, e.g., Jeannine E. Olson, *Deacons and Deaconesses through the Centuries*, rev. ed. (Saint Louis, Mo.: Concordia, 2005), 28–105; Barnett, *Diaconate: A Full and Equal Order*, 43–131; C. T. Dimont, "Charity, Almsgiving (Christian)," in *Encyclopaedia of Religion and Ethics*, ed. James Hastings (Edinburgh: T&T Clark, 1908–1927), 3:382–85; and J. van Lonkhuijzen, "De geschiedenis van het diaconaat," in *Het diaconaat*, ed. P. Biesterveld, J. van Lonkhijzen, and R. J. W. Rudolph (Hilversum: J. H. Witzel, 1907), 36–104.

2. Irenaeus, *Against Heresies* 1.26.3; 3.12.10; 4.15.1.

a defense. Subsequent authorities in the early church also saw the seven as deacons.[3] As could be expected, the deacons had responsibilities for caring for the poor, widows, and orphans, although they sometimes betrayed the trust placed in them.[4]

Consistent with the participation of the entire congregation in choosing the seven in Acts 6, the *Didache* or *Teaching of the Twelve Apostles* (which may date from as early as 70–80) instructed the congregation to be involved in the election of deacons. "Select, then, for yourselves bishops and deacons worthy of the Lord."[5] This selection was to take place according to the biblical criteria found in 1 Timothy 3. Indeed, these norms were upheld, for example, by Polycarp, a personal disciple of the apostle John; Athanasius of Alexandria (c. 295–373); John Chrysostom (c. 347–407); and others.[6] The biblical involvement of the congregation in the election process meant that in the first period of the church, those chosen to the office of deacon were selected by people who knew their strengths and weaknesses. It also meant that the diaconate and the congregation it served had a close and meaningful relationship.

The congregations that chose their deacons were also directly engaged in helping the poor, sick, and disabled and in providing the deacons with the necessary means to minister to those in need. Inspired by Matthew 25:31–46, the early church fed the hungry, gave drink to the thirsty, welcomed strangers, clothed the naked, and visited the sick and the imprisoned. They also buried the dead

---

3. See, e.g., Francis Martin and Evan Smith, eds., *Acts*, Ancient Christian Commentary on Scripture (Downers Grove, Ill.: InterVarsity, 2006), 70–71.

4. *The Shepherd of Hermas*, Similitude 9.26.2. Carolyn Osiek, *Shepherd of Hermas: A Commentary*, ed. Helmut Koester, Hermeneia (Minneapolis: Fortress, 1999), 249.

5. *Didache* 15.1. K. Niederwimmer and H. W. Attridge, *The Didache: A Commentary*, Hermeneia (Minneapolis: Fortress, 1998), 200 and 53 for views on the date of the *Didache*. See also G. W. H. Lampe, "Diakonia in the Early Church," in *Service in Christ: Essays Presented to Karl Barth on His 80th Birthday*, ed. James I. McCord and T. H. L. Parker (Grand Rapids: Eerdmans, 1966), 61.

6. See Peter Gorday, ed., *Colossians, 1–2 Thessalonians, 1–2 Timothy, Titus, Philemon*, Ancient Christian Commentary on Scripture (Downers Grove, Ill.: InterVarsity, 2000), 174–76.

and had compassion on widows and orphans. With these expressions of love, Christians brought much joy and encouragement into the lives of many, including those outside the fellowship of the church. Indeed, the non-Christian world was astounded by the love shown to those less fortunate in their own midst, whom they easily neglected.[7] For example, when a pestilence broke out during the persecution under Emperor Gallus (c. 252), the pagans abandoned their sick and dead for fear of contagion, but the Christians, who were being persecuted, took care of the sick of their enemies and buried their dead as well. Christians showed the same love to non-Christians who were suffering from poverty, despite the hostility shown to the church. More instances of such Christian charity can be given. The love of Christians, even for those who hated them, was preached by their deeds.[8]

The deacon was regarded as a representative of Christ. As Ignatius of Antioch put it in the second century, the deacons are "entrusted with the service of Jesus Christ," and "Let everyone respect the deacons as Jesus Christ."[9] Polycarp wrote in a similar vein: "Be subject to the presbyters and deacons as to God and Christ." Also, he described the deacons as "ministers of God and of Christ, not of humans."[10] One implication of this view of the office of deacon is that it is not subordinate to another ecclesiastical office, a view consistent with that found in the New Testament, as

---

7. Helen Rhee, *Loving the Poor, Saving the Rich: Wealth, Poverty, and Early Christian Formation* (Grand Rapids: Baker Academic, 2012), 107–27.

8. Rhee, *Loving the Poor*, 128–31; Philip Schaff, *Ante-Nicene Christianity A.D. 100–325*, vol. 2 of *History of the Christian Church*, 3rd ed. (Grand Rapids: Eerdmans, 1910), 375–76; and van Lonkhuijzen, "De geschiedenis van het diaconaat," 80–83.

9. See, respectively, *Ignatius to the Magnesians* 6.1; and *Ignatius to the Trallians* 3.1; William R. Schoedel and Helmut Koester, *Ignatius of Antioch: A Commentary on the Letters of Ignatius of Antioch*, Hermeneia (Philadelphia: Fortress, 1985), 112, 140.

10. *Polycarp to the Philippians* 5.2–3, in Bart D. Ehrman, ed. and trans., *The Apostolic Fathers, Volume 1*, Loeb Classical Library (Cambridge, Mass.: Harvard University Press, 2003), 338–41.

we have seen in chapter 5. Ministerial order was not conceived of at this time in terms of status or rank, but in terms of function.[11]

Change came, however, as the church moved away from apostolic times. In the second century already there was a tendency to centralization with an ecclesiastical hierarchy as well as the notion that the deacon should be the servant of the bishop. Part of this development may have been because the church centralized funds in order to meet the challenges of ministering to widespread poverty, which plagued society especially in the third century. Furthermore, the toleration of Christianity in 313 and Constantine's favoring the church meant that the Christian faith was becoming the official religion of the Roman Empire. When the church became a state church, the centralization of power was inevitable, and by the fourth century, ecclesiastical hierarchy was clearly entrenched. The Council of Nicea (325) decreed in canon 18, "Let the deacons keep within their proper bounds, knowing that they are the ministers of the bishop and inferior to the presbyters."[12] The result was that care for the poor was organized by bishops, and deacons lost their diaconal function and became preoccupied with liturgical and other tasks. Indeed, with the transition of the Lord's Supper into the Mass, the offering of Christ, the bishop was the high priest, the presbyters were the priests, and the deacons were the Levites, or helpers.[13]

With the growth of hierarchy, the congregation no longer participated in the election of deacons and was excluded from the entire process leading to the ordination of men to the diaconal office. And as the congregation lost its input into the diaconate, it also lost its primary place in meeting the needs of the poor. The diaconal office basically ceased to function as the primary official

---

11. Barnett, *Diaconate: A Full and Equal Order*, 50–52.

12. J. Stevenson, ed., *A New Eusebius: Documents Illustrative of the History of the Church to A.D. 337*, rev. W. H. Frend (*London*: SPCK, 1987), 343. Also see Lampe, "Diakonia in the Early Church," 57–58, 61–62.

13. Jaap van Klinken, *Diakonia: Mutual Helping with Justice and Compassion* (Grand Rapids: Eerdmans, 1989), 62; also Rhee, *Loving the Poor*, 139–51.

means of alleviating poverty in the church. It became a stepping-stone, an apprenticeship, toward the priesthood.

This development did not mean that the poor were neglected, but they were no longer the first concern of the deacon or of the congregation. Instead, Christian benevolence was channeled through the bishop, who was expected to give freely of his revenues.[14] By the time of Emperor Julian in the fourth century, hospitals and houses of refuge were founded to provide for the helpless—not only the sick but also orphans, widows, the aged, and strangers who had no place to go. These establishments were at times supported by the state, but they later became the sole responsibility of the church and operated under the oversight of bishops. Many of these institutions eventually became independent. In any case, the office of deacon and the official participation of the congregation no longer functioned in a biblical way in caring for the poor.

Another important degeneration away from scriptural norms was the growing belief in the meritorious nature of giving to the needy. The idea that relieving poverty offered atoning value had deep roots in the early church. Already, Polycarp had written, "Giving to charity frees a person from death."[15] During subsequent centuries, the biblical basis for giving to the poor, love for one's neighbor, was gradually replaced with the motivation of saving one's soul. This also led to the belief that giving to the needy could atone for the sins of those who had already died, thus shortening their stay in purgatory. By the Middle Ages, the chief motive for giving to the poor was to gain entrance to eternal life.

All through the Middle Ages until the time of the Reformation, the office of deacon ceased to function in any biblical way. Although

---

14. For legal reasons, bequests made to the church ended up as the wealth of the bishop. He was master over the funds. See Peter Brown, *Through the Eye of a Needle: Wealth, the Fall of Rome, and the Making of Christianity in the West, 350–550 AD* (Princeton, N.J.: Princeton University Press, 2012), 487–88.

15. *Polycarp to the Philippians* 10.2 (quoting Tobit 4:10; 12:9); in a similar vein, *Didache* 4.6; Ehrman, *Apostolic Fathers*, 346–47, 424–25; also see Lampe, "Diakonia in the Early Church," 53–54; and Rhee, *Loving the Poor*, 73–102.

caring for the poor continued to be an important responsibility of the bishop, the exercise of charity "was mostly the fruit of private initiative: generous donors of every rank and station, monasteries and religious orders, commons, and lay brotherhoods."[16] This was the time when orders such as the Knights Hospitallers were founded and established hospitals. These facilities provided help for a wide range of needs: the sick of course, but also the destitute, blind, and hungry could find refuge there. It is not surprising that they were sometimes called "Hostel of God" (*Hôtel-Dieu*). Another institution that helped the poor was the monastery, which was set up with high ideals of self-denial so that its resources could go for the support of the less fortunate: the poverty-stricken, sick, and hungry. Also, the guilds, associations of craftsmen, assisted those in need. All these institutions did much good in meeting the many needs of the indigent.

An important impetus for all this charitable activity, however, was the belief that giving to the poor was one of the most effective meritorious works that one could do. This meant that, apart from notable exceptions, for many donors the chief purpose of charity was earning eternal life. On the whole it did not really matter who might be at the receiving end, but it was important that as many as possible were helped. After all, those who received assistance were expected to pray for the salvation of the souls of those who aided them. There was thus little incentive to try to eradicate poverty, and the number of beggars grew. Indeed, being a poor beggar was often considered a positive Christian ideal. Furthermore, those with some money could "pay" the less fortunate to pray for their eternal well-being and, in the process, earn credit with God. Not surprisingly, the best interests of the needy were usually not a priority, and

16. G. Barrois, "On Medieval Charities," in *Service in Christ: Essays Presented to Karl Barth on His 80th Birthday*, ed. James I. McCord and T. H. L. Parker (Grand Rapids: Eerdmans, 1966), 66. For what follows on medieval times, see Olson, *Deacons and Deaconesses*, 63–92; van Lonkhuijzen, "De geschiedenis van het diaconaat," 87–104; and Dimont, "Charity, Almsgiving (Christian)," 384–85.

aid was often given haphazardly and without careful planning. As a consequence, in spite of the great wealth of the church and of many private individuals, poverty and beggary flourished. With the deacon and the congregation no longer officially ministering to the poor, the diaconal ministry of the church was ready for reformation.

The Heritage of the Reformation

The Reformation of the sixteenth century brought about enormous change. There are especially three areas in which the consequences of the Reformation were profound for the office of deacon. First, the proclamation of the gospel that a person is righteous before God by faith alone and not by good works took away the rationale of self-interest that maintained a beggar class so that donors could receive prayers in exchange for their good works. A Christian must give to the poor to be sure, but only out of love for God and neighbor and not out of self-interest.

Second, the Reformation rejected beggary as a positive Christian ideal as well as the monastic aspiration of the contemplative life and doing good works. The Reformers taught that a person's daily calling is just as godly and noble a task as any office in the church. Every occupation, if done in humble obedience to God, is pleasing to Him and is of great value. The combined effect of understanding the futility of earning salvation by good works and work as a noble calling from God undermined beggary and had positive economic consequences.[17]

Third, with respect to ecclesiastical offices, the Reformation had a renewed biblical vision for the office of deacon and worked to restore that office to its original task of helping the poor. No longer was the diaconate to be a servant of the bishop and a stepping-stone to the priesthood. The deacon had his own office from God

---

17. See, e.g., James Atkinson, "Diakonia at the Time of the Reformation," in *Service in Christ: Essays Presented to Karl Barth on His 80th Birthday*, ed. James I. McCord and T. H. L. Parker (Grand Rapids: Eerdmans, 1966), 80–85. Also see McKee, *John Calvin on the Diaconate*, 99–100.

that he had to fulfill. It was restoring the deacon to his original calling that proved to be the most difficult. Although Luther wanted deacons to function on the model of Acts 6, it was the civil authorities who ended up organizing relief for the poor.[18] The same happened in Huldrych Zwingli's city, Zurich. Even Martin Bucer in Strasbourg and John Calvin in Geneva were unable to restore the diaconal office to its rightful biblical place in the congregation because government took on the role of providing for the needy. It was especially Calvin, however, who led the way to eventually restoring the diaconate according to the biblical model.[19] Since Calvin's thinking on the diaconal office had enormous impact both on the Continent and in the English-speaking world, we will consider it at this point.

John Calvin

In agreement with the early church and other Reformers such as Luther and Bucer, Calvin, in his commentary on Acts 6 (1552), understood the seven to refer to the first deacons. They are an example for us today. In the first edition of his *Institutes* (1536), he wrote with reference to Acts 6: "Would that the church today had such deacons."[20] The only other passage he cited in this edition to

---

18. Olson, *Deacons and Deaconesses*, 107–11, 177.

19. Olson, *Deacons and Deaconesses*, 118–29. Although Bucer influenced Calvin's thinking on the diaconate while he lived in Strasbourg from 1538 to 1541, Calvin eliminated many of the liturgical functions that Bucer had assigned to the deacons. Glenn S. Sunshine, "Geneva Meets Rome: The Development of the French Reformed Diaconate," *Sixteenth Century Journal* 26 (1995): 331–32. For the dominant government role in Geneva and the very limited sense that the deacon was an ecclesiastical office, see Herman A. Speelman, *Calvin and the Independence of the Church*, trans. Albert Gootjes, Reformed Historical Theology (Göttingen: Vandenhoeck & Ruprecht, 2014), 118–22.

20. For Luther, see "The Babylonian Captivity of the Church (1520)," in *Luther's Works: Word and Sacrament II*, ed. Jaroslav Jan Pelikan, Hilton C. Oswald, and Helmut T. Lehmann (Philadelphia: Fortress, 1999), 36: 116; for Martin Bucer, see *De regno Christi*, in Wilhelm Pauck, ed., *Melanchton and Bucer*, Library of Christian Classics (Philadelphia: Westminster, 1969), 183, 289, 307; also see Willem van't Spijker, *The Ecclesiastical Offices in the Thought of Martin Bucer*, trans. John Vriend and Lyle D. Bierma, Studies in Medieval and Reformation Thought (Leiden: E. J. Brill, 1996), 434 ; for Calvin, *Institutes*

justify the diaconate as an office ministering to the poor rather than assisting the priest liturgically was 1 Timothy 3:8–12.

Later, Calvin distinguished between two diaconal functions: "of providing what is necessary for the poor, and of devoting care to their attention." He made this distinction in his 1540 commentary on Romans 12:8, which reads in part: "He that gives, let him do it with simplicity;... he that shows mercy, with cheerfulness."[21] He subsequently mentioned, with some hesitation, "two distinct grades" of deacons in his *Institutes* (4.3.9) from the 1543 edition on. There he explained Romans 12:8 thus: "Since it is certain that Paul is speaking of the public office of the church, there must have been two distinct grades. Unless my judgment deceive me, in the first clause he designates the deacons who distribute the alms. But the second refers to those who had devoted themselves to the care of the poor and sick." Then instead of referring to 1 Timothy 3 as he had in the first edition of the *Institutes*, he substantiated his twofold understanding of the diaconal office by saying that those deacons who visit the poor and sick are "the widows whom Paul mentions to Timothy" (1 Tim. 5:9–10). He then added: "Women could fill no other public office than to devote themselves to the care of the poor." It appears that Calvin's twofold diaconal office was "a logical way to relate the ecclesiastical administration of Acts 6:1–6 with the women chosen in 1 Tim. 5:3–10 to care for the poor and sick." In this way Calvin could accommodate the fact that a woman, Phoebe, was called a deacon in Romans 16:1.[22]

---

of the Christian Religion [1536], trans. and annotated by Ford Lewis Battles (Atlanta: John Knox, 1975), 235. Unless otherwise noted, quotations from Calvin's *Institutes* are from *Institutes of the Christian Religion*, ed. John T. McNeill, trans. Ford Lewis Battles, Library of Christian Classics (Philadelphia: Westminster, 1960).

21. John Calvin, *The Epistles of Paul the Apostle to the Romans and to the Thessalonians*, ed. D. W. Torrance and T. F. Torrance, trans. Ross Mackenzie, Calvin's Commentaries (Grand Rapids: Eerdmans, 1960), 270. The translation of Romans 12:8 is as found in the McNeill edition of the *Institutes* (4.3.9).

22. McKee, *John Calvin on the Diaconate*, 200; also see Elsie Anne McKee, "Calvin's Exegesis of Romans 12:8—Social, Accidental, or Theological?," *Calvin Theological Journal* 23 (1988): 11–18. In his commentary on Romans 12:8, Calvin also mentioned

Calvin maintained this distinction of two kinds of deacons in his Ecclesiastical Ordinances, which the General Council of Geneva promulgated in 1541. Much of the diaconal work and social welfare in Geneva was centered on the general hospital, and the two kinds of deacons Calvin described neatly fit into the roles of the procurators and the hospitallers of the city hospital. He wrote, "The one deputed to receive, dispense and hold goods for the poor, not only daily alms, but also possessions, rents and pensions; the other to tend and care for the sick and administer allowances to the poor."[23] As the number of indigent increased due to the influx of impoverished refugees, special funds were established for these foreigners, and those who administered them were called deacons.

These special diaconal funds were used for a wide variety of needs. With respect to the French Fund, financed by gifts that came from a variety of resources outside Geneva, "the money was used for the poor, but it also sent books and pastors into France and paid a man to transcribe Calvin's sermons as he preached, a project that was hoped would raise money for the poor through their eventual sale."[24] It is interesting to note that under Bucer, who influenced Calvin's thinking significantly, diaconal assistance was given for a

---

widows showing mercy in the context of diaconal care. With respect to the widows of 1 Timothy 5:9, Calvin stated, "These widows had a church office, as we see by the last chapter to the Romans, where he commends a widow, whom he calls, minister of the church of Cenchrea." John Calvin, *Sermons on the Epistles to Timothy and Titus*, 16th–17th Century Facsimile Editions (1579; repr., Edinburgh: Banner of Truth, 1983), 475 (the spelling has been updated).

23. John Calvin, "Draft Ecclesiastical Ordinances," in *Calvin: Theological Treatises*, ed. J. K. S. Reid, The Library of Christian Classics: Ichthus Edition (Philadelphia: Westminster, 1954), 64. On the role of the hospital in Geneva and the unlikeliness of Calvin's interpretation being a case of socially induced eisegesis, see, respectively, McKee, *John Calvin on the Diaconate*, 106–8, 126–27, and 197–200. Cf. Robert M. Kingdon, "Calvin's Ideas about the Diaconate: Social or Theological in Origin?," in *Piety, Politics, and Ethics: Reformation Studies in Honor of George Wolfgang Forell*, ed. Carter Lindberg (Kirksville, Mo.: Sixteenth Century Journal Publishers, 1984), 167–80.

24. Olson, *Deacons and Deaconesses*, 128. Also see McKee, *John Calvin on the Diaconate*, 109–13. For a detailed account of the French Fund, see Jeannine E. Olson, *Calvin and Social Welfare: Deacons and the Bourse Française* (Selinsgrove, Pa.: Associated University Press, 1989).

wide range of needs. Besides satisfying the obvious needs of those stricken with poverty, such as food, clothing, and shelter, deacons, according to Bucer, should give assistance, for example, to a promising student so that he could study, to a poor girl so that she had a dowry and could get married, or to an enterprising and capable individual so that he could start his own business.[25]

Consistent with the ecclesiastical framework in which Calvin worked, he connected offerings for the poor with the worship service. It is probable that Calvin's Strasbourg liturgy provided for alms to be collected as a token of gratitude when celebrating the Lord's Supper. Calvin believed that no one was to appear before God empty-handed (see Deut. 16:16). Indeed, he was convinced that "no meeting of the church should take place without the Word, prayers, partaking of the Supper, and almsgiving." Due to circumstances, however, it was not until 1568, about four years after his death, that the collection of alms was linked to the worship service in Geneva. Boxes were placed at each church door so that people could give alms after the service. Men would be stationed at the exits to exhort people to give. Before this arrangement, Calvin had yielded for practical reasons to meeting the city's charitable needs with funds generated by ecclesiastical property that had been dedicated by a previous generation to the church, but had since then been claimed by the state. However, collecting funds for the needy eventually became part of the regular worship order of the great majority of Reformed churches.[26]

With respect to choosing deacons, Calvin, in his commentary on Acts 6:1–6, regarded the ordination of the seven as "an example," so "choice is permitted to the church" in determining those who serve as deacons. "The appropriate method is for those who are to

---

25. Pauck, *Melanchton and Bucer*, 315.
26. The quotation is from Calvin, *Institutes*, 4.17.44. See further McKee, *John Calvin on the Diaconate*, 50–65; J. K. S. Reid, "Diakonia in the Thought of Calvin," in *Service in Christ: Essays Presented to Karl Barth on His 80th Birthday*, ed. James I. McCord and T. H. L. Parker (Grand Rapids: Eerdmans, 1966), 108.

enter on any public office in the Church to be elected by common votes" according to the criteria that the apostles set out. "Nothing indeed may be done except by the consent and approbation of the people." But the pastors are "to hold in check the impulses of the people, to prevent their enthusiasm running away with them."[27] Since during Calvin's lifetime diaconal work in Geneva was done by the offices of the procurator and hospitaller, his ideal of having direct congregational involvement in choosing deacons was not realized. Indeed, the Ecclesiastical Ordinances indicate that like the elders, those doing official diaconal work had to be appointed by the governing authorities of Geneva in consultation with the ministers, keeping in mind the biblical criteria for the diaconal office.[28]

When it came to ordination, Calvin rightly regarded the office of deacon as ecclesiastical, so he was in favor of including the laying on of hands at their ordination in accordance with the practice mentioned in Acts 6:6. However, it appears that in practice no laying on of hands took place in Geneva when deacons were ordained. In his sermon on Acts 6:1–3, he commented that the apostles laid hands on those elected as deacons and then wrote: "And even today it would not be a bad idea if we had this ceremony."[29]

Calvin had high regard for the diaconal office, as he considered it to be holy, spiritual, and with an integrity of its own. In this respect the diaconal office is no less than that of a minister or preacher. The deacon is not a subordinate of the minister of the Word. Commenting on Acts 6:2 he wrote: "We know what a holy thing it is to be careful for the poor." In his sermon on 1 Timothy 3:6–7, he observed that the office of deacon, as manifest in the procurators and hospitallers, was generally seen as a secular office even by those holding it: "For if they thought, see, God has called us to an office, and to a holy

---

27. John Calvin, *The Acts of the Apostles, 1–13*, ed. D. W. Torrance and T. F. Torrance, trans. John W. Fraser and W. J. G. McDonald, Calvin's Commentaries (Grand Rapids: Eerdmans, 1965), 157, 161.

28. Calvin, "Draft Ecclesiastical Ordinances," 63–65.

29. As quoted in McKee, *John Calvin on the Diaconate*, 155.

state, it is joined with the office of the ministers and preachers, and those that have charge to govern the Church of God: it is certain, that men would walk otherwise in it than they do, with a great deal more reverence than we see." Calvin saw the holiness and dignity of the office in that "the alms that men offer nowadays are sacrifices to God, therefore they must be distributed by such as God accepts for such an office." Deacons "have not only an earthly office, but a spiritual charge which serves the Church of God, and therefore they must be near the ministers of the Word of God, and them that have charge as well by doctrine, as by reproof to maintain the people of God in fear and honest life." The "deacons pertain to the spiritual government which God has established." They "have the treasures of the church to dispense."[30] Indeed, as those "holding the mystery of the faith" (1 Tim. 3:9), deacons are to give biblical "advice and comfort, if they are not going to neglect their duties."[31] Although Calvin was not able to realize the establishment of a consistently biblical diaconate in Geneva, elsewhere this did take place as a result of his teaching on the office of deacon.

The Restoration of the Diaconal Office

Calvin's understanding of the diaconate spread throughout much of Europe. In France, where Reformed churches were basically an unorganized group of individual churches, deacons were often in positions of leadership along with the elders, and some even preached. This situation changed when the first national synod was held in Paris (1559). It adopted a church order that restricted the task of the deacons to distributing the alms of the church with the advice of the consistory. They were not to preach or administer the sacraments, but they were part of the consistory along with the

---

30. Calvin, *Sermons on Timothy and Titus*, 293–95. The spelling has been updated in the material quoted. On the issues raised, also see Reid, "Diakonia in the Thought of Calvin," 106–7; and McKee, *John Calvin on the Diaconate*, 181.

31. John Calvin, *The Second Epistle of Paul the Apostle to the Corinthians and the Epistles to Timothy, Titus and Philemon*, ed. D. W. Torrance and T. F. Torrance, trans. T. A. Smail, Calvin's Commentaries (Grand Rapids: Eerdmans, 1964), 229.

elders and pastors. Also, this church order specified that the congregation was to choose elders and deacons as part of the process of instituting a church, but where a church was already instituted, the consistory would choose these office-bearers. The Synod of Paris approved and the Synod of La Rochelle (1571) adopted the French Confession of Faith (1559), which recognized three ecclesiastical offices: pastor, overseer, and deacon (art. 31).[32]

In England, Jan Laski (or John of Lasco), a Polish nobleman appointed by King Edward VI as superintendent of the independent Protestant congregation of foreign exiles in London (1550–1553), succeeded in realizing many of Bucer's and Calvin's ideals regarding the diaconate. The congregation chose the deacons and supported the diaconal work by giving their gifts for the poor during the worship services. The way the diaconate worked in this congregation became a model for other Reformed churches to follow. When Edward VI died and Bloody Mary came to the throne, Laski and his congregation had to flee from London, and these Reformed principles of the diaconate spread, especially to the Netherlands. With the return of toleration under Queen Elizabeth, the Reformed congregation of exiles was reestablished in London and even had daughter congregations elsewhere in England.

Due to many factors, however, the Church of England did not restore the office of deacon according to the Reformed understanding. The offices of the church were bishop, priest, and deacon, the last office being transitional to the priesthood. The form for the ordination of deacons in the 1559 Book of Common Prayer describes the task of the deacon as assisting the priest in divine

---

32. For the text of the French Confession of Faith, see Jaroslav Pelikan and Valerie Hotchkiss, eds., *Creeds and Confessions of Faith in the Christian Tradition: Volume II, Part Four: Creeds and Confessions of the Reformation Era* (New Haven, Conn.: Yale University Press, 2003), 383. For French developments regarding the diaconate, see Sunshine, "Geneva Meets Rome," 329–46; Glenn S. Sunshine, *Reforming French Protestantism: The Development of Huguenot Ecclesiastical Institutions, 1557–1572*, Sixteenth Century Essays & Studies (Kirksville, Mo.: Truman State University Press, 2003), 94–119; Speelman, *Calvin and the Independence of the Church*, 150–52.

service, especially with Holy Communion, reading Holy Scripture and homilies in the congregation, and instructing the youth in the catechism. The list of duties ends with those pertaining to the sick and the poor.[33]

A key document of the Reformation in Scotland was the First Book of Discipline (1560), which set out the basics of the doctrine and organization of the Scottish church. It also reestablished the diaconal office. Members of the congregation had the responsibility to share in the process of nominating and electing the deacons, whose task it was to gather and distribute the alms of the church. The Second Book of Discipline (1578) reaffirmed that diaconal task but stipulated that deacons were to be elected by the presbytery with the consent of the congregation. There was no longer a mention of congregational involvement in nominating deacons.[34]

With respect to the Low Countries, the deacons of the Reformed church ministered to the poor, but how they functioned differed according to the local political circumstances. In some places they took a leading role in municipal charity, and in other places they took care of church members while the city provided for

---

33. For the form for ordination for the 1559 Book of Common Prayer, see *The Forme and Manner of Making and Consecrating Bishops, Priestes and Deacons* (London: Robert Barker, 1634), http://justus.anglican.org/resources/bcp/1559/BCP1559.pdf. The 1559 edition best characterizes Anglicanism as a middle way between Geneva and Rome. John E. Booty, ed., *The Book of Common Prayer, 1559: The Elizabethan Prayer Book* (Charlottesville, Va.: University of Virginia Press, 2005), 329–30. For the line of thinking based on 1 Timothy 3:8–13 that there are two types of deacons, an assistant minister and a caretaker of the poor, see McKee, *John Calvin on the Diaconate*, 173–76. For a brief overview of the history, see Olson, *Deacons and Deaconesses*, 155–60.

34. James K. Cameron, *The First Book of Discipline with Introduction and Commentary* (Edinburgh: Saint Andrew Press, 1972), 174–79 (eighth head); James Kirk, *The Second Book of Discipline* (Glasgow: Covenanters Press, 2005), 179 (3.7), 201 (7.22), 207–8 (8.5–7). Both the first and second books of discipline envisaged a comprehensive role for the diaconate in collecting and distributing revenue in support of the ministry, the schools, and the poor. But there is little indication of any sustained attempt to fulfill such a wide range of responsibilities. Their primary task was the relief of the poor. Kirk, *Second Book of Discipline*, 208n142.

the others.[35] Calvin's idea of two distinct grades of deacons, based
on his understanding of Romans 12:8 and probably influenced by
the Genevan context, found some acceptance there at first, but that
approval was short-lived. The Colloquy of Wesel (1568), important
for organizing Dutch Reformed churches, agreed that two types of
deacons, as understood by Calvin, would be profitable especially
in larger congregations, but subsequent assemblies, the Synod of
Emden (1571) and the Synods of Dort (1574, 1578), made no mention of this distinction.[36] The Belgic Confession (1561), adopted
by the Reformed churches in the Netherlands during the sixteenth
century, speaks only of the offices of pastors, elders, and deacons
(art. 30).[37] And so the Reformed understanding of the diaconate
spread in different ways and in different countries, laying a foun-
dational heritage on which Reformed and Presbyterian churches
could build.

Summary and Conclusions

In apostolic times the office of deacon focused on helping the needy
and showing the love of Christ in many varied ways. The congregation was involved both in choosing deacons according to biblical
criteria and in helping the poor and needy. Congregations met not
only needs resulting from financial poverty but also those that could
arise from sickness, hunger, and imprisonment.

As the church moved from apostolic times, several factors led
the deacon to become the servant of the bishop. The diaconal office
became more concerned with liturgical matters and developed into
a stepping-stone to the priesthood. As ecclesiastical hierarchy devel-

---

35. Olson, *Deacons and Deaconesses*, 162–63. For an account of the development
of the diaconate in the Dutch Reformation, see Charles H. Parker, *The Reformation of
Community: Social Welfare and Calvinist Charity in Holland, 1572–1620*, Cambridge
Studies in Early Modern History (Cambridge, U.K.: Cambridge University Press,
1998), 111–22.

36. Van Lonkhuijzen, "De geschiedenis van het diaconaat," 154–59.

37. Also, the French Confession of Faith (1559) did not speak of two types of
deacons.

oped, the congregation had no say in the election of deacons, and their participation in taking care of the needy eroded. The bishop was expected to give of his revenues to help the indigent. Indeed, giving to the needy was considered to have meritorious and atoning value. By the Middle Ages, a chief impetus for having pity on the needy was that showing such charity helped to earn salvation and eternal life.

The Reformation sought to bring the church back to a more biblical view of the diaconate. Especially important was the work of John Calvin. He stressed the ecclesiastical nature, holiness, and dignity of the office, which was to be focused on helping the poor. Political conditions in Geneva, however, prevented him from fully realizing his ambition to have a consistent biblical diaconate in which the congregation would choose the deacons and support their work by giving alms in church. Elsewhere in Europe his influence resulted in the office being restored more closely to the biblical norms. This influence eventually reached many places in the world wherever Reformed and Presbyterian churches were established.

CHAPTER 8

Women and the Diaconate

In chapter 6 we concluded that there is little justification for certainty that women were ordained in the office of deacon during New Testament times. The question arises whether there is evidence of female deacons in the period immediately following New Testament times. If so, what did that mean, and what was involved? In the previous chapter we saw that Calvin considered women eligible for the office of deacon. How was his view received elsewhere as the Reformed faith spread? How do we approach the issue of female deacons today? The literature on this topic is vast. This chapter attempts to address these questions in a summary manner by looking at the following areas: the early Christian church, Reformed and Presbyterian churches from the Reformation to the twentieth century, and the twenty-first century.

The Early Christian Church

There is no evidence that women were ordained to the diaconal office in the first two centuries of the early Christian church.[1] That changed in subsequent centuries. The church in the eastern part of

---

1. A famous letter from Pliny the Younger to the Emperor Trajan (AD 11–113) has been interpreted as referring to a female deacon. But this is far from certain. See Aimé Georges Martimort, *Deaconesses: An Historical Study*, trans. K. D. Whitehead (San Francisco: Ignatius Press, 1986), 25–26; and Kevin Madigan and Carolyn Osiek, eds. and trans., *Ordained Women in the Early Church: A Documentary History* (Baltimore, Md.: Johns Hopkins University Press, 2005), 26–27. The late first-century *Didache* or *Teaching of the Twelve Apostles* specifically instructed, "Select, then, for yourselves

the empire had female deacons starting in the third century. This reality is reflected in the exegesis of biblical passages that could be understood to refer to female deacons, and were so interpreted. For example, with respect to Romans 16:1, which describes Phoebe as "a deacon [diakonos] of the church in Cenchreae," Chrysostom, bishop of Constantinople (c. 354–407), noted that Paul indicated "her status by calling her 'deacon.'" Also, he explained the "women" mentioned in 1 Timothy 3:11 as those who "hold the rank of deacon." Other Eastern commentators, like Theodore of Mopsuestia (c. 350–428) and Theodoret of Cyrrhus (c. 393–456), offer a similar interpretation of this passage.[2] It is understandable that commentators who lived in an area with female deacons would more readily read the relevant biblical texts as referring to them. But what exactly was the status of female deacons in the Eastern church?

The earliest church order that describes the office of female deacons is the third-century Syrian church order called *Didascalia Apostolorum*. Chapter 16 explains why it was necessary to have women in the diaconate. First, they would be able to visit females who lived in pagan households. You could not send a male deacon to visit a woman, especially if it could mean helping them in sickness and corporal works of mercy. Second, female assistance was needed at the baptism of women. This sacrament was by immersion, was received nude, and involved anointing the entire body. It was improper for a man to do that. If there was no woman deacon available, then only the female convert's head would be anointed. Third, although women did not normally teach, the deaconess was to instruct and educate newly baptized women so that they would be preserved in holiness and purity. These three reasons for female deacons indicate that the pressure of social conditions and the need to maintain modesty appear to have made a female diacon-

---

bishops and deacons worthy of the Lord, mild-tempered men." Niederwimmer and Attridge, *Didache*, 200.

2. Madigan and Osiek, *Ordained Women*, 14–15, 19–20.

ate necessary.[3] The fourth-century *Apostolic Constitutions*, which is a compilation of church orders and includes the *Didascalia*, mentions the ordination of a deaconess. It included the laying on of hands by the bishop and appears to mirror the ordination of male deacons. But there is no mention of such an ordination in the *Didascalia Apostolorum*, suggesting that women were then appointed to be deacons rather than ordained.[4]

To put the matter of deaconesses in the Eastern church in perspective, we must note two facts. First, the institution of deaconesses in Eastern churches appears to have been much more limited than the abundant documentation we possess might lead us to believe. Even within Syria and elsewhere in the eastern Mediterranean, it appears that not all churches had female deacons. Furthermore, they were not accepted in Egypt or by the ancient Maronites in Lebanon or by the Armenians. They were also unknown to the Slavic peoples. In addition, the tasks of a deaconess could differ. Where protecting feminine modesty at baptism or visiting and evangelizing women were not issues, female deacons were introduced for other reasons—for example, as a degree of honor to consecrate a candidate into religious life, such as heading a convent.

---

3. Martimort, *Deaconesses: An Historical Study*, 37–44; Madigan and Osiek, *Ordained Women*, 108–9; and Olson, *Deacons and Deaconesses*, 41–42. Indeed, Epiphanius, who became bishop of Salamis in 367, bluntly stated that "deaconesses are instituted solely for service to women, to preserve decency as required." Martimort, *Deaconesses: An Historical Study*, 112–15. When a female was baptized, the bishop or priest would stand outside the baptistry or behind a curtain and from that position pronounce the baptismal formula. John Wijngaards, *The Ordained Women Deacons of the Church's First Millennium* (Norwich, U.K.: Canterbury Press, 2011), chapter 8.

4. Madigan and Osiek, *Ordained Women*, 113–16; Francine Carman, "Women, Ministry, and Church Order in Early Christianity," in *Women and Christian Origins*, ed. Ross Shepard Kraemer and Mary Rose D'Angelo (New York: Oxford University Press, 1999), 318; Olson, *Deacons and Deaconesses*, 42. Also see H. G. Davies, "Deacons, Deaconesses and the Minor Orders in the Patristic Period," *Journal of Ecclesiastical History* 14 (1963): 4; Martimort, *Deaconesses: An Historical Study*, 69–70, 75. For arguments that the ordination of a deaconess was not the same as that of a deacon, see Martimort, *Deaconesses: An Historical Study*, 146–64, esp. 156; for counterarguments see Wijngaards, *Ordained Women Deacons*, chapters 5–12.

Second, by the end of the eleventh century, deaconesses had basically disappeared from the Eastern church. When Christianity was first legalized early in the fourth century (313), there were predominantly adult baptisms as many joined the church. By the fifth and sixth centuries, however, such baptisms were in decline with more and more infants receiving the sacrament. With this development the predominant mode of baptism changed from immersion to the pouring or sprinkling of water, and the importance of a key function of the deaconess decreased. This circumstance contributed to their eventual disappearance from the Eastern church.[5]

With respect to the Western church, there is no positive evidence that there were women deacons until about the sixth century. In commenting on 1 Timothy 3:11, Ambrosiaster (active c. 366–384) stated that only heretics would want to ordain women as deacons. But when Pelagius (c. 354–420) commented on the same passage, he interpreted it as referring to female deacons. He commented that the women "be selected similarly to the way in which deacons are chosen. Apparently he [the apostle] is speaking of those who still today in the East are called deaconesses." While such a statement indicates that the Eastern church had female deacons in the past and still had them in his time, it says nothing about female deacons in the Western church.[6] Repeated official prohibitions to ordain female deacons, however, indicate that the issue was alive, and ordinations may have taken place in the Western church. The Councils of Nîmes (396), Orange (411), Epaon (517), and Orleans (533) forbade their ordination. In 1017, however, Pope Benedict VIII wrote to the bishop of Porto recognizing the office of deaconess and conceding the validity of women's ordination to it. So the office

---

5. Martimort, *Deaconesses: An Historical Study*, 127–43, 165–83.

6. See Madigan and Osiek, *Ordained Women*, 12–21. For the need for caution due to lack of evidence for concluding that the Western church had female deacons during the first five centuries, see Martimort, *Deaconesses: An Historical Study*, 187–96.

of a female diaconate existed in some form in the Western church, but it was clearly not readily accepted.[7]

The problem of protecting modesty for those receiving baptism nude seems to have been resolved in the Western church through the employment of a special order of widows. These widows had the same functions in women's baptisms that in the East had been assigned to deaconesses.[8] The origin of this order of widows is found in the early church's understanding of 1 Timothy 5:9–10, which speaks of widows being enrolled, or put on a list.[9] In chapter 6 we saw that such enrollment could imply that these particular widows were committed to doing specific tasks in the church as the need arose. There are indicators that an order of widows existed in the second century and that their function was to pray and to visit the sick (cf. 1 Tim. 5:5, 10). Polycarp (c. 69–155) highlighted their task of spiritual intercession by calling the widows "the altar of God," an image that underlined their selfless dedication to God. Ignatius's (c. 35–107) mention of "virgins called widows" could indicate that the term "widows" had an ecclesiastical meaning, suggesting an order in the church.[10] In any case, by the beginning of the third century, the order of widows held an important place in the church. The *Didascalia Apostolorum* lists the widows with the

---

7. For the relevant texts, see Martimort, *Deaconesses: An Historical Study*, 193; and Madigan and Osiek, *Ordained Women*, 145–47.

8. The fifth-century Statua Ecclesiae Antiqua, canon 100. See Martimort, *Deaconesses: An Historical Study*, 194; and E. Hatch, "Widows," in *A Dictionary of Christian Antiquities*, ed. William Smith and Samuel Cheetham (London: John Murray, 1880), 2:2036.

9. E.g., Martimort, *Deaconesses: An Historical Study*, 23. J. N. D. Kelly writes of "an officially recognized order of widows" in Ephesus and that the reference in 1 Timothy 5:9 "is the first clear allusion in Christian literature to the existence of such an order." Kelly, *Pastoral Epistles*, 112. Also see Thurston, *Widows*, 44–55; but cf. Marshall and Towner, *Commentary on the Pastoral Epistles*, 578.

10. Jean Daniélou and Henri Marrou, *The First Six Hundred Years*, trans. Vincent Cronin, The Christian Centuries (London: Daton, Longman and Todd, 1978), 118–19; on widows as altar also see Thurston, *Widows*, 69–73, 106–13; on "virgins called widows," suggesting an order, also see Schoedel and Koester, *Ignatius of Antioch*, 252; cf. Thurston, *Widows*, 63–65.

bishops, deacons, presbyters, and deaconesses. The enrolled widows were not ordained, but appointed. Their primary duty was to pray for the church and their benefactors, but they were also to do good works such as making clothes for those in distress (cf. Acts 9:36–43) and visiting the sick. They worked under the supervision of the bishop and were forbidden to teach or to baptize.[11]

Eventually, however, female deacons were beginning to take over the tasks of these widows. The exact relationship between widows and female deacons is problematic. In the Western church, Pelagius, in his commentary, identified the widows who could be enrolled in 1 Timothy 5:9–10 as "the women who are being considered for ordination as deaconesses" even though the office is not specifically mentioned in that biblical passage. However, his contemporary in the Eastern church, Theodore of Mopsuestia, noted in his commentary that what is said in 1 Timothy 5:9 "applies only to the order of widows and not to deaconesses, as some believe."[12] The plausible suggestion has been made that the "office" of widow merged with the functions of the deaconesses, or we could say that the deaconesses took over the duties of the widows. With the rise of asceticism, the order of widows became the origin of monastic orders for women. Gradually the order of widows and the function of the deaconesses were absorbed into the monastic movement. By the twelfth or thirteenth century, female deacons had disappeared from Europe, and by the eleventh century in the Eastern church. There may have been a revival of the ritual of the blessing of the deaconess in some convents in the fourteenth and fifteenth centuries, but the parish deaconess was a thing of the past.[13]

---

11. Daniélou and Marrou, *First Six Hundred Years*, 163; Thurston, *Widows*, 92–105; Olson, *Deacons and Deaconesses*, 39–41. For their not being ordained, also see Martimort, *Deaconesses: An Historical Study*, 41–42, 50–51; and Madigan and Osiek, *Ordained Women*, 114–15.

12. Gorday, *Colossians, 1–2 Thessalonians, 1–2 Timothy, Titus, Philemon*, 200.

13. For the merging of functions, see Olson, *Deacons and Deaconesses*, 55 (cf. Martimort, *Deaconesses: An Historical Study*, 52); Thurston, *Widows*, 105, 114; for the

From the Reformation to the Twentieth Century:
Reformed and Presbyterian Churches

In chapter 7 we saw that Calvin wanted widows to serve in the office
of deacon. He based his thinking on 1 Timothy 5:9–10, seen in conjunction with Romans 12:8 and 16:1. Calvin broke new ground with
his exegesis, but he was not able to realize his wish in Geneva and
did not insist on it. We need to remember that Calvin considered
the widow-deacon to be of a second grade or second order, with the
male deacons being the first order. Their office was established in
Acts 6, and they had the authority of administering aid to the poor.
In other words, the female deacon was a subordinate type of deacon who actually ministered to the needy and nursed the sick under
the direction of the male deacons. These women were not ordained,
although Calvin recognized that they had an office or official function in the church. He thus described Phoebe's position as an office
(Rom. 16:1), linking her standing to the widows of 1 Timothy 5,
whom he characterized as "this honorable order of widows."[14]

Calvin's idea of widow-deacons did have some influence in
Reformed and Presbyterian churches elsewhere in Europe, but
overall there was little enthusiasm for a diaconal office for women.
Let us consider some highlights in the Reformed and Presbyterian
ecclesiastical worlds.

Reformed Churches
French Calvinist Lambert Daneau, who did not consider widows
serving as deaconesses to be prescriptive, held that "these women,
however, are assigned to a limited office and are inferior to the

---

monastic development, see Thurston, *Widows*, 114–15; Olson, *Deacons and Deaconesses*,
75–77, 89–90; Martimort, *Deaconesses: An Historical Study*, 217–40.

    14. Calvin, *Institutes*, 4.3.9; McKee, *John Calvin on the Diaconate*, 211–16. Elsie
Anne McKee, "Church Offices: Calvinist Offices," in *The Oxford Encyclopedia of the
Reformation*, ed. Hans J. Hillerbrand (New York: Oxford University Press, 1996),
338; Calvin, *Romans and Thessalonians*, 320–21. The phrase "this honourable order of
widows" is found in his commentary on 1 Timothy 5:11. Calvin, *Second Corinthians,
Timothy, Titus and Philemon*, 257.

deacons to whom they are subject, whom they obey and to whom they render account of their vocation." His views are typical of the second generation of Reformed thinking in the sixteenth century. Furthermore, for most, the widows as deaconesses remained a devout wish, which could not be acted on due to cultural pressures. Caring for the sick and poor was left to others.[15] There were, however, exceptions.

One of these exceptions was the Colloquy of Wesel (1568). This was an unofficial gathering of about sixty Reformed ministers, elders, and deacons convened for the purpose of laying the foundations for a Reformed church federation in the Netherlands. The decisions they made, therefore, had the character of advice to the churches. The Articles of Wesel, which sought to give direction for a Reformed church order, also dealt with the office of deacon. After noting that it was not possible to prescribe a certain number of deacons for a congregation since circumstances differed, the Articles stated that "especially in the more important cities, it will not be unsuitable to establish two kinds of deacons, some of whom will devote themselves to the work of collecting and distributing alms.... The others have especially the care of the sick, wounded, and captives" (art. 5.5–6). A little later, we read: "In certain places it will also be suitable, we think, that women of approved faith and probity and advanced age be admitted to this office, according to the example of the apostles" (art. 5.10). It would appear that these female deacons would be especially concerned with caring for the sick, wounded, and prisoners. Since it was only a colloquy that produced these articles, they were not binding on the churches.[16]

---

15. For the Daneau quotation, see McKee, *John Calvin on the Diaconate*, 218; also see 222.

16. The translation of the quotation is from McKee, *John Calvin on the Diaconate*, 221. The original Latin text is found in F. L. Rutgers, comp. and ed., *Acta van de Nederlandsche Synoden der zestiende eeuw* (1889; repr., Dordrecht: J. P. van den Tol, 1980), 26. The original Latin term translated "office" is *munus*. It has been suggested that it could be better translated as "duty" or "task," indicating that an ordained office was probably not in view, for which one would expect the Latin *officium*. G. Van Rongen, "'Widows' and

The first official synod of the Reformed churches in the Netherlands, convened at Emden in 1571, made no mention of female deacons in their church-orderly decisions. However, in 1573 the congregation of Wesel had four ordained women deacons to care for the poor, sick, and expectant mothers. The consistory chose them for one-year terms, after which they could be selected for the office again. In 1575 there were nine deaconesses. Difficulties arose in 1578 because of confusion about the New Testament meaning of widows and deaconesses. There were objections that the sixty-year age limit of 1 Timothy 5:9 had not been honored. The issue came to the Classis of Wesel, which decided in 1580 that the age limit set by the apostle should be honored, but exceptions could be made if there were other compensating qualities in the candidate. To be sure of the propriety of being flexible with the biblical directive, the classis took the issue to the next synod. It came to the Synod of Middelburg in 1581 by asking the assembly whether it would not be advisable to reintroduce the office of deaconess in the churches. The Synod responded in the negative "because of various inconveniences which could follow." If situations arose in which it was not proper for male deacons to care for sick women, then their wives or other capable women could be called in to help. With this decision the Reformed churches in the Netherlands had officially decided not to ordain women deacons. Deaconesses, however, continued to function in some congregations, apparently in an unofficial capacity.[17]

Deaconesses in Ancient and Recent History: Part Three," *Una Sancta* 38, no. 19 (1991): 388. However, evidence for this suggestion is wanting. Indeed, as A. Wolters pointed out in private correspondence (October 10, 2014), in Calvin's *Institutes*, 4.3.4–12, dealing with offices, "The English translation by Ford Lewis Battles has the word 'office' 18 times. In 10 cases this reflects the Latin 'munus,' in 6 cases 'officium,' and in 2 cases 'function.'" Calvin therefore uses the terms interchangeably. For the unofficial character of the Colloquy of Wesel, see Parker, *Reformation of Community*, 112.

17. For the original Dutch text of the question and decision, see Rutgers, *Acta van de Nederlandsche Synoden*, 417, 437; on the unfolding events, see G. Huls, *De dienst der vrouw in de kerk. Een onderzoek naar de plaats der vrouw in een Presbyteriale kerkorde*

Deaconesses continued serving in Wesel until 1610, when the care of the poor was reorganized so that it became a joint church and government responsibility. Also, women deacons ministered for some time in Goch (just to the west of Wesel) and Den Hoorn on the North Sea island of Texel. The Reformed church in Amsterdam already had deaconesses in 1566, and in 1578 there were three. The same number was appointed in 1582. Given the decision of the Synod of Middelburg, these deaconesses were volunteers who did not necessarily satisfy the norms of the widows of 1 Timothy 5. They worked in close cooperation with the deacons. This congregation had deaconesses until the eighteenth century. They were normally appointed by the consistory on the basis of the deacons' proposal. By 1713 this was the only church to have female deacons. After the French Revolution, deaconesses disappeared in Amsterdam as well, in part because the civil government took over the responsibility of caring for the poor.[18]

In the middle of the seventeenth century, Gisbertus Voetius and others pleaded for deaconesses who were not ordained into an ecclesiastical office as a help for the deacons. This line of thinking eventually resulted in the establishment of special diaconal homes in the nineteenth century in the Netherlands and Germany where nonecclesiastical deaconesses would minister to the sick and the poor. Attempts at the end of the nineteenth century to reintroduce the deaconess as an ecclesiastical office, as once practiced in Wesel, failed.[19]

In the twentieth century, the Dutch Reformed Church (*Hervormde Kerk*) opened the office of deacon to women in 1936, but the decision was rescinded a year later because of widespread opposition from those who considered it to be in conflict with Scripture.

(Wageningen: Veenman Zonen, 1951), 89–91; Koen Kyungkeun Lim, *Het spoor van de vrouw in het ambt*, Theologie en Geschiedenis (Kampen: Kok, 2001), 22–23.

18. Lim, *Het spoor van de vrouw*, 23–24; Huls, *De dienst der vrouw*, 91–93; H. Bouwman, *Het ambt der diakenen* (Kampen: Kok, 1907), 44–45.

19. Lim, *Het spoor van de vrouw*, 25.

Due to changing times and contexts, however, opposition waned, and all the offices were opened to women in 1957. The Reformed churches in the Netherlands followed on this course, deciding that in principle women could be admitted to any ecclesiastical office in 1966, and because there was relatively little opposition, full unconditional access to ecclesiastical office was eventually granted in 1985.[20] Their sister church, the Christian Reformed Church in North America, followed suit in 1995 by opening all offices to women. The Reformed Church in America had already allowed for the ordination of women as deacons in 1972. The Netherlands Reformed Churches in the Netherlands admitted women to the office of deacon in 1995 and to all offices in 2004.[21]

In France today there is virtually no functioning ecclesiastical deaconess office serving a local Reformed congregation. This office has been superseded by the ordination of women as pastors and by the movement to integrated women's ministry. Furthermore, the financial situation of many churches has discouraged the development of this office for males as well as females.[22] In Canada the church order of l'Église réformée du Québec allows for the ordination of female deacons, but whether the practice is biblically justified is currently under discussion.[23]

20. Lim, *Het spoor van de vrouw*, 78–81, 181–82, 247, 264.

21. For the Christian Reformed Church, see *Agenda for Synod 1995* (Grand Rapids: Christian Reformed Church in North America, 1995), 726–32 (art. 79), http://bit.ly/1Udx9XU; for the Reformed Church in America, see Edwin G. Mulder, "Full Participation a Long Time Coming!," *Reformed Review* 42 (1989): 224–46; for the Netherlands Reformed Churches in the Netherlands, see their decision made in 1995, *Akta Landelijke Vergadering Nederlands Gereformeerde Kerken Apeldoorn 1994–1995*, 26–28, http://www.ngk.nl/kerkverband/landelijk/archief-lv/.

22. Paul Wells, private correspondence with the author, August 12, 2014.

23. Paulin Bédard, minister in l'Église réformée du Québec, noted in a private communication (August 11, 2014) that "our church order says (my [Bédard's] translation): 'The congregation may call to the office of deacon any member having the qualities according to the biblical criteria as mentioned in Acts 6:3; Rom. 16:1, 2, and 1 Tim. 3:8–13' (Art. 2.4.3). This has been understood as leaving the possibility for deaconesses. But at this moment, two of our churches (Quebec City and St-Georges) have come to the conclusion that we should not have deaconesses, based on biblical

Presbyterian Churches

Many of the eminent divines who formed the Westminster Assembly considered the widows of 1 Timothy 5:9 to be church officers, but none argued for their ordination into the diaconate. Consistent with Calvin's thinking, they considered Phoebe to be a deaconess (Rom. 16:1) in the sense of the servant widow of 1 Timothy 5; they did not view her as holding the office of male deacons. To be a deaconess did not therefore necessarily entail ordination.[24] By the early nineteenth century, there was almost universal neglect of the diaconal office. Efforts were made, however, to reinstate the office, and deacons were eventually elected and ordained. In 1888 the General Assembly of the Church of Scotland approved restoring the biblical office of the diaconate for women, and the Kirk Session of Bowden, near Melrose, set apart the first deaconess to this office. It was not until 1988 that the first men were commissioned as deacons, thus finally completing the restoration of the diaconate as visualized in 1888.[25] The Free Church of Scotland and the Free Presbyterian Church of Scotland have no deaconesses.[26]

In North America, there were early proponents of female deacons. The Southern Presbyterian Robert L. Dabney was in favor of appointing women as deaconesses, but apparently not in ordaining

---

arguments. The subject has not been raised at the synodical level yet. There are deaconesses in Repentigny (east of Montreal) and they have been ordained. The church order does not stipulate any difference in function, authority, or calling between male and female deacons."

24. Brian M. Schwertley, *A Historical and Biblical Examination of Women Deacons*, ed. Stephen Pribble (Southfield, Mich.: Reformed Witness, 1998), 36–40.

25. M. I. Levison, "Diaconate, Deacons, Deaconesses," in *Dictionary of Scottish Church History and Theology*, ed. Nigel M. de S. Cameron (Downers Grove, Ill.: InterVarsity, 1993), 241. Olson, *Deacons and Deaconesses*, 260.

26. For the Free Church, see the Policy for the Admission of Congregations in *Reports to the General Assembly of the Free Church of Scotland 2014*, 23, http://free church.org/resources/assembly-reports/; for the Free Presbyterian Church, see, e.g., the "Male/Female Distinctions" under "Frequently Asked Questions," http://www.fp church.org.uk/about-us/frequently-asked-questions/#office.

them.[27] Indeed, the Book of Church Order of the Southern Presbyterian Church (adopted in 1879) stated that "where it shall appear
needful, the Church Session may select and appoint godly women
for the care of the sick, of prisoners, of poor widows and orphans,
and in general for the relief of distress."[28] This essentially describes
the duties of a deaconess as Calvin understood them. Benjamin B.
Warfield of Princeton wrote that "it need not be denied that the
office of deaconess is a Scriptural office although it must be con-
fessed that the Biblical warrant for it is of the slenderest."[29] The
first Presbyterian church to ordain women as deacons was the
Reformed Presbyterian Church of North America (Covenanter) in
1888. While this decision was considered to be in harmony with
the New Testament, it came about because of the influence of
nineteenth-century feminism.[30] The United Presbyterian Church
of North America allowed for the ordination of women as deacons in 1906, and the Presbyterian Church in the United States of
America, also called the Northern Presbyterian Church, enacted a
provision allowing for female deacons in the early 1920s. The Associate Reformed Presbyterian Church approved the ordination of
women as deacons in 1969.[31]

Several churches recognize women's diaconal gifts without giving them an official office in the church. The Reformed Presbyterian
Church Evangelical Synod decided in 1977 "to affirm the right of a
local church to have a separate body of unordained women who
may be called deaconesses."[32] The Presbyterian Church in America
in its Book of Church Order (chapter 9) allows for the appointment

27. Frank J. Smith, "Petticoat Presbyterianism: A Century of Debate in American
Presbyterianism on the Issue of the Ordination of Women," *Westminster Theological
Journal* 51 (1989): 54.

28. Benjamin B. Warfield, "Presbyterian Deaconesses," *The Presbyterian Review* 10
(1889): 287–88.

29. Warfield, "Presbyterian Deaconesses," 283.

30. Schwertley, *Women Deacons*, 52–63.

31. Smith, "Petticoat Presbyterianism," 59, 62, 70.

32. Smith, "Petticoat Presbyterianism," 67.

of godly men and women to assist the deacons, but they are not officers of the church and, as such, are not subjects for ordination.

In Korea, Presbyterian churches have had female deacons for a long time. Rather than feminism, the cultural concerns regarding the appropriateness of males ministering to females has influenced this practice. These women deacons are clearly distinguished from the male deacons, who are ordained for life service with the laying on of hands. Female deacons are not ordained and have a one-year term. They function as assistants to the male deacons. Their key responsibility is to build up the church's congregational life, especially working with and for the well-being of the women in the church. There are a large number of such unordained female deacons, and, in the case of the Presbyterian Church (Koshin), they comprise almost one-fourth of the communicant members. An older woman who has served as a deacon can become an "exhorter" (*kwon-sa*). Although these exhorters are not ordained and are thus outside the formal structure of the church, they exert enormous influence. Normally, they are consulted in making important decisions.[33]

Into the Twenty-First Century

How can a church best resolve the issue of women and the diaconate? Of paramount importance is what Scripture tells us. We have seen in chapter 6 that the available evidence for ordained women deacons is either meager or nonexistent in the New Testament, depending on how it is evaluated. The early history of the post-apostolic church similarly gives little justification for an ordained female diaconal office in the church. Nevertheless, due to Calvin's

---

33. Soon-Gil Hur, "Women in Office: Especially About 'Deaconesses,'" in *Proceedings of the International Conference of Reformed Churches, October 15–23, 1997. Seoul, Korea* (Neerlandia, Alberta: Inheritance, 1997), 142–43; Su Yon Pak, "Women Leaders in Asian American Protestant Churches," in *Religious Leadership: A Reference Handbook,* ed. Sharon Henderson Callahan (Thousand Oaks, Calif.: Sage, 2013), 300. The ratio of the female deacon to the communicant members in the Presbyterian Church (Koshin) is based on the statistics of the official website of Koshin, which was accessed by Heon Soo Kim on May 29, 2014.

views, the matter of deaconesses has been an issue in the history of Reformed churches, especially in the Netherlands. However, as we saw earlier in this chapter, that notion gained little traction basically because the biblical data did not convince the churches of the necessity of female deacons, and the idea that women should be ordained as deacons died out. Now, however, the issue has the attention of those in Reformed and Presbyterian circles, undoubtedly due to current cultural influences of feminism and women's rights movements. It is therefore appropriate to pause for a moment and consider some of the issues associated with discussions or debates on this question.

In chapter 7 we saw that Scripture teaches women are not to have authority over men in the church of God and ordaining women into the office of deacon would contravene this principle. Calvin's linking the widows of 1 Timothy 5 to the office of deacon has led some to place the widow-deacon on the same level as male deacons. But that had not been Calvin's intent. He clearly stated that there were two grades of diaconal service, with the widows occupying the second subservient grade. It would therefore be helpful to disassociate completely the widows of 1 Timothy 5 from the male diaconate.

On the other hand, it is clear that the apostle Paul, under the inspiration of the Holy Spirit, instructed Timothy to enroll certain widows in what appears to have been a diaconal service of some sort. These instructions show one possible way to involve women in diaconal service—namely, to enroll godly widows sixty years and older for the service of love and good works in the congregation where they already had a good name (1 Tim. 5:9–10). The practice of the church in the past in applying this passage has been mixed, especially with respect to the age limit. J. N. D. Kelly observes, "The fourth-century *Apostolic Constitutions* (III.i.1 f.) accepted the same age-limit for widows, although it is interesting to observe that some texts of the late third century *Didascalia* (III.i) reduce it to fifty."[34]

---

34. Kelly, *Pastoral Epistles*, 115.

We find the same ambivalence in the sixteenth century. As mentioned earlier in this chapter, the Classis of Wesel decided in 1580 that the churches should honor the sixty-year-old age limit, but exceptions could be made "if other qualities required by Paul were found" in the widow.[35] It would be best if there is to be an official commission or enrollment of widows according to the guidelines of 1 Timothy 5 that the apostolic guidelines be honored for the reasons the apostle gives. These reasons have continuing validity (1 Tim. 5:11–14). Such a list of widows can serve as a valuable resource for the deacons, who may need the help of a woman with much life experience. There are those who argue that such servant-widows should be officially ordained as deaconesses. However, this notion goes beyond what Scripture clearly mandates. As we saw in chapter 6, there are no conclusive reasons for equating the enrollment of 1 Timothy 5:9 with ecclesiastical ordination into the office of deaconess.[36]

There are other ways to use women's gifts to support the deacons' work. A church may ask gifted women of whatever age or status to give unofficial assistance to the deacons wherever it would be desirable because of modesty and propriety. A deacon, elder, or minister may encounter situations where such feminine help would be most desirable, such as with personal private issues best understood by another female. There would then be no reason to limit requesting diaconal assistance from women who are sixty and older. That such can be the case is evident from 1 Timothy 3:11. We saw that this passage likely refers to the wife of a deacon. To be able to support her husband's work by doing diaconal work she should be reverent, not a slanderer, but temperate, faithful in all things (1 Tim. 3:11). However, we also saw in chapter 6 that the ambiguity inherent in the term "women" (rather than "their women/wives") may be intentional so as to include other likewise gifted women who could

---

35. Lim, *Het spoor van de vrouw*, 23.
36. For further discussion on this, see Schwertley, *Women Deacons*, 149–55.

support the work of the deacons.[37] Indeed, the apostle urged Titus that older or mature godly women of no specified age teach and train young women to be good wives and mothers (Titus 2:3–5). Such teaching can surely be relevant for the diaconal ministry, especially when dealing with dysfunctional marriages and families.

As long as it does not have official ordination in view, a church has considerable freedom as to how it engages the help of women in the diaconate. A church can simply leave the matter to the discretion of the office-bearers themselves to involve appropriate women as helpers as needed, or a consistory or session can appoint certain qualified women to assist the deacons as needed on the analogy of 1 Timothy 3, or a consistory can decide to enroll widows according to the criteria of 1 Timothy 5. In any case the diaconate should make use of the gifts within the congregation as much as possible in executing their task, and that most certainly includes the gifts of women.

Summary and Conclusions

The first evidence for female ordination into the diaconate in the early Christian church is found in the third century in the eastern part of the Roman Empire. Women deacons were needed to protect female modesty at baptisms, to minister to sick women, and to teach new female members of the church the basics of Christianity to preserve their purity. The involvement of female deacons in the church was, however, by no means universal in the East, and by the end of the eleventh century it had disappeared. Although women

---

37. A noteworthy quote from a report on women in church office with respect to 1 Timothy 3:11: "Having denied the ordained status of the 'women' (K.J.V. 'wives') of this verse, it is all too easy to say no more. That is a shame, because whether these women were wives of elders or deacons or both, it is clear that Paul had 'deaconing women' in view. They were recognized as special assistants to the ordained officers of the church." Davis et al., "Report of the Committee," 350. E.g., a Reformed church in Harlingen, The Netherlands, has had officially appointed deaconesses to assist the deacons under official ecclesiastical supervision since 1888. C. van der Leest, "Een eeuw diaconessen in Harlingen," *Dienst* 39, no. 2 (1991): 12–24.

deacons are not clearly attested in the Western church until the sixth century, the issue of the female diaconate was discussed and possibly practiced. But the ordination of women was not widely supported and was frequently prohibited in ecclesiastical councils in the fourth and fifth centuries. An order of widows existed from the second century on. These women were appointed—not ordained—for diaconal tasks. Eventually female deacons began to take over their duties, and in the end the order of widows became the origin for female monastic orders. By the thirteenth century women deacons working in the church had disappeared.

Calvin's notion of a second-rank deacon in the form of unordained widows did not really catch on in the sixteenth century. An important exception was a decision made at the Colloquy of Wesel that supported the idea, and the church at that place, along with a few others, had female deacons. The Reformed Churches in the Netherlands, however, decided in 1581 not to have an office of deaconess. Unofficially, female diaconal workers continued to labor in Amsterdam until the eighteenth century. In the twentieth century, several Reformed churches in the Netherlands and America opened up the office of deacon to women.

In the Presbyterian world, women deacons were not an issue until the nineteenth century. In 1888 the Church of Scotland opened up the diaconate to women, and in the United States, the Reformed Presbyterian Church did the same. Other Presbyterian churches followed.

There has been resistance to the ordination of women in the office of deacon in conservative churches, but feminism and women's rights movements have put the issue back on the ecclesiastical agenda. There is no biblical warrant for the ordination of women. It would, however, be proper to enroll widows according to the criteria of 1 Timothy 5, but churches need not be limited to that. A church has considerable freedom in enlisting women's help in the diaconate.

PART FOUR

The Current Functioning of the Office

CHAPTER 9

The Official Position of the Deacon Today

What is the ecclesiastical position of the deacon? Is the diaconate really an ecclesiastical office? If so, what is involved in being ordained to this office? Is there more to it than providing for the poor? How does this office relate to those of the teaching and ruling elders? Does the deacon belong in the session or consistory? Should this office be involved in matters of oversight or the proclamation of the Word? The legacy of the Reformation has not always given consistent answers to these questions. This chapter therefore considers the office of deacon, ordination and length of service, auxiliary duties, and the relationship of the deacon and the elder.

The Deacon as an Office-Bearer
The Office
First, we must reaffirm that the deacon indeed holds an ecclesiastical office. There are some who are questioning whether deacons really do have an office—that is, an authoritative ordained function—or whether their position is just a matter of appointment to a special task in the church.[1]

As we saw in chapter 4, the first men charged with providing for the poor in Acts 6 were chosen by the community of believers and were ordained with the laying on of hands for the specific task

---

1. See, e.g., Van Bruggen, *Ambten in de apostolische kerk*, 114–18. His influence is also felt in North America. Cf. the minority report in Davis et al., "Report of the Committee," 370–73, cf. 354.

of providing for the needy who were being overlooked. The laying on of hands indicates ordination to a special office (cf. Acts 13:3; 1 Tim. 4:14; 2 Tim. 1:6).[2] A further indication that a special office is in view is evident from the manner in which elder and deacon are mentioned together, as two offices (Phil. 1:1), each having their specific qualifications for service (1 Tim. 3:8–13). Among the criteria for the deacon is the ability to rule or manage his children and his own household well (1 Tim. 3:12). The original Greek term for "rule" (*proistēmi*) is used for giving authoritative leadership, suggesting that the deacon must be able to give that sort of leadership. The word translated as "rule" is employed elsewhere for giving leadership to the congregation over whom such brothers have been set (1 Thess. 5:12; 1 Tim. 5:17). All of this suggests that the deacon holds an ecclesiastical office with authority to do the tasks entrusted to him.

One objection has been that if the New Testament speaks of an office for the diaconate, why do we never read of the appointment of deacons the way we do with elders? When the apostle Paul and Barnabas traveled through Asia Minor preaching the gospel, they "appointed elders in every church" (Acts 14:23). Also, the apostle Paul commanded Titus to appoint elders in every city in Crete (Titus 1:5). We do not read of deacons in this manner. It is hazardous to argue from silence—from what is not written. But it could be that these appointments indicate that the first need of a church is the office of the elder. A church cannot do without this office. As a church gets established and needs arise, then deacons come into the picture. This seems to indicate that initially elders might have done some diaconal work and, following the principle of Acts 6, seen to it that deacons were ordained when the needs warranted it. Such practices are still basically followed in mission contexts where the missionary might be multitasking until the Lord gives the nec-

---

2. See further Van Dam, *The Elder*, 129–34; for a historical exegetical discussion of laying on of hands and its relationship to ecclesiastical office in Acts 6, see McKee, *John Calvin on the Diaconate*, 139–58.

essary gifts in the congregation to enable the ordination of elders and deacons.[3]

On the basis of Acts 6 we can be certain, however, that the task of taking care of the poor required ordination to office. As we saw in chapter 7, the early church therefore understood ordination as normative for initiating deacons into ecclesiastical office. Although the biblical office of deacon got derailed through its long history to the time of the great Reformation, the rediscovery of the diaconal office in the sixteenth century is a great treasure for the church today. So how does a man today become a deacon? What is involved in entering into this office?

Ordination into the Office

Scripture clearly sets forth the requirements for the diaconal office. Deacons must be "reverent, not double-tongued, not given to much wine, not greedy for money, holding the mystery of the faith with a pure conscience. But let these also first be tested; then let them serve as deacons, being found blameless. Likewise, their wives must be reverent, not slanderers, temperate, faithful in all things. Let deacons be the husbands of one wife, ruling their children and their own houses well" (1 Tim. 3:8–12). Also, they must be "men of good reputation, full of the Holy Spirit and wisdom" (Acts 6:3). Chapter 5 discussed these prerequisites.

Since the diaconal office is ecclesiastical, the congregation needs to be involved in the process leading to ordination (cf. Acts 6:2–3). In Presbyterian and Reformed churches, church members may propose to the session or consistory candidates for the diaconal office. Since the congregation is well positioned to know its own members, congregational involvement is important to ensure that the best-qualified men are recommended. The congregation is subsequently presented with a slate of candidates from which they can elect the necessary number of deacons. The consistory or session,

---

3. On these issues, see Knight, *Pastoral Epistles*, 175–76.

having heard the preferences of the congregation, then appoints
the elected brothers to the office. If after a predetermined length of
time no lawful objections are brought forward, the ordination can
take place according to the prescribed ecclesiastical form. The one
entering into the office then knows that he has been called by God
through the agency of the congregation to serve his people.

Should the ordination of deacons involve the laying on of
hands? Often the laying on of hands is employed only with the
ordination of a minister or teaching elder and, in some cases, the
ruling elder as well. In churches that are heirs of the Reformation,
there is a history behind this restricted and ambivalent use of the
laying on of hands because of Roman Catholic abuse and misap-
propriation of the rite.[4] The ordination of the seven to minister
to the poor in Acts 6 would, however, justify ordaining deacons
with the laying on of hands. This was also the practice in the early
church, both Eastern and Western.[5] Calvin considered it to be "a
rite consistent with order and dignity, seeing that it was used by
the apostles." He noted also that "although there exists no set precept for the laying on of hands, because we see it in continual use
with the apostles, their very careful observance ought to serve in
lieu of a precept."[6] Consistent with Calvin's direction, the Colloquy of Wesel (1568) determined that the laying on of hands can
be used with the ordination of ministers, elders, and deacons, but
left churches free to decide whether to actually use this rite. However, the church order adopted by the Synod of Dort (1618–1619)
directed that only the minister would be ordained with the laying
on of hands.[7] In its 1578 Second Book of Discipline (3.12), the
Scottish church indicated that all those admitted to ecclesiastical

4. Van Dam, The Elder, 134–35.
5. Paul F. Bradshaw, Maxwell E. Johnson, and L. Edward Phillips, The Apostolic
Tradition: A Commentary, Hermeneia (Minneapolis: Fortress, 2002), 64–65.
6. See, respectively, Calvin, Acts 1–13, 163; and Calvin, Institutes, 4.3.16; cf. 4.19.6.
7. The Articles of Wesel, 2.11, 4.7, and 5.2. For the Dutch text, see P. Biesterveld
and H. H. Kuijper, Kerkelijk handboekje (Kampen: J. H. Bos, 1905), 8, 18, 20; for the
original Latin, Rutgers, Acta van de Nederlandsche Synoden, 15, 23, 25. The Church

office are to be ordained with the imposition of hands.[8] Later, this rite was restricted to ministers.[9] More recently, there is a growing acknowledgment in both Reformed and Presbyterian churches that the use of the laying on of hands in ordaining deacons is justified. Practical considerations, however, have been used to argue against this.[10]

Length of Service
In Presbyterian churches deacons can be ordained for lifetime service, but it is possible to ordain for a limited term of service. Reformed churches usually ordain for a limited time only, usually two or three years. What accounts for these differences?

Order of Dordt, article 4; cf. articles 22 and 24. Biesterveld and Kuijper, *Kerkelijk hand-boekje*, 226, 231, 232.

8. Kirk, *Second Book of Discipline*, 178–82.

9. An indication of this development is found in Alexander Henderson, *The Government and Order of the Church of Scotland* (Edinburgh, 1641), 10, 13–15, where the minister is ordained with the laying on of hands upon his head, but not the elders and deacons. Samuel Miller recounted how, in about 1812, ordination of elders and deacons with the imposition of hands was considered an innovation. Samuel Miller, *An Essay on the Warrant, Nature and Duties of the Office of the Ruling Elder in the Presbyterian Church* (1832; repr., Dallas: Presbyterian Heritage Publications, 1987), 282.

10. For example, laying on of hands in ordaining deacons is found in *The Book of Church Order of the Presbyterian Church in America*, 6th ed. (Lawrenceville, Ga.: The Office of the Stated Clerk of the General Assembly of the Presbyterian Church in America, 2007), chapter 24-6; *The Book of Church Order of the Orthodox Presbyterian Church* (Willow Grove, Pa.: The Committee on Christian Education of the Orthodox Presbyterian Church, 2011), 71; *Kerkorde van de Protestantse Kerk in Nederland* (Zoetemeer: Boekencentrum, 2013), article 6.10, http://www.pkn.nl; for the Reformed Churches in the Nederlands (Liberated) see R. D. Anderson, "On the Laying on of Hands," *Ordained Servant* 13 (2004): 47–48. Because ministers in Reformed churches are ordained for life, the laying on of hands is restricted to that office. It is noteworthy, however, that the late Professor J. Kamphuis, who taught church polity, wished to see the laying on of hands used in the ordination of deacons. Kamphuis, *Altijd met goed accord*, 128. As a practical consideration, in larger congregations the annual ordinations of deacons to a fixed term can result in liturgical difficulties and diminish the appreciation for this rite. These arguments were used in a report to Synod Kampen 1975 (Reformed Churches Liberated) on the revision of the church order. *Acta van de Generale Synode van de Gereformeerde Kerken Kampen 1975* (Enschede: Boersma, 1975), 278.

The New Testament does not speak of a temporary ordination to the office of deacon; neither does it say that lifelong or an indefinite length of service is necessary. Reformed churches influenced by Calvin have generally opted for a definite term of office. Practical considerations played a key role. The French Reformed churches adopted their Ecclesiastical Discipline at the first national synod in Paris in 1559, according to which the diaconal office "is not perpetual" (art. 22).[11] The Reformed churches in the Netherlands made similar decisions. The Colloquy of Wesel (1568) considered it beneficial that a deacon serve for one full year with the possibility of being relieved from office after a half year if circumstances warranted, and that new deacons be chosen each year. The Colloquy recognized that faithful service in the office was very demanding and could be at great cost to the deacon's domestic life (chap. 5, §17). The Synod of Emden determined that deacons serve for two years, but made an allowance: "However, the Church, and especially those under the cross, may keep their freedom to appoint them for a longer or shorter period, as may seem appropriate and necessary" (art. 15). Subsequent synods decided likewise.[12] Practical reasons were of great weight in setting fixed terms of office, but they could also result in requiring lifelong service, as happened in Noord-Holland prior to 1587, because there was not a sufficient number of candidates for the office.

The Dutch refugee congregations in England met together at a conference in 1560 to decide on a common approach for the length of tenure for elders and deacons. The practice in most congrega-

---

11. Bernard Roussel, "La *Discipline* des Églises réformées de France en 1559: un royaume sans clergé?," in *De l'Humanisme aux Lumières, Bayle et le protestantisme*, ed. Michelle Magdelaine et al. (Paris/Oxford: Universitas/Voltaire Foundation, 1996), 189; for what follows, see H. Bouwman, *Gereformeerd kerkrecht* (Kampen: Kok, 1928), 1:603–7.

12. For the Colloquy of Wesel, the Synod of Emden, and subsequent synods, see Bouwman, *Gereformeerd kerkrecht*, 1:603, 606. The translation of the Emden decision is found in "Acts of the Synod…held in Emden," http://www.dutchrevolt.leiden.edu /english/sources/Pages/15711004.aspx. The original texts are found in Rutgers, *Acta van de Nederlandsche Synoden*, 27, 62–63.

tions was indefinite tenure, and this became the norm. The reasons for this decision included the argument that in Scripture those who served faithfully as deacons were not removed from their office, but were "moved up" to the ministry of the Word as Stephen and Philip had been (Acts 6:8–14; 21:8). Furthermore, as apprentices in every-day life are trained with a view to a long period of service, for which experience is important, so also it is not profitable for a congregation to be served constantly by inexperienced deacons. Perhaps the key reason for indefinite tenure was that these refugee congregations were under the supervision of the Church of England, which was hierarchical and did not favor congregational input for the election of office-bearers.[13]

In any case, the Reformed churches in the Netherlands clearly opted for definite tenure. An underlying reason was the fear of hierarchy. With a regular rotation of office-bearers that included deacons, the office-bearers were less likely to be able to exercise unbiblical dominion over the congregation. Also, as more people were knowledgeable of what the office entailed, they could help guard against the ecclesiastical tyranny that had arisen in the Roman Catholic Church.[14]

Given the times, it is not surprising that in Scotland as well, a definite one-year term (with the possibility to be elected for two more) was the norm for deacons in the First Book of Discipline (1560), so that none should usurp a perpetual dominion over the church (sixth head) or presume upon the liberty of the church. Another consideration was that such a short term interfered less with a person's ability to earn his livelihood (eighth head).[15] The Second Book of Discipline (1578) does not say anything specifically about the length of service for which a deacon is elected, unlike the eldership, which one may not leave (chap. 6.6). Though elected for life, however, elders were not expected to serve continuously since

13. Bouwman, Gereformeerd kerkrecht, 1:603–5.
14. Bouwman, Gereformeerd kerkrecht, 1:608.
15. Cameron, First Book of Discipline, 164, 175, 179.

attending to their daily calling and earning a living could necessitate temporary relief.[16] The principle of ordination implying lifelong service appears to have been applied to the diaconal office as well. The Westminster Assembly's Directory for Church Government (1645) affirms that the elder is ordained "not for a limited time; yet the exercise of their office may be so ordered…that their civil employments be least hindered thereby." Similarly, this document goes on to state that the continuance of the deacons in their office "is to be determined…so as may least hinder their civil employments," implying that like the elder, the deacon is ordained for life.[17] But, since lifelong service is not a clear biblical mandate, it is not surprising that indefinite tenure is not a fixed rule among Presbyterian churches.[18]

Auxiliary Duties of the Office
Churches of the Reformation recovered the primary biblical task of the deacon—namely, to provide for a wide variety of needs and so preserve the joy of salvation in the community of believers. Chapters 4 and 5 dealt with that central duty, and the next two chapters will be looking at how the deacon executes this task.

In addition to caring for the needy and ensuring joy in Christ, other duties became associated with this office, and we will mention two. The first is diaconal participation in the administration of the Lord's Supper. This role has been justified from Acts 6, because the serving of tables has been associated with this sacrament. Although this can be disputed since Acts 6 says nothing explicitly about the

---

16. Kirk, *Second Book of Discipline*, 192n90.

17. Wayne R. Spear, "The Westminster Assembly's Directory for Church Government," in *Pressing Toward the Mark: Essays Commemorating Fifty Years of the Orthodox Presbyterian Church*, ed. C. G. Dennison and R. C. Gamble (Philadelphia: Committee for the Historian of the Orthodox Presbyterian Church, 1986), 90. For ordination implying lifelong tenure, see John Macpherson, *Presbyterianism* (Edinburgh: T&T Clark, 1949), 99.

18. E.g., having indefinite tenure only, *Book of Church Order of the Presbyterian Church in America*, chapter 24-7; giving the option of either lifetime service or limited terms, *Book of Church Order of the Orthodox Presbyterian Church*, 67.

Lord's Supper, deacons were involved as assistants in administering the Lord's Supper in the early Christian church. This diaconal participation is quite apt. The Lord's Supper pictures the joyous fellowship of believers with Christ and with one another, a goal of the work of mercy, and it reminds us of Christ's sacrificial love, which should be mirrored in the diaconal service to each other in the communion of saints (1 John 4:11, 19). In Calvin's administration of this sacrament, the minister took the bread and wine, then passed them on to the deacon, who passed the elements on to the people. The participation of the deacons is seen today when they prepare the Table and provide the bread and wine. The connection between the diaconal office and the sacrament is also evident from the collection for the needy taken at the Lord's Supper celebration in some Reformed churches that commemorate the Lord's death around a physical table on which offering receptacles are placed. The beautiful aspect of this practice is that it pictures that deacons distribute what believers have given out of love for salvation in Christ.[19]

A second duty that has been assigned to the office, although not consistently so, is caring for the material assets of the church. This responsibility can relate to the church's general finances, the missionary finances, and the church properties. It is argued that ordained men handled finances in Scripture: the Levites in the Old Testament; the ordained seven in Acts 6; Barnabas and Paul, who brought relief to the church in Jerusalem; and the elders who received the money (Acts 11:30). It may be appropriate for deacons to handle the church finances or have the oversight over them, but

---

19. For the participation of deacons in the administration of the Lord's Supper in the early church, see Paul L. Gavrilyuk, "The Participation of Deacons in the Distribution of Communion in the Early Church," St. Vladimir's Theological Quarterly 51 (2007): 255–75; for Calvin, the Ecclesiastical Ordinances, 1545 edition, see W. Balke, "Het avondmaal bij Calvijn," in Bij brood en beker: leer en gebruik van het heilig avondmaal in het Nieuwe Testament en in de geschiedenis van de westerse kerk, ed. W. van't Spijker et al. (Goudrian: De Groot, 1980), 223–24; for the current connection of deacon to the Lord's Supper, see C. Trimp, Zorgen voor de gemeente: het ambtelijke werk van ouderlingen en diakenen toegelicht (Kampen: Van den Berg, 1986), 173–76. This chapter is available in English, titled "The Lord's Supper and Deaconry," at http://bit.ly/28JyeSz.

whether Scripture mandates dealing with a church's material goods in this manner is not clear. Certainly it cannot be demonstrated that churches delegating financial and property matters to committees comprised of those who are not office-bearers contravene God's Word. A church can determine that given the enormous task deacons already have, it may not be advisable to give them these added responsibilities.[20]

If the work of the deacon is to focus on providing for the needy, why have deacons historically been involved in the work of church oversight and discipline? How do the offices of elder and deacon relate to each other?

The Deacon and the Session or Consistory

Historical Background

Since the time of the sixteenth-century Reformation, deacons have been closely associated with the work of the elders, but how closely was not always clear or consistently agreed upon. In his Ecclesiastical Ordinances (1541), Calvin asserted that the deaconry as an office was instituted by the Lord "for the government of his church." After mentioning the ecclesiastical offices, including the deacon, the Ecclesiastical Ordinances continue: "Hence if we will have a Church well ordered and maintained we ought to observe this form of government." Calvin, however, did not include the deacons in meetings of the elders with the minister since this body was to supervise the life and doctrine of the church.[21]

In France the first attempt to define the duties of the deacon and the elder was in the Articles Polytiques (1557). The churches

---

20. For arguments in favor of having deacons deal with the church's finances, see, e.g., C. N. Willborn, "The Deacon: A Divine Right Office with Divine Uses," *The Confessional Presbyterian* 5 (2009): 192–93; and Roger Schmurr, "Deacons and/or Trustees?" *Ordained Servant* 4, no. 1 (1995): 20–22. Canadian Reformed Churches typically have a committee of administration appointed by the church council that manages the property and finances of the church. One does not need to be an office-bearer to serve on such a committee. See, e.g., https://langleycanrc.org/committee-of-administration.

21. *Calvin: Theological Treatises*, 58, 64, 70; Calvin, *Institutes*, 4.11.6.

obviously struggled to set forth what was biblical. The roles of deacon and elder overlapped. Deacons were charged with catechizing, watching diligently over the morals of the flock, and rebuking vice and scandal. Elders were to help with rebuking. Funds that deacons collected for the poor were distributed by either deacons or elders. Along with disciplinary and charitable duties, deacons had liturgical roles such as praying and reading Scripture in public assembly. Clearly the French churches struggled to disassociate Roman Catholic ideas from the diaconate. The deacon was almost an assistant pastor.[22]

A more consistently Reformed direction was initiated at the first national synod held in Paris in 1559, which adopted a church order. According to it, elders and deacons served in the senate of the French church with the minister of the Word presiding. The senate was distinguished from the consistory, which is mentioned in the same article. The senate should be understood as the equivalent of what the Belgic Confession (1561) in article 30 calls the senate or council of the church, which there as well is comprised of the elders, deacons, and pastors. Thus, the council could be distinguished from the consistory, which does not have deacons.[23] In any case, all possible ambiguity was put aside when in 1571 the synod held in Rochelle decided that the ministers and elders formed the consistory, and the deacons could attend when the consistory deemed it beneficial. However, in the following year, the synod at Nîmes determined that deacons may and must be present at the consistory

---

22. Sunshine, "Geneva Meets Rome," 333–36; Speelman, *Calvin and the Independence of the Church*, 150–52.

23. Jean Aymon, *Tous les Synodes Nationaux des Églises Réformées de France* (La Haye: Charles Delo, 1710), 1:5 (art. 24), second pagination. This article reads in part (my translation): "The elders and deacons are the senate [Senat] of the church over which the ministers of the Word should preside. The office of the elders will be to assemble the people, to report scandals to the consistory [Consistoire]." The authentic French text of the Belgic Confession, article 30 also uses the term *Senat*, which is generally rendered "council" in English: "Elders and deacons who, together with the pastors, are as the council of the church." J. N. Bakhuizen van den Brink, *De Nederlandse Belijdenisgeschriften*, 2nd ed. (1940; repr., Amsterdam: Ton Bolland, 1976), 126.

meetings to offer their advice, "as hitherto in these difficult times we have happily employed them in the government of the churches, and called them forth into the eldership. And for time to come all deacons thus chosen or continued, shall jointly together with the pastors and elders have the rule and conduct of the churches." Here the task of deacons as being part of the government of the church is emphasized. They assisted the elders but remained deacons.[24]

Given the close ties between Protestant France and the Netherlands, it is not surprising that some similar developments took place there. According to the Synod of Emden, deacons formed part of the consistory of the church, together with the elders and ministers of the Word (art. 6). However, the Synod of Dort (1574) explained in the church order it adopted (art. 4) that the Emden decision meant that the ministers and elders would meet by themselves. The deacons would meet to deal with their care for the needy. However, in places where there were few elders, deacons could be admitted to the consistory if that body so desired. The church order adopted by the Synod of Dort (1618–1619) stated that a consistory consists of ministers and elders, but if the number of elders is small, deacons may be part of the consistory (arts. 37–38).[25] This possibility was made a definite rule in 1905 for the Reformed Churches in the Netherlands when they decided in their Synod of Utrecht that if a consistory consisted of less than three elders, the deacons must be reckoned as part of the consistory.[26]

One could conclude from this that a basic guiding Reformed principle was that deacons participate in the government of the

24. Aymon, *Tous les Synodes*, 1:104 (art. 12), 1:115 (art. 17), second pagination. The translation, with some adjustments of capitalization, is from Kirk, *Second Book of Discipline*, 99. Also see the commentary in A. D. R. Polman, *Onze Nederlandsche Geloofsbelijdenis: verklaard uit het verleden geconfronteerd met het heden* (Franeker: Wever, n.d.), 4:27–28.

25. For Emden, see Rutgers, *Acta van de Nederlandsche Synoden*, 58; for Dort, see, respectively, Biesterveld and Kuijper, *Kerkelijk handboekje*, 63, 235–36.

26. W. B. Renkema, R. J. W. Rudolph, and J. C. de Moor, *Kerkenordening der Gereformeerde Kerken in Nederland, gelijk deze op de Generale Synode te Utrecht in 1905 is herzien* (Wageningen: Vada, 1909), 79.

church. This principle was reflected in their being part of the council of the church, with the ministers and deacons (Belgic Confession, art. 30). The different church orders attempted to explain how this principle was to be practiced without compromising the distinctive of the diaconal office.

The history of the Presbyterian branch of the Reformation also shows some ambivalence in determining the best way to deal with the position of the deacon as contrasted with the elder. According to the first Book of Discipline (1560), the deacons "may also assist in judgment with the Ministers and the Elders," indicating that they would be part of the session of the church and share in disciplinary tasks. But the second Book of Discipline (1578) denied the deacons a place on "the presbyteries or elderships" and church courts generally. Their office was a financial and not a disciplinary one. They were allowed to continue to sit on the kirk session, although the practice was far from uniform.[27] The Form of Presbyterial Church Government agreed upon by the assembly of divines at Westminster in 1645 "affirmed the diaconate as practised in Scotland."[28] Presbyterian churches honoring that heritage have no deacons on their sessions, but the board of deacons typically meets with the session from time to time to confer on matters of common responsibility.[29]

The Place of the Deacon

As churches in the days of the Reformation adjusted to the resurrected office of deacon, it is not surprising that there were questions about how they could best function biblically in the church. Scripture does not give us a neatly packaged church order. At the same time, it does give us enough information so that we can derive the necessary principles and apply them to today's context and situation.

---

27. Cameron, *First Book of Discipline*, 178–79; Olson, *Deacons and Deaconesses*, 156; Kirk, *Second Book of Discipline*, 98–99, 208.

28. Levison, "Diaconate, Deacons, Deaconesses," 241.

29. E.g., *Book of Church Order of the Orthodox Presbyterian Church*, 14–15, 17; *Book of Church Order of the Presbyterian Church in America*, chapters 9–4, 12–1.

Both the Reformed and Presbyterian systems are defensible from Scripture. The issue in view here is whether deacons belong in the session or consistory of the church. What is the way most consistent with the biblical givens?

We noted in chapter 5 that there is a close link between the office of proclaiming the Word and of helping the needy. Each office is a ministry (*diakonia*). There is a common identity that binds them together. Both minister to God's people in the service of the risen Christ. The elder does so with the Word; the deacon does so by providing relief to those in need. Each office has its distinctive role and place. The one is not superior or subordinate to the other. There is a strong bond between these offices in terms of their administering Christ's love and mercy by word and deed, so it can be expected that these offices work in close cooperation with each other.

From the few times that the office of deacon is mentioned in the New Testament, we get the sense that such a close collaboration was indeed a reality. When the apostle Paul addressed the Philippian Christians, he specifically mentioned together "the bishops [overseers] and deacons" (Phil. 1:1). That close bond between the offices is also evident in 1 Timothy 3, where the qualifications for the office of elder are followed by the words that "likewise deacons" (v. 8) need to meet certain criteria. The offices belong together, and their qualifications are thus mentioned together and related the one to the other. The close relationship between proclamation and helping the poor is evident in Acts 6 also. Although deacons are not mentioned by name in that chapter, the seven provide diaconal service in close conjunction with the apostles. They work side by side for the cause of Christ to ensure the joy of salvation in the congregation.

So should deacons be part of the consistory or session? In answering that question several things must be kept in mind. The body of elders is mentioned only once in Scripture. In 1 Timothy 4:14 we read of "the eldership," "the council of elders" (ESV), "the body of elders" (NIV), or "the presbytery" (NASB), words translating the original Greek *presbuterion* (related to the Greek word for elder). This is the only biblical occurrence of the term as applied to the Christian church. It is used elsewhere for the Jewish Sanhedrin (Luke 22:66; Acts 22:5), but here clearly refers to Christian elders as a group.[30] They have the authority to ordain to office by the laying on of hands (1 Tim. 4:14). As the term indicates, deacons are not part of this entity. One can therefore argue that this is an indication they should not be part of the consistory or session.

The elders have a specific role and authority in the church. While deacons have the authority to request, collect, and distribute monetary gifts to the needy, the office of the elder is a ruling office that comes with governing authority and a responsibility for all that occurs in the flock (Acts 20:28; 1 Tim. 3:5; Heb. 13:17). It is for this reason that deacons in both Reformed and Presbyterian churches give an account of their activities to the elders.[31] This does not mean that the deacons are subordinate to the elders in the sense of an ecclesiastical hierarchy. Both elders and deacons have their own specific authority, task, and office in the service of Christ, the head of the church, to whom they are ultimately responsible. But the elders, as shepherds of the flock, have a duty to see to it that all things are done in good order in the congregation. The elders are to exercise this responsibility without lording over others but with a serving attitude as befitting those in the service of the chief Shepherd (1 Peter 5:2–4; cf. 1 Cor. 14:40). The official oversight of the elders includes the diaconal work because a fitting and orderly way of doing things includes accountability.

Although the deacons should not typically be officially part of the consistory or session, it is imperative that the offices work closely together for the well-being of the congregation. After all, they are in the one service of Christ, and the spiritual needs of a congregation

---

30. The early Christian church later used the term to describe a council of elders. See the references in Towner, *Timothy and Titus*, 324.

31. E.g., *Book of Church Order of the Presbyterian Church in America*, chapter 9–4; Idzerd Van Dellen and Martin Monsma, *The Church Order Commentary* (Grand Rapids: Zondervan, 1941), 118–19.

are often entangled with monetary issues—overlapping areas of concern for the elders and deacons. Consultation between the offices is therefore necessary, and meetings of the consistory with the deacons should take place. However, it is important that each office retain its own authority and responsibility. This means that in combined meetings, elders can give their advice to the deacons, but the insight of the deacons weighs heavily, and it is up to the deacons to make the final decision on matters pertaining to their office after having heard the counsel of the elders. Likewise, if elders ask deacons for advice in pastoral issues, the input of the deacons is needed, for they are together in Christ's service. But the elders' take on the matter at hand has considerable weight, and they should have the final say. Elders do not become assistant deacons, and deacons do not become assistant elders. Each office remains distinct from the other and responsible for matters within its jurisdiction.

When it comes to organizing a new congregation with a limited number of office-bearers or working in a small existing church with only two elders and a deacon, common sense would suggest that close cooperation is necessary. There is much wisdom in the old saying that it takes three people to properly discuss a matter and come to a decision, especially if there is disagreement (see Prov. 15:22). It is therefore the better part of prudence when there are such small numbers to include deacons in the regular meetings of the consistory. But it should be clear that the decision for close collaboration is simply due to circumstances and ideally will last only for a limited time. Such close working together can be justified in part because the qualifications for the office of elder and deacon do overlap considerably, as is evident from 1 Timothy 3:1–13.[32]

We offer here a final comment on the place of the deacon. Many churchgoers sometimes have the impression that the office of deacon is somewhat less important than the office of elder. This

---

32. See W. W. J. Van Oene, *With Common Consent: A Practical Guide to the Use of the Church Order of the Canadian Reformed Churches* (Winnipeg: Premier, 1990), 186–87; Kamphuis, *Altijd met goed accord*, 135–37.

perception can be fueled by the practice of choosing elders from those who are serving or have served as deacons. This custom can be traced back to the first or second centuries after the apostles. But such a practice should not suggest the interpretation that being an elder is more important than being a deacon. Calvin acknowledged that "the diaconate may sometimes be the nursery from which presbyters are chosen," but hastened to add that the diaconal ministry is "worthy of no small honor, for it is not a menial task but a highly honorable office."[33] Indeed, both offices are in the service of the risen Christ. The ministry of mercy is so important that, through the work of His Spirit, the Savior moved His apostles to raise up a special office to see to it that everyone in the congregation could experience the joy of salvation and release from the bondage and oppression of poverty, loneliness, and want. It can therefore happen that, in view of keeping the ministry of mercy equipped with the best possible office-bearers, a church consciously chooses candidates for the diaconate from those who have served as elders in the past.

A strong diaconate is a great blessing to the church, for not only does it show Christ's love and compassion in practical and tangible ways, but it also frees the elders to concentrate on their task of shepherding and spiritual oversight in the service of the Head of the church. Where possible the elders and the deacons are to cooperate with each other for the well-being of the flock (cf. Phil. 2:3–5). Since both offices are in Christ's service and ultimately are responsible to Him, there can be no sense of the one being superior to the other.

Summary and Conclusions

Although some people question whether the deacon is really an ecclesiastical office-bearer, the biblical evidence affirms he is. Those who were first given the task of caring for the poor were ordained

---

33. Calvin, *Second Corinthians, Timothy, Titus and Philemon*, 229.

with the laying on of hands (Acts 6:1–6) and were closely associated with the elders (Phil. 1:1). Furthermore, the requirements for this office are clearly spelled out (1 Tim. 3:8–13).

Following the pattern set in the early church, the congregation should be involved in the process that leads to ordination under the supervision of the consistory or session (Acts 6:2–3). In this way God calls men to ecclesiastical office with the participation of the congregation. Although the laying on of lands with the ordination of a deacon has biblical sanction, Presbyterian and Reformed churches do not universally practice this rite.

According to the biblical example, the duties of a deacon should focus on caring for the poor and needy, whether the needs be financial or otherwise. All must share in the joy of redemption. Besides this central task, deacons have been assigned responsibilities with respect to the Lord's Supper and the church's finances.

Historically, establishing a right relationship between the deacons and elders took some time. However, there is now general agreement that elders and deacons each have their own specific field of labor, and they should not encroach on the responsibilities of the other office. However, they should meet together as necessary to discuss mutual concerns, keeping in mind the limits and distinctive of each respective office.

Finally, the diaconal office is in no way inferior to that of the elder. Both are honorable offices and ministries in the service of Christ, to whom each is ultimately responsible.

CHAPTER 10

Enabling and Prioritizing

Before discussing the actual work of the deacons, we need to consider how deacons can best be enabled and equipped to do their office. Another issue related to the diaconate is the question of priorities. What is the place of the family, church members, and the state with respect to meeting the needs of the poor? This chapter will therefore deal with the following issues: enabling deacons and establishing priorities for meeting different needs.

Enabling the Deacons

For the deacons to do their task properly, two things stand out as necessary. Deacons must be equipped for the office, and they need the necessary material resources to care for the poor. The question arises, then, whether the gifts mentioned in Acts 6 and 1 Timothy 3 could be or should be further supplemented or reinforced through some special training in preparation for ordination into the office. Subsequently, we will consider how deacons acquire necessary financial resources, highlighting the privilege of giving for this work and raising the issue of tithing.

Special Training?

Newly elected candidates for the diaconate can feel intimidated by the prospect of being ordained into this office. Often relatively little attention is paid to educating and equipping deacons or those aspiring to this office. Unlike elders, who tend to be older and armed with years of spiritual growth and maturity in the faith, those chosen to be deacons can be younger and may wish they had a clearer understanding of the office and its expectations. This raises the question whether some sort of special training should take place before a person becomes a deacon and officially takes up his task.

Such training would enhance the gifts the prospective deacon has and help ensure that only the best would be ordained for this office. A special training program that is open to all those interested in serving in the diaconal office would give the office-bearers an opportunity to observe the different talents and aptitudes of those taking the course. Such observation would help them to make well-grounded judgments in proposing a list of candidates to the congregation from which deacons are to be chosen. Since making diaconal vows before God and His people at the ordination service is a serious commitment, shouldn't those chosen to serve as deacons be as well prepared as possible? These are undoubtedly good arguments for some sort of training prior to ordination, and, not surprisingly, some churches have required that such instruction take place.[1]

Special training, however, cannot be mandated on the basis of Scripture. Chapter 5 outlined the biblical requirements for the office, and these suffice to qualify men for ordination. After being ordained on that basis, a deacon would nevertheless benefit greatly from ongoing training. That instruction starts with the first visits a deacon makes with a more experienced colleague. A seasoned partner can share much wisdom with a deacon beginning his duties. Further education can also take place in meetings of the elders with the deacons and in meetings of deacons only when these groups take time to discuss diaconal issues, possibly with the help of a book or other literature that participants read ahead of time. Additional

---

1. For arguments in favor of a special training program, see William Shishko, "Reforming the Diaconate," *Ordained Servant* 1 (1992): 43–45, 63–66; for an example, William Shishko, "A Training Program for Deacons," *Ordained Servant* 9 (2000): 62–70.

training can be accomplished by diaconal conferences, workshops, and other educational opportunities that should be open to all who are interested, and not just deacons. Such instruction can be beneficial. Exercising the diaconal office takes much wisdom and insight given the difficult practical questions deacons can face. Any help from colleagues and relevant experts should be welcomed and gratefully used.[2]

Regardless of how training occurs, it is extremely important that maturing young men be exposed from an early age to a culture of loving Christian service that is encouraged and stimulated as much as possible in the home, in catechism classes, in regular preaching on the Lord's Day, and, where possible, in Christian schools. Part of this exposure includes studying what Scripture says about helping the less fortunate and growing in appreciation for the privilege of serving in Christ's church. In this way the seeds for future diaconal service can be sown and young men encouraged to better acquaint themselves with the office and its requirements. Thus, young men will grow in necessary knowledge, confidence, and Christian character and so make themselves available for eventually being called to serve in the ministry of mercy.

In summary, special training and education for the diaconate is highly desirable in whatever form it takes, prior to or subsequent to ordination. The key factor, however, is to recognize the diaconal gifts God has given to the congregation and ensure that the right men are ordained for the office. Such gifts can be encouraged and developed if a love for helping others is cultivated both inside and outside the home during the formative years of Christian young men. In addition to the necessary qualifications for the office, the deacon requires the resources to meet the needs of the poor.

---

2. On preparation for deacons, see De Jong, *Ministry of Mercy for Today*, 102–7.

A Rewarding Privilege

The congregation makes diaconal work in its midst possible by sharing its resources with these office-bearers (see Acts 4:32–37; Rom. 12:13). It is both a privilege to give for this work (2 Cor. 8:4) and a holy obligation. As Christians we are to give out of love, willingly, for the Lord and our neighbor. We know that everything we have really belongs to God, who has given it to us to use for His glory during our time here on earth. But as Christians we also know the privilege of giving in love because of God's grace working in us (2 Cor. 8:1–2). Our Savior became poor, leaving heaven's glory to take on the likeness of sinful flesh (Rom. 8:3) so that we may be rich, living in Christ and being His precious possession. If we by grace share in Christ and are thus rich in Him, then we will give what we can to others. Nothing that we do for Him in loving our neighbor can be too much, for this is a fruit of God's transforming grace in us (2 Cor. 8:9).[3] It is therefore highly appropriate that the congregation give for the diaconal work in gratitude for Christ's work during Sunday worship when the gospel is proclaimed. Giving on the Lord's Day has been the custom of the church from the beginning (1 Cor. 16:2).

It is beneficial to consider the Lord's promises that accompany such giving for the needy in love and gratitude through the ecclesiastical ministry of the deacons. Put differently, acting on the biblical principles of giving, as seen in chapter 3, pleases the Lord, and His favor rests on those who so seek the well-being of fellow believers.

Scripture teaches that God loves a willing and cheerful giver (2 Cor. 9:7). He responds to such giving by ensuring that those who give will never come short, for whoever sows bountifully will also reap bountifully. When we give willingly, God sees to it that we will have more than enough for ourselves and even plenty left over for good causes. Also, the Lord assures us that the church will have sufficient funds to provide for the needy. God's people will be

---

3. See Fred B. Craddock, "The Poverty of Christ: An Investigation of II Corinthians 8:9," *Interpretation* 22 (1968): 158–70.

rich enough to be generous in every way so that thanksgiving will be given to God (2 Cor. 9:6–11). Giving according to God's wishes does not make the Christian poor, but enriches. Indeed, "he who has pity on the poor lends to the LORD, and He will pay back what he has given" (Prov. 19:17; cf. 28:8). The Lord promises those who give willingly and freely to the poor that He will bless them in everything they do (Deut. 15:10). The ultimate outcome is that the Lord's provisions are sufficient to keep the joy of redemption in the fellowship of believers so that people are not burdened by poverty or want of whatever kind.

This truth also functions on a larger scale, beyond an individual congregation. A congregation that helps another in need may experience a time when the once-needy congregation now comes to their aid. As the apostle Paul wrote to the Corinthian believers when encouraging their giving for the poor in Jerusalem: "Now at this time your abundance may supply their lack, that their abundance also may supply your lack—that there may be equality. As it is written, 'He who gathered much had nothing left over, and he who gathered little had no lack'" (2 Cor. 8:14–15). Obviously a church should not give assistance expecting that their help can be reciprocated in the future. Christ said that we should do good without expecting anything in return (Luke 6:35). Rather, the point is that it is unacceptable for one congregation to have plenty and another to suffer want. That principle would hold true if the Corinthian church were to be in need. Then they could expect help from others. God wants fairness in distributing available riches to His church. There should be no unsatisfied need among His people. This fundamental point is illustrated in Exodus 16 in Israel's collection of manna in the wilderness. Some gathered more manna, some less, but God saw to it that "when they measured it by omers, he who gathered much had nothing left over, and he who gathered little had no lack. Every man had gathered according to each one's need" (v. 18). Through His miraculous intervention, God ensured that everyone had what they needed, thus articulating the principle that there should be no want among His people.[4]

Should We Tithe?

When it comes to giving to the church, including the diaconate, the question of tithing is often raised. How much should Christians give? Are they obligated to tithe 10 percent of their income, and should it be net or gross income?[5] Those who maintain that tithing is obligatory today typically have arguments based on Scripture to make their case. Tithing was required in the Mosaic law and formed part of Israel's offering to the Lord (Num. 18:21–32; Deut. 12:5–19; 14:22–27). The Lord underlined a lasting principle when He accused Israel of robbing Him by not honoring the command to tithe and by promising that if they brought the whole tithe, then He would open the windows of heaven and pour out so much blessing that there would not be enough room for it (Mal. 3:8–10). Furthermore, tithing was practiced even before God gave the Mosaic law (Gen. 14:20; 28:22) and thus should be considered a universal requirement that God's people honor today. In addition, the apostle Paul seems to allude to tithing when he urges the Christians in Corinth that each one of them should "lay something aside, storing up as he may prosper" (1 Cor. 16:2).

It has been correctly pointed out that these arguments are not convincing. Scripture does not mandate Christians to tithe today. Just because tithing was practiced before the time of Moses does not mean that tithing should be practiced today. Tithing was also part of

---

4. See the discussion in Harris, *Second Epistle to the Corinthians*, 592–93.

5. Helpful in framing the main issues are two popular articles: John J. Mitchell, "Tithing, Yes!," *Presbyterian Guardian* 47, no. 9 (1978): 6–7; and Jack J. Peterson, "Tithing, No!," *Presbyterian Guardian* 47, no. 9 (1978): 8–9. For more detail, see James D. Quiggle, *Why Christians Should Not Tithe: A History of Tithing and a Biblical Paradigm for Christian Giving* (Eugene, Ore.: Wipf & Stock, 2009); Andreas J. Köstenberger and David A. Croteau, "'Will a Man Rob God?' (Malachi 3:8): A Study of Tithing in the Old and New Testaments," *Bulletin for Biblical Research* 16 (2006): 53–77; and Andreas J. Köstenberger and David A. Croteau, "Reconstructing a Biblical Model for Giving," *Bulletin for Biblical Research* 16 (2006): 237–60.

the Mosaic law. That law has been fulfilled in Christ, so Christians are no longer under that obligation (Matt. 5:17; Hebrews 4–10). Similarly, animal sacrifice, another pre-Sinaitic ordinance that later formed part of the Mosaic law, has been fulfilled in Christ. No one would argue that such sacrifices are still required of us today. The same argument holds that tithing is no longer a divine requirement today. Furthermore, it is striking that although the New Testament says much about giving, it is silent with respect to tithing. When the Corinthian Christian is urged to set aside a sum of money in keeping with his income on the first day of the week (1 Cor. 16:2), no mention is made of a specific amount, and certainly not of a tithe. Rather, the point is to give in accordance with what one is able to give and to do so on a regular basis.

When it comes to giving, the New Testament stresses that God's people who have been redeemed of mere grace are obligated to put everything they have in God's service. Scripture does not speak in terms of percentages for those living in the final age. Rather, it relates how members of the church at Jerusalem "sold their possessions and goods, and divided them among all, as anyone had need" (Acts 2:45). God's grace enabled the Macedonian churches, which were in difficult circumstances, to give even beyond their ability (2 Cor. 8:2–3). Like the Macedonians, we can give sacrificially since everything we are and have belongs to the Lord. We are to present our bodies as "a living sacrifice, holy, acceptable to God" (Rom. 12:1). "Do not forget to do good and to share, for with such sacrifices God is well pleased" (Heb. 13:16). Calvin put it well: "God certainly always commands that we relieve our brethren's necessities, but he nowhere lays it down how much we ought to give, so that we can make a calculation and divide between ourselves and the poor. He nowhere binds us to specific times or persons or places but simply bids us be guided by the rule of love."[6] Indeed, and when we follow the rule of love, we do whatever we can for the needy. We are

---

6. Calvin, *Second Corinthians, Timothy, Titus and Philemon*, 110. On Calvin's views, also see McKee, *John Calvin on the Diaconate*, 248–53.

not limited to a certain percentage, so that once we have given that amount we can say that we have done enough. God claims everything for His service, including the diaconate, and He so judges our giving. If we have the readiness to give, God will accept our gift according to what we have and not according to what we do not have (2 Cor. 8:12). The Lord does not ask the impossible. We are to give as we are able and to do so on an ongoing basis (Acts 11:29; 1 Cor. 16:2). As noted, it is both a joy and a holy privilege to give to the poor.[7]

The Diaconal Offering

Since giving to the poor is a holy privilege and part of our service to God, it is most appropriate that offerings for the poor are held during the official Sunday worship service. This appears to have been the custom of the apostolic church. The Corinthian Christians were urged: "Now concerning the collection for the saints, as I have given orders to the churches of Galatia, so you must do also: On the first day of the week let each one of you lay something aside, storing up as he may prosper, that there be no collections when I come" (1 Cor. 16:1–2). The first day of the week was the day of the resurrection and was used for worship (see John 20:19; Acts 20:7; Rev. 1:10). Paul's mention of the "first day" suggests that he was referring to the Christians' gathering for worship, since there would have been no need to specify the day if this money were simply set aside at home. Since the term "collection" in the original refers especially to the voluntary giving of money for a sacred purpose, it is quite possible that the Corinthian believers gave money during the worship service as part of the liturgy. So on the first day of the week, regular giving in proportion to one's income became the norm. This is still the case today.

---

7. On the extent of giving as seen, e.g., in Luke 12:33 ("sell what you have and give alms"), see chapter 3 of this book under the heading "Christ's Teaching about Service to the Poor."

Bringing offerings in the form of monetary gifts is an important part of worship. As we offer up our sacrifice of praise to God, we must not neglect to do good and to share what we have, "for with such sacrifices God is well pleased" (Heb. 13:15–16). Offerings the deacons collect during the worship service should therefore be for the diaconal ministry and not for the regular items on the church budget. The latter can be collected outside the worship service in whatever way is deemed best. Responding to the gospel by giving to the ministry of mercy is an important element in worship and the Sunday liturgy.[8] With respect to diaconal giving, Christ teaches that "when you do a charitable deed, do not let your left hand know what your right hand is doing, that your charitable deed may be in secret; and your Father who sees in secret will Himself reward you openly" (Matt. 6:3–4). In light of the warning not to make a show of our generosity, using bags to take the offering for the needy is more conducive to the secrecy that Christ demands than using an open plate. The argument that using an open plate results in collecting more money does not convince. Such reasoning could be an indication of the poor spiritual health of a congregation that needs an open plate to raise the necessary funds. Also, in the manner of gathering alms, the church should safeguard the principle that a Christian's giving should be determined and influenced by his love for his neighbor in thankfulness for Christ's gift of love—and not in order to be seen by men.

---

8. Research has shown that 80 percent of offerings taken in worship services in the Netherlands went for the internal use of the congregation rather than to the poor. This is not how it should be. Van Well, *Diaken in de praktijk*, 74. One common way to collect funds for the church's regular operating expenses is for members of the congregation to place their regular voluntary financial contributions in special receptacles found at the back of the auditorium as they come to worship. It is difficult to object to offerings for special and urgent Christian causes during a worship service, but any such collection should be additional and not displace the diaconal offering. For Calvin on almsgiving as an expression of worship, see chapter 7 of this book under the heading "John Calvin" and McKee, *John Calvin on the Diaconate*, 244–45.

Priorities for Meeting Different Needs

Gathering the necessary funds for diaconal use is only one aspect of meeting the needs of the poor. Another question is whether the deacons should necessarily be the first ones to address particular needs within the congregation. Such needs can be monetary. However, there may be needs that cannot be resolved with money, such as combating loneliness, offering encouragement, assisting the sick, or helping to find employment. How does the responsibility of the family relate to that of the deacons in providing necessary help? Who has the first responsibility? What about the place of the congregation or the state and their duties toward the needy? It is necessary to determine priorities for meeting different needs.

The Family

In chapter 2 we saw that in Old Testament Israel, the family had the first responsibility for meeting the needs of those who were oppressed by poverty, bad debt, widowhood, fear, and loneliness and as a result could not experience the joy of the freedom of the children of God. The basic principle of the family having the first responsibility to provide any necessary assistance carried over into the New Testament church.

An important passage regarding this is 1 Timothy 5:3–4: "Honor widows who are really widows. But if any widow has children or grandchildren, let them first learn to show piety at home and to repay their parents; for this is good and acceptable before God." Here the apostle stresses the obligation of children to their parents and grandparents, which normally cannot be passed on to others, such as the church community. Caring for family members is their responsibility first. Godly children will do everything they can to provide the support the family member needs, whether material or otherwise. Parents have a right to this support, for it is pleasing to God (Ex. 20:12; Matt. 15:1–9; Eph. 6:2). In this way, children can repay their parents for some of the care they received. All this needs to be learned—it does not come automatically. As the original language indicates, this kind of care is an ongoing process, for children can easily become reluctant to take on such responsibilities.

In 1 Timothy 5:8, this familial duty toward parents is repeated and broadened to all relatives: "If anyone does not provide for his own, and especially for those of his household, he has denied the faith and is worse than an unbeliever." A person's first duty is to members of his household—that is, those relatives who actually live with him. Widows would be included either as relatives or as members of one's household.[9] If a Christian, knowing that God expects him to honor his father and mother, does not do what an unbeliever will instinctively do—namely, take care of needy parents—then he is worse than an unbeliever. Such an indictment underlines how serious the responsibility to provide for one's parents is. More than those living in the same household are in view, however. The conditional clause has a broad reach: "if anyone does not provide for his own." This is a general statement, but we may assume that the closest relative of one needing assistance should be first in line to give necessary help. In any case, the apostle underlines the point that outside the relationship of parents and children, the siblings of those in need and other family members could have some responsibility toward the one requiring help (cf. the principles in Lev. 25:25, 47–49; Prov. 17:17).

Later in 1 Timothy 5, the apostle essentially repeats an earlier admonition: "If any believing woman has widows in her care, she should help them and not let the church be burdened with them so that it can help those widows who are really needy" (v. 16).[10] This stresses the principle that those closest to the needy should be first in line to provide help. A female member of the household would be most effective for seeing to the needs of a widow

9. Marshall and Towner, *Commentary on the Pastoral Epistles*, 590; Bruce Winter, *Seek the Welfare of the City: Christians as Benefactors and Citizens*, First Century Christians in the Graeco-Roman World (Grand Rapids: Eerdmans, 1994), 67–70.

10. My translation. Most translations follow a Greek text that excludes the phrase "man or," which is found in the KJV and NKJV.

or widows (mother and mother-in-law) and should carry most of the responsibilities. Not surprisingly, she is singled out here. Since the early Christian church did not have many wealthy members, an important practical consideration is that the church should not be burdened unnecessarily. The implication is that if the family is not able to provide financially or otherwise, then the church community will.

There are many blessings associated with assisting family members. Those helping their next of kin in love will strengthen the familial bond (Col. 3:13–14), will experience God's favor and blessing (Prov. 11:24–25; 2 Cor. 9:6–7), and will appreciate all the more the material blessings they already have from the hand of God. It is indeed "more blessed to give than to receive" (Acts 20:35).

Special situations can arise that make it difficult, if not impossible, for the family to help. In chapter 1 we saw that an Israelite who moved from his original social setting could be considered a sojourner in his new abode. Such a person would have lost the support of his family should he need assistance (see Judg. 19:16–21). In our mobile Western society there are many "sojourners" and "strangers"—individuals or families—who have moved and settled far from their original family setting for economic or other reasons. When unemployment and poverty or some other calamity strikes, such as serious physical or mental sickness, and if no relief from the current distress is on the horizon, what should be done?

Since Scripture places a high premium on family involvement, those in need should immediately contact relatives back home. If they do not do so, the deacons of their local church should. These relatives know the needy one and can develop an appropriate approach to the problem. It is probably best that a young single individual return to home base and receive the necessary emotional, mental, and material support there. If returning to the immediate family is not possible or realistic, then other options need to be considered. If the person is experiencing emotional or mental difficulties—this too is an affliction—then it is almost impossible for the distant family to give the necessary help. The local faith community or some other type of support services would have to find another solution. If the problem is financial—although a problem is rarely just financial—the local deacons of the afflicted family's church should fully inform the closest relatives who live at a distance what has transpired and seek their advice and assistance. Then the deacons and family can properly develop a plan of support. If such close consultation with the family does not happen, then the brothers and sisters in the faith community where the needy are members are first in line to exercise their responsibilities directly to those in need. The family of flesh and blood is out of reach, and the family of God, the local church, must take up the task.

The Church Community
When we consider the local congregation's involvement in providing support for the needy, we should not immediately think of the deacons. Individual members of the congregation have a duty as well, and it properly precedes official diaconal involvement. After all, the special offices are to activate the gifts of all believers (see Eph. 4:11–16). When we recall that the Old Testament people of God had no diaconal office and that all members of the community were responsible for the well-being of the needy, it becomes clear that the community of believers should be the first to exercise their gifts for the common good. Only if that does not occur, or if the needs are too great for the family or individual to resolve, should deacons be officially involved. Such involvement of the special diaconal office is the defining pattern of Acts 6. Only when needs were not met did specially appointed people get involved (Acts 6:1–6).

This principle of all believers having responsibility was already evident in the early days of the Pentecost church: "All who believed were together, and had all things in common" (Acts 2:44). The image of the church as a body underlines the same point. The apostle Paul noted how God has put the body of the church together in such a way that He gave greater honor to the parts that were lacking so that there should be no division in the body, "but that the members should have the same care for one another. And if one member suffers, all the members suffer with it; or if one member is honored, all the members rejoice with it" (1 Cor. 12:24–26). Elsewhere we read that the congregation is "one body in Christ, and individually members of one another. Having then gifts differing according to the grace that is given to us, let us use them: if…ministry, let us use it in our ministering;… he who gives, with liberality;… he who shows mercy, with cheerfulness…distributing to the needs of the saints, given to hospitality" (Rom. 12:5–8, 13). Similarly, "as each one has received a gift, minister it to one another, as good stewards of the manifold grace of God" (1 Peter 4:10). Notice that each member of the church has received a gift to be used to serve one another. No one is excluded. All have diaconal obligations (see 1 Corinthians 12–13). Consistent with this responsibility are the words of the apostle John: "Whoever has this world's goods, and sees his brother in need, and shuts up his heart from him, how does the love of God abide in him?" (1 John 3:17; cf. James 2:15–17). Also, "through love serve one another" (Gal. 5:13), and "bear one another's burdens, and so fulfill the law of Christ" (Gal. 6:2). The example of Dorcas, who "was full of good works and charitable deeds," also comes to mind (Acts 9:36).

The communion of saints is to reflect the love of Christ. Paul writes, "Let each of you look out not only for his own interests, but also for the interests of others. Let this mind be in you which was also in Christ Jesus," who took the form of a servant (Phil. 2:4–7). So members of a congregation must humbly serve each other in sacrificial love as shown by the Savior. Such a high standard underlines the depth of the commandment to "love your neighbor as yourself" (Matt. 22:39). Indeed, "do not forget to do good and to share, for with such sacrifices God is well pleased" (Heb. 13:16).

When deacons do address a need, they do well to engage the members of the congregation as much as possible. Deacons are to give leadership by activating the gifts of the congregation for the benefit of the body of Christ. Scripture urges us, "Let us consider one another in order to stir up love and good works" (Heb. 10:24).

Finally, we should note that since the family has the first responsibility toward a person in need, whatever help the members of the congregation give should not undermine the family support system.

The State

The New Testament does not specifically address the issue of whether the state has responsibilities for the poor. In the days of the early Christian church, there was no state-funded safety net for the needy that was in any way comparable to what is offered in much of the Western world today.[11] The indigent in the congregation relied on family, fellow believers, and deacons for all the financial and related support they needed. The situation is different now. How should we regard the place of the state today in helping the needy?

God's Word tells us that the ruling authorities are to uphold justice and are God's servants for the good of a state's citizens (Rom. 13:4). We saw in chapter 2 that the state, the king in Old Testament times, had responsibilities toward the poor and needy (Psalm 72). Pagan rulers also were expected to provide for the oppressed (Dan. 4:27). There is therefore no reason to deny that government has that responsibility now. Today Western governments address the needs of the poor through different means, including income redistribution, by way of income taxes and welfare legislation. State measures to help the poor should be kept to a minimum so as not to undermine the responsibility of the individual, his family, and support communities in society, especially the church.[12] However, the process of secularization has meant that the majority of North American citizens no longer attend church regularly and do not have normal access to ecclesiastical diaconal assistance. Also, churches

---

11. For charitable initiatives in the Greco-Roman world, see Bruce W. Longenecker, *Remember the Poor: Paul, Poverty and the Greco-Roman World* (Grand Rapids: Eerdmans, 2010), 60–107.

12. For other ways that government can justly meet the needs of the poor, see Cornelis Van Dam, *God and Government: Biblical Principles for Today: An Introduction and Resource* (Eugene, Ore.: Wipf & Stock, 2011), 42–46.

have not always been faithful in taking care of the needy in their own flocks. The state has had to step in to help the poor. We can bemoan this state of affairs,[13] but the reality is that government checks have become a vital lifeline for church members as well as those outside the church. And Scripture does not forbid needy Christians to accept government funds. This money did not originate with the government, but with taxpayers. Ultimately, however, a government check is a provision from God's hand. Nevertheless, accepting state funds puts neither the congregation nor the deacons out of work with respect to showing mercy and love to needy neighbors. All the state can give is money, but Christ, through His congregation and office-bearers, has much more to offer those in need.

Money does not satisfy all the wants of the poor. Indeed, we must be careful not to define needs in purely monetary terms. Those dependent on government checks need more than cash. They need the ongoing empathy, support, and encouragement of fellow believers as they go through their time of dependency on others. They need to experience the love of Christ as families, church members, and the deacons minister to them. Besides those financially challenged, the needy include those who are burdened by sickness, loneliness, disabilities, and other issues that threaten their joy in Christ. Recognizing how much Christians can give in spiritual guidance, in support, and in showing God's love puts the limited help of the welfare state in a more realistic light. Government can never replace or take over the diaconal ministry of the church or its deacons, nor should the church or the deacons ever be open to that possibility. It would be a denial of the diaconal office.[14]

---

13. Even Abraham Kuyper said, "Never forget that all state relief for the poor is a blot on the honor of your Savior." Abraham Kuyper, *The Problem of Poverty*, ed. James W. Skillen (Washington D.C./Grand Rapids: The Center for Public Justice/Baker, 1991), 78. As we saw in chapter 7 (notes 17 and 18), the civil authorities also took on the role of providing for the poor in the time of the Reformation.

14. The encroachment of the state into the task of the deacons became the subject of debate when the welfare state started to show itself. For an overview of the history and issues involved in North America, see, e.g., George Grant, *Bringing in the Sheaves:*

There are real problems with state welfare that need to be recognized.[15] Well-meant government programs to fight poverty have rendered many poor people both dependent and helpless. Also, state programs have contributed to undermining the family unit. There is often little regard for or concern about the impact that welfare legislation has on this basic building block of society. It is frequently assumed that neither the nuclear nor the extended family has much of an obligation to help a teenager or young adult living away from home or an elderly relative in need. The state will provide should destitution threaten. One result of this type of thinking is that family members have become mobile and feel no moral compulsion to remain geographically near to their next of kin should they need help. Another problem with government programs to help the needy is their inefficiency and general ineffectiveness in providing the necessary emotional or relational support. Official relationships, for example, between employment counselors and job seekers or between government home caregivers and those they care for do not necessarily make for friendships that create emotional support. Furthermore, government agencies have a difficult time judging whether they are dealing with deserving or undeserving poor. Research has shown that generous government welfare can mean that the poor have no incentive to find work, but that wise financial incentives can help welfare recipients get off government support.[16]

Replacing Government Welfare with Biblical Charity, 10th ed. (Franklin, Tenn.: Ars Vitae, 1995), 15–40; De Jong, *Ministry of Mercy for Today*, 192–207; for the Netherlands, J. C. L. Starreveld, "The Visible Love of Christ: The Diaconate in the Nineteenth Century," *Diakonia: Quarterly for Officebearers* 23, no. 1 (2009): 4–16.

15. For what follows, see Schluter, "Welfare," 187–92; Grant, *Bringing in the Sheaves*, 33–40; and Michael Bauman, "What Went Wrong with Welfare: How Our Poverty Programs Injured the Poor," in *Welfare Reformed: A Compassionate Approach*, ed. David W. Hall (Phillipsburg, N.J.: P&R, 1994), 41–63.

16. For welfare-discouraging work, see Michael Tanner and Charles Hughes, *The Work versus Welfare Trade-Off: 2013: An Analysis of the Total Level of Welfare Benefits by State* (Washington, D.C.: Cato Institute, 2013); for positive results of financial incentives encouraging work, see Charles Michalopoulos et al., *Making Work Pay: Final Report on the Self-Sufficiency Project for Long-Term Welfare Recipients* (Ottawa: Social Research and Demonstration Corporation, 2002).

Government welfare programs should involve and mobilize the family unit as much as possible and create incentives for family members to assist, for example, in finding jobs for the unemployed or home care for ailing indigents and aging parents. It is a marvel of the communion of saints that fellow church members can often help in these and related areas as part of the family of God. Church networks of assistance can be astoundingly effective either through congregational or official diaconal means. This reality also emphasizes the need for diaconal ministries to cooperate with government agencies wherever possible.

Such cooperation assumes that deacons are knowledgeable about the relevant laws that could affect their work. It is important that deacons be fully aware of government programs that needy members of the church are benefiting from. There should be no financial duplication between the government and the church in addressing needs. Furthermore, if deacons know what is available from the state in terms of special programs, such as retraining the unemployed or rehabilitation, they can refer members of their flock to such aids. As a general rule, if at all possible, deacons should take care of their own poor and needy and work closely with the state if circumstances warrant it. If there are extreme needs that deacons cannot meet in their own church, then they can seek help from the diaconates of other congregations. As noted earlier, congregations need to take care of each other. When the church at Jerusalem was suffering want, support came from other churches (Acts 11:29; Rom. 15:25–28; 1 Cor. 16:1–4; 2 Corinthians 8–9).[17]

Summary Listing of Key Principles

The office of deacon requires much wisdom and discretion. The biblical qualifications for the office found in Acts 6:3 and 1 Timothy 3:8–13 should therefore be taken seriously. Furthermore, if at all

---

17. See the discussions on state and diaconate in De Jong, *Ministry of Mercy for Today*, 203–7; Gerard Berghoef and Lester DeKoster, *The Deacons Handbook: A Manual of Stewardship* (Grand Rapids: Christian's Library Press, 1980), 221–25.

possible, those aspiring to the office or those already in the office should have special training and education available to them to further enhance their gifts and make the execution of their office that much more beneficial for God's people.

It is both a privilege and a holy obligation for church members to enable the deacons to do their work by providing the necessary financial resources. God loves a cheerful giver who gives from love for God and his neighbor out of the abundance he has been entrusted with. There is no need to limit our giving to 10 percent. We may make all our resources available. The Lord claims everything for His service, including the work of the deacons.

When it comes to diaconal care, all members of the congregation are responsible to love their neighbor, including those who have material needs. There are priorities regarding who ought to be first to give assistance. The family has the first responsibility to provide help, followed by the church community, first as individuals and then as deacons. Deacons can utilize the different gifts in the congregation to meet the needs of the poor, lonely, afflicted, and sick. Although there are real problems associated with state support for the poor, Scripture does give government responsibilities for the needy and does not forbid believers from benefiting from state aid.

CHAPTER 11

The Diaconal Ministry within the Congregation

As noted in chapters 2 and 3, the basis for believers helping each other is the command to love God and your neighbor as yourself. Love is always open-ended. We can never give too much love. But how can deacons best put that command into practice? Connected with this is the need to keep joy in the fellowship of believers. No one should be deprived of that joy because of unmet needs and want. So what is the biblical—and therefore realistic— way forward for deacons in their service to their fellow church members so that this love can be properly channeled to the greatest effect? To come to a biblical approach, we first need a brief review of the original context of the diaconal office, an issue dealt with in detail in chapter 4, and then consider how this office can best function within the local church. This chapter therefore discusses the original context of diaconal care, diaconal visitation, some typical scenarios, proactive strategies, and challenges and biblical guidelines.

The Original Context of Diaconal Care

Reflecting for a moment on the circumstances leading to the establishment of the diaconal office will help us consider more profitably the work of the deacons. For many, poverty was an immediate life reality in the young Pentecost church, because when the poor became Christians, they lost the financial benefits of being part of the synagogue. The believers' prompt response was to share their resources. They sold their possessions and goods and gave to those in need (Acts 2:44–45). They understood their obligations from Christ's instructions, as taught by the apostles (Acts 2:42), and from their application of the principles of Old Testament law to their situation. After all, the Spirit had been poured out and had written the law on their hearts (see Jer. 31:33). There was a vibrant communion of joy in which the poor shared: "Now the multitude of those who believed were of one heart and one soul; neither did anyone say that any of the things he possessed was his own, but they had all things in common" (Acts 4:32). All this was to be motivated by genuine love for neighbors. When Ananias and Sapphira tried to use the occasion of selling their possessions to boost their own standing and exalt themselves in the eyes of the congregation, they were severely punished (Acts 5:1–11).

It is important to realize that all this sharing and caring took place without the office of deacon. In accordance with the teaching of the Old Testament, the Pentecost congregation realized that it was the duty of God's people as a whole to take care of the poor and to ensure communal joy. Only when the needs of those who were suffering want and affliction were not being met were seven men specially ordained to ensure the proper distribution of food and to meet the various needs of the believers (Acts 6:1–6). Unlike Old Testament times, there was now a special office with regard to the poor, needy, afflicted, and oppressed in the congregation.

The absence of deacons in Old Testament times holds a powerful message for us today in at least two ways. First, the fact that there was no diaconal office in ancient Israel underscores the primary responsibility of the members of the congregation to take care of the needy and afflicted. Concretely this means, as we saw in the previous chapter, that church members should not refer a need in the congregation to the deacons too quickly. Rather, individual church members should first consider whether the matter can be dealt with by those who have first become aware of an issue, without involving the diaconal office. Second, it is a great privilege to have the office of deacon. When circumstances changed and the church was no longer identified with a single nation living in a separate country, Christ graciously gave to His church a tremendous help in the office of deacon. It is an aid that we may gratefully avail ourselves of.

Before we discuss deacons helping the needy, we must consider who those receiving aid are. They include the indigent, who are financially challenged and need monetary assistance. But the ministry of the deacons should go far beyond those lacking material possessions. As we have seen in the chapters considering the biblical data from both Testaments, those considered poor have a wide variety of needs. They encompass those who have experienced an unexpected calamity that has impaired them physically or psychologically. Also, people who have been intimidated, exploited, or oppressed are to be helped. In short, anyone within the communion of saints who is not able to experience the joy and freedom of God's children should be assisted. After all, God had set His people free from the bondage of Egypt and, in the fullness of time, from the bondage and dominion of sin and Satan. All must enjoy the delight of deliverance. Anything taking away from that joy, such as the burden of poverty, loneliness, sickness, or mental or physical disabilities, warrants diaconal attention and care. Christ emphasized the seriousness of meeting these needs when He spoke of the final judgment. People will be separated according to whether they gave food and drink to the hungry and thirsty, welcomed the stranger, clothed the naked, and visited the sick and those imprisoned. The reason, Christ said, is that "as you did it to one of the least of these My brethren, you did it to Me" (Matt. 25:40). When it is motivated by love, help given to brothers and sisters for Christ's sake is considered done to Christ Himself.

As noted in the previous chapter, the family has the first responsibility to make provision for unmet needs. After that, the congregation is next to help. It is important to comprehend fully how vital congregational participation is. In a vibrant communion of saints, especially in a larger church, the members of the congregation will often know of needs in the fellowship of believers before the deacons become aware of them. The Lord expects church members to meet those needs if at all possible without necessarily involving the deacons. After all, we are to do to others as we would have them do to us and love our neighbor as ourselves (Matt. 7:12; 22:39).

In light of these obligations, how can deacons best do their work? In what follows, we will consider diaconal visitation, some typical scenarios, proactive strategies, challenges deacons face, and basic principles that should govern diaconal labor. In the next chapter, we will deal with the problem of diaconal responsibility and the poor outside the church.

Diaconal Visitation

An important component for effective deacons is visiting the members of the congregation in their homes on a regular basis. The frequency of such visits can vary due to local circumstances. Since a deacon will possibly make many special visits, a visit once every three years to every member of the congregation should be achievable. A deacon ordained for a definite term would try to visit everyone under his care early in his ministry. Diaconal visits are different from elder visits. The elders have spiritual oversight of the flock, encourage a life of holiness, and warn the wayward, and their visits are directed to those ends. The diaconal visit has a different purpose.

The deacon's first aim for a visit is to get to know those entrusted to his care and to give those he visits the opportunity to feel comfortable with him. A relationship of mutual trust is absolutely essential for any diaconal ministry to be blessed. Deacons must know those to whom they are to minister, and vice versa. A visit gives deacons the opportunity to fully explain the nature of their ministry and remove any possible misunderstandings. The result of diaconal visits is that church members feel free, should it be necessary, to go to their deacons for help and support. In a day when material and spiritual support is available from many nonecclesiastical organizations, it is important when there is a need that church members think of the deacons and the help the church can offer.

Once deacons have established a good rapport and relationship, a second purpose comes into focus. A diaconal visit can ascertain whether church members have any needs, financial or otherwise, that are not being met. This purpose requires that the deacon have much wisdom and sensitivity for the feelings of church members. Deacons should respect a person's or a family's privacy. In any case, deacons must convey something of the love of Christ, reaching out to those they are visiting and wanting to provide whatever help is needed. In the course of a visit, the deacons may discover that there are real monetary concerns, but the individual or family has been too shy or embarrassed to ask for help. Ideally deacons can see or anticipate needs and offer to help rather than waiting for those in need to come to them. Deacons can see to it that help is given in such a way that those receiving it do not feel guilty or awkward, but receive assistance as an indication of Christ's love. Poverty in middle-class churches in the Western world is not common anymore. But this circumstance does not mean that there are no needs in a congregation. For example, a wealthy family may be experiencing great difficulty coping with sickness or loneliness, and that imperils their joy and freedom in Christ. Deacons can see to it that such a need is met by counseling and encouragement from God's Word. If necessary, spiritual support from gifted members of the congregation can be arranged. This brings us to a third purpose.

A diaconal visit can also include asking whether an individual or family has gifts they can use for the benefit of the congregation. Or, put differently, deacons can determine what a family or person is doing for the well-being and joy of the communion of saints when they ask, "What is your service for building up the body of Christ in love?" (see Eph. 4:12). In this way, the deacons can discover the talents and gifts of love and compassion that reside in the congregation. And they not only discover them, but they also put them to work. Without the deacons' stimulus and encouragement, these gifts might never be discovered or put to use. We must emphasize that deacons are ordained to minister and serve the entire congregation, not just the materially poor. Deacons can play a vital role in ensuring that all members of the church use their gifts to combat not only material needs but also all other needs that can stand in the way of sharing in the joy of the freedom of the children of God.

It is therefore most worthwhile and necessary for deacons to visit the entire congregation on a regular basis, and not just those members with obvious material and spiritual needs. With regular visitation, they become familiar with their charges and can spot needs and problems before they become too great. They demonstrate Christ's love and mercy when they approach those who seem to be in need rather than waiting for them to make an official request. Furthermore, simple, regular visitations can be valuable for those experiencing the negative effects of the culture of individualism that is so prevalent in our times. If deacons periodically visit church members and stimulate the service of love throughout the congregation, they can do much to ensure that no one in the church will feel lonely, bypassed, or left out. In this way, the joy and warmth of mutual love and fellowship will continue to characterize the church in a loveless and cold world. Consequently, the church will be an attractive beacon of hope and joy in a secular, sinful world that is not able to offer such cheer.

It is advisable that two deacons visit together. This is not mandatory, and there can be circumstances in which a deacon visiting alone is more appropriate. The advantage of having two go is that they can benefit from each other's insights when they evaluate their visits and when they determine the nature of any follow-up. Furthermore, if two visit, the deacon with less experience can learn from the more experienced deacon, and they can discuss issues together. In the process of such collaboration, the more experienced deacon can be training the less experienced one.

It is profitable to divide the congregation into wards or sections, with two deacons assigned to each ward. Each deacon will then have half the ward for his special care. In this way, the deacon and those in his trust can get to know each other and build a good relationship. Also, the deacon can visit those with special needs as often as necessary, share in their sorrows and joys, and administer Christ's love to them.

Confidentiality is critically important when dealing with those struggling with special needs. Such people often feel vulnerable and they need to be absolutely sure that their confidence in the deacons is not misplaced.[1]

Some Typical Scenarios

In their regular work, deacons face many different needs and situations. It is a great encouragement to those facing various challenges that the deacons come in their official capacity as Christ's office-bearers. The message is clear: the Lord and His church have not forgotten them. We have seen that the family of those who are hurting should be involved first in addressing needs. Obviously, the more family can do to help, especially concerning practical issues, the less deacons need to do. The following scenarios picture a wide range of circumstances possibly involving deacons officially, but deacons may not necessarily be doing all these things if family is involved. As shepherds of the flock, elders also can be expected to be involved in many of these situations.

Unemployment. Losing a job can be difficult to handle, both emotionally and financially. Deacons can ensure that the unemployed person's financial needs are taken care of through work or government benefits. Should that not be the case, or if the means are insufficient, the deacons can help. Finances, however, are often not the chief concern for the unemployed, especially if there are poor prospects for new employment in their chosen vocation due to technological change or globalization. Having a fulfilling rhythm in life, feeling the sense of worth that comes with being able to provide for a family, and being able to help others suddenly change to a certain emptiness, a lack of self-esteem or sense of failure, and a depressing consciousness of being dependent on others. Deacons can minister to such people and encourage them with biblical counsel. God does

---

1. A resource for diaconal visitation is W. Huizinga, *Deacons Go Visiting!: Studies on the Work of the Deacons* (Armadale, Australia: The Reformed Guardian, 2003).

have a plan for them and has not abandoned them. They have gifts that can be used. If necessary, deacons can point the job seeker to government or private resources or possibilities for new employment or retraining for another line of work.

Sickness. Chronic sickness and failing health are huge challenges for any family. Diaconal visits to provide encouragement from the Scriptures and give practical help go a long way toward meeting some of the needs people experience in such situations. Practical help can include setting up a congregational schedule to provide transportation and meals as necessary, ensuring that the sick can listen to church services either live or via recordings, and arranging visits as required. Deacons can also provide monetary assistance should the sick person suffer loss of needed income.

The Elderly. People suffering from the consequences of old age may need help coping with the daily tasks of living on their own. Deacons should minister to these people, organizing help from the congregation as necessary and ensuring that their basic needs are being met. They can make the elderly aware of programs or help available to them, be a sounding board as they discuss the future, and help them decide whether they should go into a retirement community that provides minimal care or into a nursing-care facility.

Death. The death of a loved one has enormous repercussions, and deacons should be involved in ensuring that needs are being met. If the deceased was the breadwinner for a family, financial issues may be important, along with the need to accompany and encourage the grieving family with the gospel. If a widow or widower is now on her or his own, the problem of adjusting to a more lonely life can be helped by diaconal visits, especially if no family is close by. As necessary, the deacons may plan social events to bring lonely, aged people together and so encourage them to use their gifts to minister to each other's needs.

Disabled Persons. Although there is generally much help available for those with mobility issues, deacons should be aware of the needs of those confined to wheelchairs and those who use walkers. Perhaps special doors and washrooms should be installed in the church, or perhaps the deacons can enlist qualified volunteers to make physical adjustment to the newly disabled person's home.

Persons with Mental Disabilities. Deacons need to watch out for people with mental disabilities to make sure that their needs as part of the communion of saints are being accommodated at their level. It is wonderful if special homes for such people can be established by agencies or organizations run by fellow Christians. These organizations deserve diaconal support as do the residents.

In all these examples, and in other situations in the church that require the help of the deacons, the family and the congregation should be challenged to do their part. Deacons should not do everything, because showing the love of Christ is a communal responsibility.[2]

Proactive Strategies

If deacons are to provide for the needy, then a logical consequence is that they also work to prevent material poverty, suffering, and want that can rob church members of the joy of salvation. Much of this work takes the form of educating God's people in relevant biblical principles. In this sense the work of the deacons will support the work of both the teaching and ruling elders.

We have already mentioned one way that deacons can educate church members: by visiting the congregation. In the intimate setting of a diaconal visit, deacons can use the opportunity to apply biblical principles directly to specific issues. This implies that the deacons are wise and have the ability to assess a situation and give sound advice. Also, deacons can give more generic instruction by highlighting principles that can assist people in a more general way. For example, a feature of our times is rampant materialism; the dollar has become known as the "almighty buck." Many people bow to the altar of this god and are enticed into the service of money.

---

2. For more on practical scenarios, see Berghoef and DeKoster, *Deacons Handbook*, 155–68.

Deacons can help make people aware that their possessions are not theirs in any absolute way. Everything that believers have in this life is given to them in trust by God to be used in a stewardly way for His glory, and this includes furthering the communal joy and freedom of the people of God. Such a biblical view of our possessions is liberating not only for the needy, who benefit materially from monetary gifts, but also for the giver. To be able to give liberally is a blessing, for one must never be enslaved to money. To be in bondage to money is a cruel captivity that robs God of a most precious possession of His—a member of the church. We cannot serve two masters (Matt. 6:24). The eighth commandment, as discussed in chapter 2, also has implications regarding this matter.

Another way for deacons to be proactive through education is to have a role, directly or indirectly, in premarital counseling. Before a Christian couple gets married is a good time to set a biblical pattern for the future. It is critically important that married couples have a clear understanding of biblical stewardship and learn to adopt a lifestyle commensurate with their income. Their expectations should be in accordance with biblical principles. Believers should keep their lives free from the love of money, live modestly, and be content (1 Tim. 6:6–9; Heb. 13:5). It is significant that one Reformed marriage form includes in the duties of the bridegroom working faithfully in his daily calling so that he may support his family "and also help those in need."[3]

Also, deacons can organize conferences for church members to discuss current issues relevant to their office and to the congregation's responsibilities. Such conferences can address matters such as a biblical view of debt, household finances, budget priorities, care for disabled persons, obstacles widows and widowers face within

---

3. This phrase occurs in the marriage form used in the Canadian Reformed Churches. *Book of Praise: Anglo-Genevan Psalter* (Winnipeg: Standing Committee for the Publication of *The Book of Praise* of the Canadian Reformed Churches, 2014), 629. For a perceptive discussion on Christian living, balancing giving for the needy and keeping for oneself, see Timothy J. Keller, *Ministries of Mercy: The Call of the Jericho Road*, 2nd ed. (Phillipsburg, N.J.: P&R, 1997), 67–79.

the congregation, and many other topics. Conferences can be educationally enriching and instrumental in creating a consensus on how best to approach contemporary issues facing the diaconate. They can also motivate church members to appropriate action.

Deacons can do only so much to prevent poverty, want, and loneliness. Their task is ecclesiastical and limited. It is up to the church membership, as residents and citizens of their community and country, society at large, and government to seek economic and social solutions to conditions leading, for instance, to poverty and sickness. But, as already indicated, deacons can provide much concrete help, encouragement, and stimulation.

Challenges and Biblical Guidelines

Deacons face many challenges in responding biblically to the various needs in the congregation. It is one thing to understand what Scripture teaches, but it is another thing to put that knowledge into practice. Deacons must seek much wisdom in prayer so that their labors can be blessed. What follows are some areas that warrant attention.

Debt

A common problem is that people are too far in debt because they have not handled money properly or understood certain fiscal realities. Scripture teaches that debt enslaves, and, as Christians, we should not be enslaved (Prov. 22:7; Rom. 13:8; 1 Cor. 6:12; 7:23). An obvious implication is that Christians should not get too far into debt. They must resist the materialistic culture and the constant striving for more. A simple lifestyle in a smaller home is preferable to a mortgage a family can barely afford. Too much debt is a recipe for many problems that can deeply impact the family negatively and can even lead to poverty if income is interrupted or lost. Having debt also limits a church member's options to help the poor. As a general rule, debts should be repaid as quickly as possible. Deacons can therefore assist in drawing up a realistic repayment plan and, if the matter is complex, call in expert help. In particularly severe cases, a wealthy person in the communion of saints could get involved by repaying debts, and then the debtor would repay that person according to a realistic schedule and without interest. Not requiring this fee would be in accord with the Old Testament prohibition of charging interest to a brother (Ex. 22:25; Lev. 25:35–38; Deut. 23:19–20) and Christ's teaching (Luke 6:34–35). Taking care of debts in this manner could result in better relational bonding within the communion of saints, and the lender is blessed with the knowledge that he is acting according to Christ's wishes and will receive his reward in the affirmation of his status as a son of the Most High (Luke 6:35).[4]

Deacons being proactive is the key, although this is not always possible. But Scripture does give guidelines regarding money and planning for the future. For example, with respect to marriage, an important part of the preparation is financial. In ancient Israel, a father contributed to the new family's finances by giving his daughter part of the inheritance. But the groom also had to prove his worth. He had to pay what probably amounted to at least a year's wages, although it could have been more, to his future father-in-law, who would eventually pass that on to his daughter. Jacob could not afford a monetary payment and ended up paying with his labor much more than a year's wages for Rachel, but he kept the rewards of his labor (Genesis 31).[5] The point is that arrangements were in place so that marriages could begin on a sound financial footing. Couples today can learn from that.

---

4. See the discussion on these issues in Paul Mills, "Finance," in *Jubilee Manifesto: A Framework, Agenda, and Strategy for Christian Social Reform*, ed. Michael Schluter and John Ashcroft (Leicester, U.K.: Inter-Varsity, 2005), 203–5; and Jonathan P. Burnside, *God, Justice, and Society* (Oxford: Oxford University Press, 2011), 232–34.

5. Victor P. Hamilton, *The Book of Genesis: Chapters 18–50*, New International Commentary on the Old Testament (Grand Rapids: Eerdmans, 1995), 289. Although the situations described in Ex. 22:16 and Deut. 22:29 are sinful, these texts show that a man had to pay a bride price to his future wife's father.

Discerning Needs

Deacons must help the poor wisely and with discernment. Not just anyone without money qualifies for assistance. For example, the apostle Paul warned against helping those who are idle and lazy. He gave the rule: "If anyone will not work, neither shall he eat" (2 Thess. 3:10; cf. 1 Thess. 4:11–12). So that lazy people would not be encouraged in their sin of idleness, the apostle strictly enjoined the church not to help them, but to warn them as a brother (2 Thess. 3:14–15). Obviously these guidelines presuppose careful investigation so that justice is done. Since the deacons are dealing with church members, it should not be difficult to evaluate needs and hopefully assist in finding suitable employment.

Everyone who is able to work has the responsibility to be productive, to provide for his own needs, and to be able to help those who are truly poor. The apostle Paul testified to the Ephesian elders how he had lived this principle. He supported himself and noted that "I have shown you in every way, by laboring like this, that you must support the weak. And remember the words of the Lord Jesus, that He said, 'It is more blessed to give than to receive'" (Acts 20:35). He also enunciated this principle in correspondence with the Ephesian church when he enjoined: "Let him who stole steal no longer, but rather let him labor, working with his hands what is good, that he may have something to give him who has need" (Eph. 4:28). Similarly, he wrote: "Let our people also learn to maintain good works, to meet urgent needs, that they may not be unfruitful" (Titus 3:14).

Needs beyond Money

Deacons must not perceive of needs too narrowly, as if providing only for the most basic necessities of life is good enough. The command to love your neighbor as yourself (Matt. 22:39) is applicable here, as is Christ's word: "Whatever you want men to do to you, do also to them" (Matt. 7:12). We must not be tightfisted, but openhanded (Deut. 15:7–8). Deacons should give all the help church members need so that they can live normal lives and never feel like second-rate church members living off the goodness of others. What they receive is from their Lord through the agency of the congregation and deacons. He owns all the church's resources, and He distributes according to needs. And when Christ gives through the deacons, He gives generously so that those who belong to Him can live the freedom and joy of the gospel (cf. Rom. 12:8; James 1:5).

The need for generosity has many practical implications. The sixteenth-century Reformer Martin Bucer counseled that beyond giving food, shelter, and clothing to those in dire need, deacons should give liberally "to endow and help marriageable girls who are honest and devout, who, because they are without dowry, are kept from marriage longer than is fair, so that they can be married in due time and joined to suitable husbands." He also advised that they should help "both by gifts and loans, faithful men who are unemployed, that they can make a living by their trade and feed their children and educate them in the Lord and show themselves more profitable citizens of the commonwealth."[6] With respect to our own context, we live in what is in many respects a godless society, and many people are in bondage to secularism. This worldview has no room for God or His will outside the church in society or in public life. Christians struggle against this enemy by, for example, sending their children to Christian schools. They see this as a need. Deacons should respect and support parents who recognize their responsibility in this regard. If such education is a need for Christians and is available, then everyone in the congregation who wishes to use it should have equal opportunity to access it. Otherwise, a church member is poor and needy in the Old Testament sense of the word and is unable to fully execute his parental responsibility. If his children attend a public school, they will be unnecessarily afflicted by secular forces. As a result, if there are parents who cannot truly afford to make use of available Christian education but

---

6. Bucer, *De regno Christi*, as translated in Pauck, *Melanchton and Bucer*, 315.

wish to do so, the resources of the congregation should be utilized through the deacons.[7]

When we consider being generous in a biblical sense in satisfying needs, we must think beyond monetary help. As we saw in the first four chapters, anything that can take away the joy of redemption and leads to oppression or affliction of any kind can be a reason for showing the love of Christ to one's neighbor. Deacons therefore have an obligation to visit those distressed by sickness and loneliness or those struggling with addictions and mental health issues. Indeed, showing such compassion is the obligation of the entire congregation, the one body of Christ. If one part of the congregation suffers, all suffer with it (1 Cor. 12:26). Individual believers can do diaconal work by using their varied gifts to visit the lonely and the sick (Matt. 25:36), to encourage and help the despondent (1 Thess. 5:11), to assist those who are challenged mentally or physically (Phil. 2:4; Heb. 13:16), to share in sorrow and grief (Rom. 12:15), to show hospitality (1 Peter 4:9), and to share the burdens of others (Gal. 6:2). In short, "as each one has received a gift, minister it to one another, as good stewards of the manifold grace of God" (1 Peter 4:10).

As we reflect on these matters, we see the relevance of Christ's words: "You have the poor with you always" (Matt. 26:11). Who those poor and needy are should never be construed too narrowly. They include the poor in spirit who know they cannot go through life without God's help and those who are poor in the eyes, or judgment, of the world (James 2:5). Although facing afflictions and poverty, these believers can realize their riches in Christ through the support of the congregation (cf. Matt. 5:3; Rev. 2:9).

Meeting Needs Equitably
It is not always easy to ensure that the needs of the poor are met equitably (2 Cor. 8:13–15). As noted in chapter 2, no one should

---

7. For more on congregational support for Christian education, see Berghoef and DeKoster, *Deacons Handbook*, 169–71.

be overlooked, and all needs should be met. This principle does not necessarily mean that everyone receives the same amount. Needs and circumstances differ, and deacons require much wisdom to ensure a stewardly use of resources and, at the same time, to make sure that all needs are met in a fair and just manner. No one should suffer want in the church. All members must feel that they truly belong. There should be no reason for people to feel like they are second class because genuine financial constraints prevent them from fulfilling their normal covenantal responsibilities. Also, church members should not be robbed of their joy in the Lord because of illness, loneliness, and other pressures. All needs should be satisfied (cf. 2 Cor. 8:15).

Working with Relatives
What should deacons do if a needy person has relatives who are able to assist him, but they refuse? We have seen in the previous chapter that the family should be first to help the needy in their midst. But if they are not willing, the needy should not suffer, and the deacons are to help. In the meantime, the deacons should continue to deal with the unwilling relatives in a careful and compassionate way and make sure that they fully understand the seriousness of their refusal. Should these relatives who ought to be contributing continue to withhold help for unbiblical reasons, the deacons will have no choice but to let the elders know. Their office is to watch out for the spiritual well-being of the flock. They need to lovingly and firmly confront obstinate family members with the Lord's demands and appeal to them to change their attitude. Their task is not to compel them to give. Support for the poor needs to be given voluntarily and in love and cannot be dictated (2 Cor. 8:8–9; 9:5). Ultimately, the issue is not the money or support that relatives should give to the poor, but their spiritual well-being when they do not show the love of Christ to their kin as the Lord would expect. This is a serious matter, because the love a Christian directs to the poor is love shown to Christ Himself (cf. Matt. 25:40), and

the Lord considers those who do not provide for their relatives as deniers of the faith and worse than unbelievers (1 Tim. 5:8).[8]

Institutionalized Care

What obligations do the deacons have toward those who need to be institutionalized in places such as homes for the mentally disabled and long-term care facilities? If it is possible to provide a Christian environment for these children of God, church members should pursue that. Deacons can encourage such initiatives and provide monetary support. History has shown that where there is willingness and a focused commitment, much can be accomplished, sometimes in cooperation with local, regional, or federal civil authorities.[9] If setting up a Christian organization and facility is not possible, Christians could volunteer in government institutions or get involved at the board level of such institutions to promote care and an atmosphere consistent with Christian norms.

Deacons can be a valuable resource to direct church members with specific needs, including unwed mothers who are estranged from their parents and siblings, people struggling with addictions, troubled youth living far from their family, and elderly members with dementia, to places where they can find help.

Deacons can see to it that members of the congregation who have the time and gifts regularly visit those who are institutionalized or are shut-ins at home. Visits encourage these believers as they realize that they have not been forgotten. Visitors can bring

---

8. It is noteworthy that in the Old Testament God did not specify legal penalties to be inflicted on those who did not help the poor. Such help could not be forced but must come from the heart in love for one's neighbor. Menso Poppius, a minister in East Friesland, "asked Calvin if one who did not give charitably should be excluded from the Lord's Supper. Calvin answered in the negative: giving must be voluntary, though it is extremely important." McKee, *John Calvin on the Diaconate*, 107n44. Cf. also De Jong, *Ministry of Mercy for Today*, 142–44.

9. See, e.g., De Jong, *Ministry of Mercy for Today*, 215–21. Two current Canadian examples of nongovernment organizations providing Christian homes for those with developmental disabilities are Bethesda (http://www.bethesdabc.com) and Anchor (http://www.anchor-association.com/index.html).

them recordings of church services on a regular basis and celebrate special events with them. James writes, "Pure and undefiled religion before God and the Father is this: to visit orphans and widows in their trouble, and to keep oneself unspotted from the world" (James 1:27). No one should live uncomforted and in bondage to sickness and special needs in the fellowship of the children of God.

As previously mentioned, deacons need much prayerful wisdom, and it is important that the entire work of diaconal service be carried out in prayer. Before a deacon goes visiting, he needs to ask the Lord for wisdom, insight, love, and compassion. During the visit he ought to bring the afflicted person's needs to God in prayer, confessing his dependency on the Lord and His mercy, thanking Him for the support He gives through His church, and praising Him for His love in Christ.

The work of the deacons should be remembered in public supplication during the worship services as well as in private prayer. This office is from God, and prayer for its ministry belongs in the official liturgy. The deacons can do their work only in the strength of the Lord by His Spirit, and it is good that the congregation be reminded of this reality as well as of their own duty in this regard. Asking the Lord for the necessary strength and insight in public worship will help the congregation minister to each other in mercy and compassion. The minister should bring specific needs to the throne of grace without compromising afflicted church members' need for privacy, asking God for help for those who are unemployed, sick, elderly, and facing various challenges. God has given gifts to each member that can be used in ministering to one another, and by His Word and Spirit, God will enable each member to discern those gifts and use them. After all, in the language of the Heidelberg Catechism (Q. 55), members are duty bound to use their gifts readily and cheerfully for the benefit and well-being of their brothers and sisters in the church (Rom. 12:4–8; 1 Cor. 12:20–27; Phil. 2:4–8).

Summary Listing of Key Principles

The Lord's command to love your neighbor as yourself (Matt. 22:39) and to do to others as we would have them do to us (Matt. 7:12) should motivate all diaconal work, whether official or unofficial. Love is to be the motivating force in providing for those who are hurting because of poverty or other issues. The original context of diaconal work indicates that a primary motivation for showing this love is to maintain the joy and freedom from want for all within the fellowship of believers.

The fact that there was no deacon in Old Testament times underlines the responsibilities of the family and members of the congregation for tending to the needs of the poor. There is no warrant for family or members of the congregation simply to refer situations in which there are needs to the deacons. They should first consider whether they can meet these needs without involving the deacons.

The work of deacons is much more effective if it takes place within the context of regular visits to those entrusted to their care. Such a practice enables the deacons to know the congregation, to build mutual trust and confidence, and to anticipate possible needs. Furthermore, such visitations will also facilitate the circulation of gifts within the communion of saints for the benefit of all.

Whenever possible, deacons should try to anticipate future needs and make preparations to that end. Home visitation can be helpful for preventing future problems, as are getting involved in premarital counseling and organizing conferences. Such educational endeavors offer great benefits in terms of making people aware of potential pitfalls and avoiding financial problems. In addition, such a proactive strategy will make church members more sensitive to potential difficulties and equip them to offer discreet help to those who need it.

No deacon should in any way encourage idleness and laziness by supporting undeserving people. God expects us to use our gifts and resources to the best of our ability. There is no place for favoritism.

Diaconal needs should never be conceived of too narrowly. Any burden that can rob church members of the joy and freedom God has given them can potentially be a diaconal concern. Put differently, poverty and need are relative concepts, and we must not say too quickly that there are no needy people in the congregation. The communal riches of the congregation, both monetary and otherwise, must be used so that all needs for normal Christian living in the joy and freedom of the Lord's salvation can be equally satisfied.

The needs of the poor should be satisfied in an equitable manner. No one should suffer want in the church. All should feel and experience that they truly belong to the communion of saints.

Wherever possible deacons should stimulate and support the establishment of institutions or agencies to provide care for those who are unable to live at home. Church members with disabilities can benefit from a Christian environment.

Prayer is extremely important in all aspects of the diaconal ministry. It is necessary that the work of the deacons be remembered in public prayer in the official worship service. This ministry concerns everyone in the congregation, and all members need God's blessing for it.

Now that we have considered the work of the deacon within the congregation, the question arises whether deacons have responsibilities to the needy outside their local church. This takes us to the next chapter.

CHAPTER 12

The Diaconal Ministry outside the Congregation

Do deacons, as ecclesiastical office-bearers, have responsibilities outside the congregation in which they were ordained? How does the church relate to the poor outside their fellowship, and what are their responsibilities to them? This chapter considers these matters and deals with the biblical evidence regarding these questions, the local scene, and the global village.

The Biblical Evidence
The Obligation
In one of his concluding admonitions to the churches in Galatia, the apostle Paul wrote: "As we have opportunity, let us do good to all, especially to those who are of the household of faith" (Gal. 6:10). From this instruction it is clear that members of a local church should prioritize care for fellow members in need, but they should also remember the needy outside the congregation when they have an occasion to show generosity.[1] This directive is consistent with the way Old Testament Israel was obliged to treat sojourners and strangers who lived in their midst. As we saw in chapter 1, although

---

1. Second Corinthians 9:13 is sometimes mentioned in support of helping the needy outside the church. In that verse, the apostle Paul writes of "your liberal sharing with them [i.e., the Jerusalem church] and all men." However, there is disagreement regarding the identity of "all men." See, e.g., the discussion in Harris, *Second Epistle to the Corinthians*, 655–56; and C. K. Barrett, *The Second Epistle to the Corinthians*, Black's New Testament Commentary (London: Continuum, 1973), 240–41.

strangers were not part of the holy nation, the Lord classified these needy people with the widows and orphans and commanded the Israelites to help them as well (Deut. 14:29; 24:19–21). God's people were not to oppress or mistreat the sojourners and strangers (Ex. 22:21; Deut. 24:14–18), but to love them (Deut. 10:18)—loving their neighbors as themselves (Lev. 19:18).

The apostle's exhortation is broad: "As we have opportunity, let us do good to all" (Gal. 6:10). This reflects the command of love. You do good whenever you can and to whomever you are able. Love is open-ended and ongoing. The good in view is, according to the immediate context, spiritual help and encouragement and bearing each other's burdens (Gal. 6:1–2), but material help is not excluded (Gal. 6:6, 9). While our love for our neighbor should be directed to fellow believers first, we are to extend our love to those outside the church as well. As the apostle Paul wrote elsewhere: "May the Lord make you increase and abound in love to one another and to all," and "always pursue what is good both for yourselves and for all" (1 Thess. 3:12; 5:15). In keeping with this show of love is the apostolic exhortation to show hospitality to strangers, which literally says, "Do not forget the love of strangers" (Heb. 13:2). The command to love includes even our enemies. As the Lord Jesus taught: "Love your enemies, do good to those who hate you.... Be merciful, just as your Father also is merciful" (Luke 6:27, 36; see also Matt. 5:38–48; Rom. 12:14, 20). There is no limit to the command to love your neighbor. The diaconal service of the congregation extends to all those who—regardless of their background, creed, or nationality—need compassion and who God, in His providence, brings to our attention.

The Lord Jesus illustrated the high demands of love that God expects from His people by His own deeds and words. He extended His compassion to those who were not of Israel. He healed a Roman centurion's servant (Matt. 8:5–13). He had mercy on the Canaanite woman and healed her demon-possessed daughter, even though He had reminded her that she was not of Israel and in effect had called her a dog (Matt. 15:21–28). Unlike many in Israel, Jesus did not hesitate to interact with Samaritans, such as the woman at

Jacob's well. She was so surprised that she said, "How is it that You, being a Jew, ask a drink from me, a Samaritan woman?" John added his own commentary: "For Jews have no dealings with Samaritans" (John 4:9). Indeed, they were virtual enemies (cf. Luke 9:51–56). But Jesus did not treat the Samaritans as they treated Him. He had compassion on them, and He healed a Samaritan leper (Luke 17:11–19). When He answered the question of who our neighbor is, He illustrated His point with a Samaritan who was a neighbor because he showed mercy (Luke 10:25–37). This parable also illustrates that we need to love whoever God places in our way.

In his sermon on Galatians 6:9–11, Calvin noted that we must do kindness to all men because God has placed us in this world with others. We share a common humanity, and if we do not provide for the needy neighbor, we are disfiguring ourselves and no longer wish to be human. He wrote, "For whilst we are human beings, we must see our own faces reflected, as by a mirror, in the faces of the poor and despised, who can go no further and who are trembling under their burdens, even if they are people who are most alien to us. If a Moor or a barbarian comes to us, because he is a man, he is a mirror in which we see reflected the fact that he is our brother and our neighbor." He continued: "Thus, we are obligated without exception to all men, because we are made of the same flesh." He then referred to Isaiah 58:7, where God expressed His expectations for His people: "Is it not to share your bread with the hungry and bring the homeless poor into your house; when you see the naked, to cover him, and not to hide yourself from your own flesh?" Calvin then commented that those who are mean and tightfisted "not only display contempt for God and reject his Word, but reveal that they are monsters because they have no regard for the brotherhood that should exist between all men."[2]

---

2. John Calvin, *Sermons on Galatians*, trans. Kathy Childress (1574; repr., Edinburgh: Banner of Truth, 1997), 624–25.

Whose Task?

Clearly, the church has an obligation to the poor outside it. But whose task is it to address those needs? Is it the task of the deacons, or of the members of the congregation? It is clear that all Christians have the responsibility to do whatever they possibly can to help those in need outside the fellowship of believers. This is an obligation that cannot simply be passed on to the deacons as a matter of course. Having a personal duty toward one's neighbor is the "default setting" in the Old Testament. Furthermore, it is striking that in the parable of the good Samaritan, Christ's illustration shows an individual addressing the needs of the neighbor. This man saw his responsibilities and acted accordingly. Does the individual responsibility of believers mean that the deacons are absolved of any duty with respect to those outside the church?

Some might think so. Two common objections are raised against official diaconal labor outside the church. First, some people say that the deacons have been ordained to work within the congregation, and not outside it. Second, injunctions such as those of the apostle Paul to do good to everyone (Gal. 6:10) are directed to all believers, and not just to the deacons. Both of these statements are true. But can we conclude, then, that deacons have absolutely nothing to do with needs outside the church? We should be careful not to create false dilemmas.

Individual believers indeed have a primary responsibility in their daily walk and talk to show the love of Christ. They can take inspiration from the example of the believers in the early Christian church who, as we saw in chapter 7, valiantly took care of those afflicted with a variety of needs to the astonishment and admiration of non-Christians. But even though the congregation is to be a diaconal body showing the love of Christ in a dark world of sin, deacons, as office-bearers in the church who represent the body of Christ in aiding the indigent, cannot be exempted from responsibilities here. The admonition of Galatians 6:10 applies to them as well. Although they have been ordained primarily to labor in the congregation, they will bear that limitation in mind and do what they can to show the love of Christ to those outside the church whom the Lord places in their path.[3] In addition, they can assist the members of the congregation in fulfilling their diaconal calling and in limited and important ways become officially involved. A basic responsibility that deacons share with other office-bearers is to help equip the saints "for the work of ministry [*diakonia*]" (Eph. 4:12). Deacons can educate and mobilize the congregation to exercise their duty to show love to their neighbor, including those outside the fellowship of believers. Furthermore, deacons can provide stimulating leadership, motivate the people of God to reach out in love, and help coordinate the efforts of the believers to minister to the needy outside the church.

When the Lord in His providence places a need in front of His people, whether inside or outside the church, then church members must respond in love and mercy. There is no other option, and deacons cannot remain on the sidelines. For example, if a member of a congregation sees a need outside the church that is beyond his ability to meet, would it not be proper to ask the deacons for advice on how best to seize the opportunity to show the love of God? Or, when a deacon sees a need outside the congregation that the church can address, will he not inform and mobilize the people of God to show the love and mercy that God expects from His people? Jesus said, "Be merciful, just as your Father also is merciful" (Luke 6:36).

---

3. It is important to note that Reformed and Presbyterian churches have historically acknowledged this diaconal responsibility to those outside the church. The Church Order of Dort (1619), e.g., states that deacons are to distribute alms to "the needy, both residents and strangers" (art. 25). Richard DeRidder, trans. and ed., *The Church Orders of the Sixteenth Century Reformed Churches of the Netherlands: Together with Their Social, Political, and Ecclesiastical Context* (Grand Rapids: Calvin Theological Seminary, 1987), 549. Consistent with this, a Reformed form for ordination exhorts deacons to "do good to all men, especially those of the household of faith." Canadian Reformed Churches Standing Committee, *Book of Praise: Anglo-Genevan Psalter* (Winnipeg: Premier, 2014), 627. In the Presbyterian tradition, "deacons are called to show forth the compassion of Christ in a manifold ministry of mercy toward the saints and strangers on behalf of the church." Form of Government, 11.1., in *Book of Church Order of the Orthodox Presbyterian Church*, 14.

A church must not be tightfisted but should be generous whenever possible as members of the church work in harmony with the
deacons to meet the responsibilities God has entrusted to them.
Such a church becomes known as a loving, generous community
that seeks to help the needy. Was this not one of the features of
the church in the days after the outpouring of the Holy Spirit that
caused the assembly of believers to gain favor with all the people
(Acts 2:44–47)?

In sum, church members have the first responsibility to extend
help to needs confronting them outside the church. Although the primary task of deacons is to address needs in the local church, they
should, however, do what they can to help the needy outside. They
should also be involved in a supporting and encouraging role and in
helping to organize ways for church members to effectively minister
to those outside the church. Deacons can financially support ministries and agencies organized by church members that seek to meet
some of the urgent needs found in the local community or in the
world at large.

How Deacons Are to Give Help

Deacons are to give help in conjunction with the gospel. As those
conveying in word and deed the love of Christ to people the Lord
has providentially placed in their path, deacons are to provide material help along with the good news of salvation. Christian deacons
who give aid to meet the temporal needs of the body and neglect
to minister to the eternal well-being of the soul misunderstand
their responsibility. The two must go together. In this way the
deacons will follow the example of Christ. When the Savior sent
His disciples out on a mission, He not only gave them the power
to drive out evil spirits and to heal the sick but also entrusted to
them the mandate to proclaim the gospel of the coming of the
kingdom (Matt. 10:1–8). Showing true mercy includes seeking
the eternal well-being of those in need. The compassion and love
Christ displayed should be an example for Christians and motivate
them to love their neighbors and share the good news with them

(cf. Eph. 5:1–2). Christians who help the poor have a wonderful opportunity for evangelism and for sowing the good seed of the Word of God. By so letting their light shine, members of Christ's church show some of the fruit of the Spirit and cause others to give glory to God (Matt. 5:16).

Deacons should give material help according to the principles of good stewardship and biblical generosity, as detailed in the previous chapter. Christian compassion dictates that deacons can provide emergency aid fairly quickly. They should not, however, be naive. They do need to ask appropriate questions before continuing to offer aid to strangers to ensure that they are not supporting sinful lifestyles (cf. Eph. 4:28). They should inquire about the needy person's total family income, whether he has requested assistance from other sources, and why he is in difficulty now. If there are unanswered questions or the deacons have doubts, they need to do more research.[4] The same approach applies to organizations requesting financial diaconal assistance. When helping those outside the church, deacons and congregation members constantly need to remember that they are giving in the name of Christ and reaching out in love to the whole person, so that they are not simply meeting material or psychological needs, but addressing the person's need for the Savior.

Finally, it should be noted that deacons are not to give help by getting involved in social and political activism to relieve the needs of the poor. That task does not belong to the diaconal office. In a democracy, though, getting involved does rightly belong to the members of the church. They can campaign for the vulnerable in society and make known to their legislative representatives policy initiatives that would help the plight of the unjustly oppressed (cf. Ps. 72:2–4, 12–14).[5] Such political initiatives can involve cooperating with others who have similar goals.

---

4. For a helpful discussion on continuing to help a stranger, see Keller, *Ministries of Mercy*, 93–105.

5. On the task of civil government, see Van Dam, *God and Government*, 34–46.

Local Diaconal Service

There are different ways of approaching diaconal ministry to those outside the congregation. Members of the congregation can simply respond to needs as they arise in God's providence. Another approach is to have a well-thought-out plan of action organized and run, for the most part, by the deacons. There could be a combination of these two. The approach a church takes depends to some extent on the human and material resources available as well as where a particular congregation is located, whether, for example, it is in a wealthy suburb or in an economically depressed area.

Believers are invaluable for seeing and hearing of opportunities for local diaconal service outside the fellowship of the congregation. Indeed, administering mercy in the name of Christ is most effectively done by church members who see needs in their daily lives and respond to them in love. The ability to do this, however, does not come naturally to all people. Some believers do not know whether they should follow up with proper resources if they discover a need. Preparation is needed. One form of preparation is to formally survey the community to determine its most urgent needs and the services available. This helps to set priorities for ministering to needs.[6]

Office-bearers can be involved in such preparations. Through appropriate preaching, a congregation can be shaped more and more by the Word and Spirit to have a heart for their neighbors. Deacons can organize educational conferences and ensure that resources are put in place. They can also make a list of talents and gifts congregational members have for different duties, ranging from snow shoveling for the neighborhood elderly to making encouraging visits to shut-ins. Needs that arise can be matched with available gifts. Resources on file should also include referral information so that those requiring help can benefit from programs run by the government or by private agencies.

---

6. Practical help on surveying is found in Keller, *Ministries of Mercy*, 145–53.

With hearts sensitized to show Christian compassion for their neighbors and with resources in place, members of the congregation can engage in a variety of opportunities to serve, including the following examples. A family with an unemployed breadwinner is not aware of programs and assistance available to them, or they need additional help to make ends meet. Neighbors are trying to cope with the death of a loved one and need a listening ear. Another neighbor struggles with the challenges of having a child with disabilities and needs relief and some time off. A new immigrant family has moved into the area and could use some help in adjusting to their new surroundings. A neighbor has had an accident and needs mobility assistance. A poor elderly couple needs help with snow removal. A neighborhood family is struggling with alcohol addiction. A sudden torrential rainfall has flooded basements, and people need clean-up assistance. Also, believers can volunteer and bring Christian cheer in nursing homes and visit the sick. Church members can consider long-term commitments. For example, in our broken world there are always children waiting for a foster home or who are available for adoption into a stable family home. Under God's blessing Christians can satisfy more than physical needs.

In many cases church members can use their gifts and talents to meet needs without involving the deacons. Simple, practical Christian help can go a long way toward resolving an issue. When an individual can no longer meet a need adequately, he can always turn to the deacons, who can call upon congregational talents and resources to provide the necessary help or turn to professional resources. Sometimes church members may need to do some research to find public programs available for certain situations that cannot be addressed by other church members. Bringing some cheer and relief to the lives of those who are hurting can be a wonderful encouragement to them as well as a golden opportunity to show the love of Christ and tell of the true joy that can be found in Him. In this way, members of a congregation can exercise their Christian calling and be a shining light in a dark world.[7]

In a different approach, deacons take the initiative for and ownership of extending help to the community. Inspired by the example of Thomas Chalmers (1780–1847), a minister in the Free Church of Scotland, the idea of official diaconal visits in the church's neighborhood has been revived.[8] The concept is to target a certain number of neighborhoods in proportion to the number of deacons available. The geographic area around the church is an obvious place to canvass as are those neighborhoods in which church members live. To begin, church members can help compile a list of known needs in the different neighborhoods where they live. With this information available, the deacons can determine how best to meet these needs. If there are opportunities to help that the church cannot officially take up, such as retraining someone for a new job, the need can be made known to appropriate individuals in the church or in the community who can address it. As the outreach develops, deacons can begin regular visits into the homes of those who require help and encouragement. The deacons should also use the gifts of visiting and encouraging found within the congregation. Another aspect of this outreach is deacons providing instruction to neighbors on topics such as how to manage money.

Deacons should visit and offer help with the intent of showing the love of Christ and so work for the propagation of the gospel. If a needy neighbor is already a member of another church, the deacons should notify the person's church of the need, and they should determine the way ahead in consultation with the other church. Through this manner of programmatic work among neigh-

---

7. An excellent resource for ministering to those outside the church is Keller, *Ministries of Mercy*. For getting started and organizing the type of diaconal service just described, chapters 8–10 are particularly helpful.

8. C. N. Willborn, "The Gospel Work of the Diaconate: A Ministry 'Proportioned in Number,'" *The Confessional Presbyterian* 10 (2014): 23–32. What follows draws from this article, which gives far more detail than space here allows.

bors, deacons can demonstrate Christian love and serve the cause of the church-gathering work of Christ. It is praiseworthy when deacons are able to organize such a ministry without taking away from their obligation to the congregation.

But can such a comprehensive diaconal program be considered an obligation or biblical norm for every diaconate? A fair question is whether this approach might be an imposition on the deacons. One response is that when the program is up and running, a deacon needs to spend only about an hour each month on this ministry, so his diaconal labors for his own congregation need not suffer or be shortchanged. However, the difficulty is that if such a program prospers, deacons would probably find it difficult to restrict their involvement to one hour a month. Showing compassion is an open-ended activity. If a deacon builds relationships with several people in a neighborhood who need considerable attention, can he really restrict his involvement to a set number of minutes every four weeks? This is a legitimate concern, particularly if the deacons cannot find the necessary gifts and talents in the congregation to relieve them of their involvement in ministering to those outside.

It seems that the first model, in which the onus for caring for the needy falls on the church members with support from the deacons as needed, would be a better approach for most churches for showing Christian compassion and love to those outside the fellowship of believers. It is important that deacons not work under the crushing burden of having too many obligations outside the church. It can be frustrating and counterproductive if deacons are not able to meet the demands for help of those outside the church without shortchanging their congregational labors, which creates intolerable tensions in the execution of their office.[9] Deacons are

---

9. It appears that this is the reason why the exhortation to the deacons to do good to everyone (Gal. 6:10) was dropped from the revised form for ordaining deacons in the Reformed Churches in the Netherlands (Liberated). Instead, the revised form now simply says that the diaconal work should result in the congregation growing "in love for each other and all people (Gal. 6:10)" (author's translation). The old form was consistent with the Church Order of Dort (1619), which noted the deacons' responsibility to those

not ordained to care for all the poor of their town or city. The Lord does not expect the impossible from His office-bearers. We should therefore not overburden the deacons and cause them to feel guilty for not being able to live up to expectations for which there is no clear biblical warrant. Although the church definitely has the obligation to do good to all men—and this obligation should not be diluted or minimized in any way—the deacon's primary focus is the congregation in which he was ordained.

The Global Village

Today there are more opportunities than ever to show Christian compassion and mercy to those who are hurting but are geographically distant. Living in a global village means that we are confronted by many calls for help from diverse parts of the globe. How should the office of deacon respond? The principle of doing "good to all, especially to those who are of the household of faith" (Gal. 6:10) suggests that helping Christians in need has priority. Indeed, being merciful to believers is showing love to Christ Himself. The Lord Jesus said that at the final judgment He would invite into His kingdom all those who had given Him food when He was hungry, given Him drink when He was thirsty, welcomed Him as a stranger, clothed Him when He was naked, visited Him when He was sick, and came to Him when He was in prison. When the righteous ask when they did these things (for they were not aware they had done all this to the Lord), the Lord will answer, "Assuredly, I say to you, inasmuch as you did it to one of the least of these My brethren, you did it to Me" (Matt. 25:40).[10] There are many Christians in the

---

outside the church; see the third footnote in this chapter. For the limitations of the diaconal office with respect to those outside, see C. Trimp, "Het diakonaat van de kerk," in *De kerk: wezen, weg en werk van de kerk naar reformatorische opvatting*, ed. W. Van't Spijker et al. (Kampen: De Groot Goudriaan, 1990), 470–71.

    10. Cf. Prov. 19:17: "He who has pity on the poor lends to the LORD, and He will pay back what he has given." The interpretation of Matthew 25:40 that only the messengers of the gospel are in view seems like an unnecessary restriction, given what the text says. See, e.g., the discussion in Hagner, *Matthew 14–28*, 744–45.

global village that require such compassion and mercy. At the same time, diaconal help should not be restricted to Christians only. The command to "do good *to all*" also stands (Gal. 6:10, emphasis added). Help for the needy in the global village can take many different forms.

Deacons in the Western world can gather funds for needy churches in the developing world, especially those with whom they have close ties. This would be in accordance with the apostolic practice of gathering money from the churches in Antioch, Macedonia, Corinth, and possibly Rome for the needy church at Jerusalem (Acts 11:27–30; Rom. 12:13; 15:25–27; 2 Corinthians 8–9). By sending financial aid to needy churches, we honor the principle of our plenty supplying their need (2 Cor. 8:14).

Also, we can give help by sponsoring refugees from war-torn parts of the world. Many Christians face horrendous persecution and oppression in the Middle East and in other Islamic parts of the world. Deacons can take advantage of government programs that enable sponsoring refugees by organizing the framework. They can then leave running the program to members of the church. While priority can be given to sponsoring Christians, deacons should consider other refugees as well. Wherever and whenever there is an occasion and the means to show Christian compassion, we should grasp these opportunities. It is an excellent way to introduce people to the gospel of God's grace. Indeed, the Lord has used such programs to bring non-Christian refugees to the faith.

Deacons can suggest that members of the congregation write to their own and possibly foreign governments or sign petitions in support of Christians imprisoned for their faith as such opportunities arise. They can also show support for people who are unjustly jailed by totalitarian regimes.

The ideal way for deacons to give help in the developing world is in association with mission and church-planting ventures, as well as in cooperation with nonecclesiastical Christian organizations within a needy country. Deacons can take care of this giving, or they can delegate these responsibilities to a special committee or voluntary association so that the diaconal priorities in their home church are not eroded. Deacons must put measures of accountability in place. Assistance can be given to such worthy causes as medical clinics, orphanages, agricultural projects, and small business start-ups. Support should be given to services that are available to all, and not just Christians. Such assistance done in Christ's name shows God's mercy to a suffering world and is one way to show the gospel in action.

When disaster strikes in a foreign country, another opportunity for diaconal service presents itself. Such diaconal work can be delegated to others, with the provision of adequate accountability. Assistance given to those suffering from terrorism, earthquakes, or a tsunami can have an enormous positive impact for the honor of God. For example, when a tsunami killed over 170,000 in the conservative Muslim population of Aceh, Indonesia, in 2004, Christian aid flooded into the area. This show of compassion in the name of Christ must have touched the survivors and shown them something of the mercy of Christ. The show of Christian compassion in the Middle East in the face of the brutality of the Islamic State has resulted in many Muslim refugees being open to and turning to Christianity in spite of the danger involved in their conversion.[11]

While the church should do everything possible to help alleviate needs in the developing world, especially considering the enormous disparity of wealth between the Western world and the developing world, we must realize that the local diaconate can make only a limited contribution. As office-bearers in the church, the deacons' attention to the global village should be primarily focused on giving practical and material help to foreign churches and Christians in need, without forgetting the needs of others. Addressing the incredible poverty of so much of the world at large in any comprehensive way is a task that is far beyond what a local diaconate can tackle by itself. Churches have therefore taken different approaches to ensure that they do what they can to meet the needs in the global

---

11. See, e.g., "Islamic State Drives Yazidis to Christ," last modified February 5, 2015, Christian Aid Mission, http://www.christianaid.org/News/2015/mir20150205.aspx.

village. Some church federations have created an official diaconal body with a full-time board that coordinates and manages all the relief and rehabilitation given by the churches it represents. Such a board makes yearly reports to the churches. Other churches have opted to leave the foreign diaconal work primarily in the hands of volunteer agencies and organizations that seek to distribute aid as effectively as possible in Christ's name. Such organizations give a full accounting of their activities and finances to all those who contribute to its work.[12]

Another way of providing help has been short-term mission trips, in which a team of Christians goes to a developing country to help out in a mission work by building a church or school or some other project. Christians should extend this type of help while making full use of the resources and gifts of the indigenous population. There are some serious potential drawbacks to short-term trips, such as a failure to understand the local culture, which can result in offending the very people a group is trying to help. Also, questions arise about whether the money involved in financing such a short-term endeavor could not have been better used elsewhere. These are serious concerns and in some cases may necessitate not taking the trip. However, on the positive side, as well as being a great encouragement to the missionaries or the permanent workers in the field, such trips do open the eyes of Western Christians to the appalling needs in developing nations and make them aware of the enormous challenges people elsewhere face. In the process, those who have such an experience find their hearts prepared for diaconal service at home, and they can become zealous for future diaconal work abroad.

---

12. The Christian Reformed Church, e.g., has a denominational agency called World Renew (formerly CRWRC), http://worldrenew.net; and the Orthodox Presbyterian Church has the Committee on Diaconal Ministries, http://opc.org/committee_dm.html. In both cases regular reports are made to the churches the organizations serve. Examples of Reformed organizations that are independent of ecclesiastical oversight are the Canadian Reformed World Relief Fund (http://www.crwrf.ca/) and Word and Deed: An International Reformed Relief and Development Agency (http://wordanddeed .org/). Both organizations report regularly to their supporters.

So although the first purpose of a short-term mission trip is not to benefit the volunteer, such a benefit is often the most lasting fruit. The long-term positive effect on those helped is usually minimal.[13]

The causes of poverty and want in so much of the world are complex and demand the kind of attention and expertise that deacons, as ecclesiastical office-bearers, are not equipped to give, nor should they be expected to be able to do so. It is therefore up to the church, as represented in its members, to address such issues by all means available. These include seeking economic justice for the impoverished areas of the world by crafting policy and legislation that encourage fair trade, working with initiatives of the World Bank and the International Monetary Fund, encouraging the funding of education for the disadvantaged, investing strategically in poor nations, promoting medical programs and institutions where such are lacking, and working directly with the poor in various ministries. The great wealth of the Western world gives Christians a tremendous opportunity and responsibility to show compassion to the poor and hurting (cf. Matt. 25:31–46). Each Christian should respond to this diaconal call according to the gifts, circumstances, and opportunities that the Lord gives.

Summary and Conclusions

Scripture clearly teaches that believers must have compassion not just for their fellow believers but for all people God in His providence puts on their life's path. The obligation to help rests first with those who encounter someone with a difficulty, whether the person is in the church or outside the fellowship. Although each person has a primary diaconal duty to his or her neighbor, deacons also have obligations. As deacons, they too should show the love of Christ to all those God puts in their path. This display of God's mercy can take many different forms, from giving emergency aid to

---

13. For a perceptive discussion on short-term mission trips, see Steve Corbett and Brian Fikkert, *When Helping Hurts: How to Alleviate Poverty without Hurting the Poor... and Yourself* (Chicago: Moody, 2009), 159–80.

a local person in need to helping organize relief in a disaster area. Deacons can also financially support ongoing ministries of mercy to non-Christians.

Believers should always give help in a way that makes clear they are motivated by the love of God for human beings who have fallen in sin. God can use works of mercy to draw people to the faith. Furthermore, biblical principles, such as sound stewardship practices, should guide all diaconal work. Deacons are not called upon to get involved in social and political activism on behalf of the needy. That task is best left to members of the church in their office and calling as Christians to be light and salt in their society.

Local diaconal work outside the church can take different forms, ranging from church members taking the initiative to show the love of Christ in their neighborhood to official diaconal involvement and ownership of benevolent outreach. A balance needs to be maintained so that deacons are able to meet their first priority in ministering to the members of the congregation.

Diaconal outreach and help in Christ's name to the global village is enormously challenging given current economic and political realities. Deacons can be involved in various ways, but their roles should be relatively modest. Ecclesiastical agencies that are at arm's length from the deacons and private organizations will lead the way in bringing help and relief in Christ's name to the many global needs.

CHAPTER 13

The Blessing of the Poor

Given the nature of their task, deacons want to make sure that there are no poor or needy in the congregation and that, as much as possible, the needs of those outside the church are tended to according to available resources. God did promise His people, Israel, before they entered the Promised Land, that if they obeyed His law, there would be no poor among them. But in almost the same breath, as if realizing Israel's inability to keep the law, God said through Moses, "The poor will never cease from the land" (Deut. 15:4–5, 11). Even the coming of the Savior did not eliminate the poor. When the disciples protested that Mary was anointing Jesus with expensive ointment and argued that its price could have been better used to help the poor, the Lord Jesus replied: "Let her alone; she has kept this for the day of My burial. For the poor you have with you always, but Me you do not have always" (John 12:7–8). The poor are here to stay until that great day when all things will be made new and poverty and want banished forever.

This seems like a dismal note on which to end a book on the office of deacon. The poor will always be there. The ministry of mercy, as embodied in the office of deacon, will always be necessary. Deacons will not be able to eradicate the blight of poverty and want. Something more than deacons is needed. The plight of the poor and needy is a consequence of the fall into sin. This origin of poverty, loneliness, sickness, and want highlights the need for redemption from these miseries and for the great deliverance that will take place on Christ's return when all misery and poverty will be history.

All this seems discouraging for the present, but the presence of the poor and the need for the deacon have a large silver lining. In His providence God gives both those who help the poor and the poor themselves the opportunity to experience His special blessings. This concluding chapter therefore considers the blessings for those helping the poor, the blessings for the poor, and the blessings for the deacon.

The Blessings for Those Helping the Poor

A blessing of having the poor with us is that ministering to them gives the giver and the recipient occasion to rejoice together in the salvation God has given—a salvation that encompasses all of life and includes relief from want. The diaconal ministry, taken up both officially and by members of the congregation, is to make sure that no one in the church lives uncomforted under the pressure of sickness, poverty, or loneliness, but that all share in the joy of salvation in Jesus Christ. It is a great blessing to be able to see and experience the results of bringing relief to those in need and sharing the joy of deliverance with them. Even though there has not yet been a complete eradication of poverty, sickness, and other needs, the diaconal ministry does give a small, joyous foretaste of the perfect happiness to come. Deacons relieve the needs of those afflicted by a variety of hardships in anticipation of that great day. This is an immense blessing to be savored and enjoyed.

There are other blessings associated with this work of mercy that are just as important. Perhaps it is because of these additional blessings that the Lord indicates that the poor will always be with us until that great day. One blessing is that the presence of the needy provides a wonderful opportunity for Christians to show their love for their Lord and Savior. As we saw in the previous chapter, when the Son of Man comes in His glory, He will let everyone know that whenever a Christian helped a fellow believer with food, drink, clothing, and visitation, he performed that service of love not just to the person to whom he ministered but to Christ Himself. As king, the Lord Jesus will say: "As you did it to one of the least of these My brethren, you did it to Me" (Matt. 25:40). That is no small matter! Those who wish to show their love for Christ can do so by ministering to the people around them who are in need of their affection, support, gifts, and compassion. In the godly poor, we meet, as it were, the Lord Himself. Indeed, the Lord places the poor on the path of believers precisely to test them, so that they can show their love to the Lord and receive His blessing. The close connection between the poor and God is seen elsewhere in Scripture: "He who oppresses the poor reproaches his Maker, but he who honors Him has mercy on the needy" (Prov. 14:31; cf. 17:5). "He who has pity on the poor lends to the LORD, and He will pay back what he has given" (Prov. 19:17). Diaconal ministry is in the service of the King who comes in His glory (Matt. 25:31).

Another blessing is that serving the poor provides a sure way to show the unbelieving world the practical light of the gospel and witness to God's love for sinners. When Israel, the Old Testament church, was obedient, the neighboring nations would be in awe and exclaim that they were "a wise and understanding people" and had God so near to them (Deut. 4:6–7). In the same way, modern neighbors need to see in the believers' acts of mercy the greatness of God. As with the early church, the church today should have "favor with all the people" (Acts 2:47). Such a positive view of the church implies that Christians minister to those outside the assembly of believers. Diaconal ministry has a definite missionary aspect, as we saw in the preceding chapter. In this way the church can be a great blessing for a neighborhood, town, or city.

A third great blessing for those who minister to people with all kinds of needs is that they become more and more aware of the sorrows and imperfections of this world and realize that ultimately they are only pilgrims here. This realization provides a healthy and biblical correction to the prevailing secular view of the importance people attach to their possessions and material wealth. What we have is temporary and ultimately not ours, but has been given to us by God in trust (Deut. 8:17–18; Luke 19:11–27). It is to be used for God's glory. After the apostle Peter enjoined that Christians love each other and show hospitality, he wrote, "As each one has received a gift, minister it to one another, as good stewards of the manifold grace of God…that in all things God may be glorified through Jesus Christ" (1 Peter 4:10–11). The apostle Paul quoted the Lord Jesus, who said, "It is more blessed to give than to receive" (Acts 20:35; cf. Luke 6:30). D. G. Peterson writes, "This saying does not mean that those who benefit from the generosity of others are less blessed than those who give. The principle is rather, 'It is better for a person who can do so to give to help others rather than to amass further wealth for himself.'"[1] Eventually we have to let go of the possessions we have gathered in this life. They are not eternal, and they pass away (1 John 2:15–17). As Christ taught in the parable of the rich fool, our lives do not consist in the abundance of our possessions. What is most important is that we are rich toward God (Luke 12:13–21). Christians have an inheritance stored up in heaven that does not decay (1 Peter 1:4; cf. Heb. 11:26), which includes deliverance from all the miseries of this present world (Rev. 21:4–5).

The Blessings for the Poor

The coming complete deliverance from all the sorrows of this life is also of great comfort and blessing for the poor. Deacons and those ministering to the needy and afflicted can come not only with material help and personal assistance but also with a message of great consolation. As we saw in chapter 3, the Lord Jesus has inaugurated the great Year of Jubilee and proclaimed the good news of liberty and comfort to the poor (Luke 4:18–21). He could therefore announce, "Blessed are you poor, for yours is the kingdom of God" (Luke 6:20). These poor included both the materially poor, as in Luke's recounting of the Sermon on the Mount, as well as those

---

1. D. G. Peterson, *Acts of the Apostles*, 573.

poor in spirit (Matt. 5:3). Indeed, the Lord mentioned the mourn-
ers, the meek, the hungry, and the weeping as also being blessed
and identified with the poor (Matt. 5:3–12; Luke 6:21). Although
Christ's kingdom has come and He is king at God's right hand
(Mark 16:19), the full blessing for the poor will be realized in perfection only on the day of His second coming. The poor, however,
already are blessed, because theirs is the kingdom of God, and the
reality that their complete blessing is in the future does not take
anything away from that. Already they are rich and can experience
the blessings of the Lord, knowing that He thinks of them (see Ps.
40:17) and is near to those who call on Him (Ps. 145:18).

In receiving the love of God through deacons and through merciful diaconal acts of church members, the needy can already savor
the rich blessings of the Lord, who does not abandon them. We
have just seen in the previous section that the Lord identifies with
them. Those who lend to the poor, lend to the Lord (Prov. 19:17).
God is the refuge, helper, deliverer, and stronghold of the poor (Ps.
14:6; 40:17; 70:5; Isa. 25:4). The needy can experience these blessings in many different ways as they receive the love of God through
the diaconal ministry. In a world burdened by sin, the afflicted may
still suffer and have physical needs, but even then the Lord tells us
that they are blessed and therefore rich.

Christ wrote a letter to the church at Smyrna in which He said,
"I know your works, tribulation, and poverty (but you are rich)"
(Rev. 2:9). Their plight indicates extreme poverty. This church
was being persecuted for the faith, and they suffered economically.
Christ is fully aware of their dire situation. Yet how is it possible
they are rich? It is possible because those riches are real. They are
poor because they identify with Christ and are persecuted. But
Christ also identifies with them, for when the church is persecuted,
Christ is attacked (see Acts 9:4)—and Christ is rich. This raises
the question of what ultimately is the real measuring rod for wealth
and poverty. What makes a person rich or poor? Is it the amount
of money and material goods one has? Are we to measure wealth
in material things, or in terms of God's priceless love in Christ,

in terms of a godly character that will endure, in terms of a faith more precious than gold and a wisdom more priceless than rubies? Are these not the riches that last? It is possible to be impoverished materially, but to be rich in Christ (see Eph. 3:8) or rich toward God (Luke 12:21).[2] As James put it: "Has God not chosen the poor of this world to be rich in faith and heirs of the kingdom which He promised to those who love Him?" (2:5).

For poor or afflicted persons struggling with issues of poverty, sickness, or disability, it is an incredible blessing to know that when it comes to what really counts, they are rich, and those riches cannot be taken away from them. That knowledge is what gives joy to the sick, the disabled, and the afflicted. In the nature of things, it is especially such Christians who are sensitive to this truth. It is of great encouragement to them. We can also see this truth reflected in the eyes of materially poor and afflicted Christians in parts of the world where there is great hardship, such as in war-torn Sudan or in the poverty-stricken townships of South Africa. Joy radiates from these believers' faces when they can worship on the Lord's Day and hear about Christ and being rich in Him. They have what counts. Paul writes, "For you know the grace of our Lord Jesus Christ, that though He was rich, yet for your sakes He became poor, that you through His poverty might become rich" (2 Cor. 8:9).

Through the blessing of diaconal ministry and being rich in faith (James 2:5), God enables the poor to go through difficult times according to His promises. The poor see through the ministering love of God's people that He does not forget them and that they can have hope for better times (see Ps. 9:18). The day will come when all sorrow will be a thing of the past. In this way God gives the poor the blessing of the strength and endurance they need to go on.

---

2. For the above, see John R. W. Stott, *What Christ Thinks of the Church* (Grand Rapids: Eerdmans, 1958), 48.

The Blessings for the Deacon

All believers who help the poor, including deacons, enjoy the blessing and joy of giving not only material help but also the good news
of salvation as an encouragement. Besides this fundamental blessing, Christ encourages His office-bearers, the deacons, through the
apostolic words in 1 Timothy 3:13. After Paul gave the requirements for the office, he concluded this section with these words:
"For those who have served well as deacons obtain for themselves
a good standing and great boldness in the faith which is in Christ
Jesus" (1 Tim. 3:13).

If deacons serve well, they will obtain a good standing for themselves. What does obtaining a good standing refer to? The original
Greek term translated "standing" (*bathmos*) literally means "step" or
"stairway" and could refer to degree or rank. Some have therefore
suggested that it means that a deacon serving well can graduate to
some sort of higher standing, such as being an elder, as if that office
is of a higher grade than that of deacon. We have seen in chapter 9
that this notion has no basis in Scripture. Like the elder, the deacon
is in the service of the risen Christ. Rather, when the apostle writes
of obtaining a good standing, he is encouraging deacons who serve
well with the prospect that because of their faithful service, they
will be esteemed in the eyes of the fellowship they are serving. The
prospect that the church will think highly of the deacon is an incentive to humbly do his duties. We are reminded of Christ's words:
"Whoever desires to become great among you shall be your servant.
And whoever of you desires to be first shall be slave of all" (Mark
10:43–44). Even though deacons do not serve with a view to such
a reward, it is encouraging and a blessing for them to know that
their unassuming work of service is a most honorable task and gives
them a high standing.

A further blessing that the apostle mentions is that those who
serve well as deacons gain "great boldness in the faith which is in
Christ Jesus" (1 Tim. 3:13). The original term translated as "boldness"
(*parrēsia*) is somewhat ambiguous and can be translated as "outspokenness, frankness" or as "confidence, boldness." The rendering one

chooses will determine where the emphasis lies. On the one hand, the rendering "outspokenness" or "boldness" can relate to the good standing that the faithful deacon achieves. Such a deacon will be outspoken and frank in ministering to the needy, admonishing and comforting as necessary from the Word of God so that the full power of the Word bears down on the lives of those concerned. Being fearful and lacking such forthrightness can be a hindrance to the work. Convicted outspokenness is only possible in faith in Christ Jesus.[3] As we have seen in chapters 4 and 5, a deacon can be expected to administer not only physical aid but also spiritual encouragement and direction from the Word of God as circumstances warrant.

On the other hand, translating the phrase in question with "great confidence" stresses the connection with the words "in the faith which is in Christ Jesus," and the focus shifts away from how the deacon interacts with others in his work and concentrates on Christ. The point is then that the deacon who serves well gains "a greater sense of confidence in God and assurance of salvation."[4]

Both understandings of the text work, and they are not necessarily mutually exclusive. Someone who grows in faith and assurance will also be more confident in interacting with others and in passing on the message of the gospel as needed. Even though there is some overlap, the main point is clear: there are encouraging blessings for faithful deacons. God will grant them a good standing, boldness, and confidence in the Lord.

Conclusion

In God's providence, the poor and needy will always be with us. But there are blessings associated with their presence. Those helping the

---

3. For this view, see P. H. R. van Houwelingen, *Timoteüs, Titus: pastorale instructie-brieven*, Commentaar op het Nieuwe Testament. Derde serie (Kampen: Kok, 2009), 93; and Ridderbos, *De pastorale brieven*, 100. They note that the term in question (*parrēsia*) is used of boldness and confidence toward people (2 Cor. 3:12; 7:4; Philem. 8).

4. Marshall and Towner, *Commentary on the Pastoral Epistles*, 497. Similarly, Towner, *Timothy and Titus*, 268.

poor have the thrill of sharing the gospel and having a small fore-taste of the perfect joy to come, when all poverty and want will be banished. Those ministering to the poor also have the privilege of showing by word and deed their love to their Savior and being a witness of Christian compassion to the larger community.

The poor who benefit from this ministry of mercy experience in practical ways the love of God and so experience a fulfillment of His promise that He will care for the needy. The believing poor also realize more and more that although they may be materially poor, they are rich beyond compare—rich in Christ and rich toward God. This realization helps them through the difficult times.

Deacons are also blessed by the presence of the poor. God promises deacons a good standing and great outspokenness and confidence in the faith that is in Christ Jesus.

Since the poor are here to stay, so are the deacons, and so is the diaconal ministry of the congregation as individual believers do what they can to minister to the needs they encounter. As church members and deacons seek to relieve the needs of the less fortunate, they realize more and more that God has not intended this world to be filled with hurts, wants, afflictions, sorrows, and tears. Has He not promised a complete redemption in Christ? Indeed, there is a new world coming where all poverty and want will be banished. God will be glorified by a renewed creation. The diaconal ministry, whether taken up officially or unofficially, is done in anticipation of better times to come. This labor of love and compassion is not easy and is sometimes downright exhausting, but it is never done in vain. It is done to God's glory in anticipation of that great day when the joy of redemption will be fully realized. Knowing that is a real blessing and encouragement for all diaconal work.

Questions for Study and Reflection

These questions are intended for those who hold the office of deacon, those who aspire to the office, and those who are simply interested in the office and are using this book as a study guide. Reflecting on the issues that these questions raise will help not only deacons but also members of the congregation to think through some of the challenges confronting deacons. May such reflection lead to a growing appreciation for the wisdom and grace of God in giving this office to the church and give some insight into how the church has wrestled in the past and at the present to do justice to the diaconal ministry. The questions usually refer to topics in the chapter under discussion.

Chapter 1: The Poor in Israel

1. People who are powerless are sometimes pictured in the Old Testament as poor and helpless. Who would the modern equivalents of these afflicted and oppressed people be?

2. How does the situation of orphans and widows today compare with their situation in ancient Israel? What can we learn from Old Testament laws regarding helping orphans and widows today?

3. Who are the sojourners and strangers in our society today? How should we regard them? How does the command to love your neighbor as yourself function in answering this question?

4. Who would you identify as foreigners? Is lack of integration in Western society enough to consider such individuals foreigners? How does that affect your attitude toward them? How does the command to love your neighbor as yourself function in answering this question?

5. Can you think of a class of people analogous to the Levites in the Old Testament? In what ways is their situation similar and different from their Old Testament counterparts?

6. Why is it helpful to know the wider political and cultural context in which God's laws regarding the poor functioned in ancient Israel? How can Christians be a light to the world in providing for the poor?

Chapter 2: Providing for the Poor

1. Why did God want to help the poor? How is the answer to that question relevant for our walk and talk today? What are some dominant themes we need to keep in mind?

2. What were some of the implications of the eighth commandment in Old Testament times? How is this commandment still applicable today in our relationship with others and our relationship with God?

3. What does it mean when we say that we are only stewards of our possessions? What impact does this have on how we regard our material goods?

4. What is the place of family in providing for their needy? What are some of the challenges we face in our fast-paced and mobile society?

5. What are some ways that society as a whole, without direct government involvement, is showing compassion for the needy? How does this compare with the situation that God wanted in

Israel? What is the place of government in providing for the needy? Is government trying to do too much, or is it doing too little? Explain.

6. Why was there no deacon in the Old Testament dispensation? Could God's people today live without this office? Discuss.

Chapter 3: Christ's Teaching on the Poor and Needy

1. How does the synagogue's emphasis on ongoing private charity along with its official, organized provision for the poor continue an important Old Testament principle?

2. Is it appropriate to compare almsgiving as a work of merit in Jewish piety with giving financial support to deacons today with the expectation of a charitable donation receipt to reduce income tax? Why or why not?

3. In what ways is the purpose of diaconal service comparable to that of the Year of Jubilee, which Christ fulfilled?

4. What are some of the practical implications for members of the congregation and for deacons of heeding Christ's call to serve rather than to be served?

5. How can we be "rich toward God" (Luke 12:21)? How does this fit in with the diaconal task?

6. What are some of the challenges in loving all those whom God places on our life's path? How can they be overcome? (Think of the parable of the good Samaritan.)

Chapter 4: Ministering to the Poor in Acts 6

1. What was the key issue in Acts 6 regarding unmet needs in the congregation? What important element was threatened by the oversight of some church members? What are some lessons for us today in terms of our motivation to help others?

2. What can members of the congregation and deacons do today to ensure that no one feels marginalized in the congregation?

3. What are some of the key arguments for seeing the seven in Acts 6 as ordained into a new office?

4. How is the procedure leading to the ordination of the seven in Acts 6 similar to how your congregation receives new deacons? What are the differences?

5. What qualities of the seven stand out as being a great blessing to the congregation? Explain.

6. What indications are there in Acts 6 that the congregation participated in meeting the needs in their midst? What are the lessons from this for today?

Chapter 5: The Office of Deacon

1. Why is there no biblical requirement for a deacon to teach? How does that distinguish his office from that of an elder? Why should a deacon nevertheless be well grounded in the faith and be "holding the mystery of the faith with a pure conscience" (1 Tim. 3:9)?

2. How soon can a recent convert become a deacon? What factors should be considered? How can a church best apply the biblical guidelines?

3. What are the qualifications for the wife of a deacon? How can she be involved in diaconal work? When is it appropriate for a

deacon to take his wife along on a visit? When is it not appropriate? Discuss, keeping in mind issues of confidentiality.

4. What are some of the implications of deacons "ruling their children and their own houses well" (1 Tim. 3:12) for the credibility and effectiveness of doing their office? Discuss.

5. What unifies the offices of elder and deacon? How are they both ministries—that is, service as servants, for God and His people?

6. How should the offices of deacon and elder relate to each other? Is one office higher than the other? Why or why not?

Chapter 6: Are Female Deacons Biblical?

1. How is Phoebe described in Romans 16:2 in the Bible translation you are using—as a servant or as a deacon? What are the pros and cons for that translation? Could it be significant that early translations such as the King James Version and the Geneva Bible used the word "servant," whereas more recently the rendering "deacon" is used in some translations?

2. Who do "wives" (literally "women") in 1 Timothy 3:11 refer to? Explain your answer.

3. When does the church have a duty toward widows? How is that obligation exercised?

4. Who were the enrolled widows of 1 Timothy 5:9? Why were they enrolled?

5. Does the diaconal office exercise authority? Discuss.

6. How were New Testament women serving the church? What is the message for today?

Chapter 7: The Testimony of the Early Church and the Heritage of the Reformation

1. What can we learn from the way the early church took care of the poor and needy?

2. How did the early church regard the position of the deacon? How did this change as the church moved away from apostolic times? How did this development affect care for the poor?

3. What became the chief motive for helping the poor prior to the Reformation? How did the Reformation change the way caring for the poor was regarded?

4. How did Calvin restore the office of deacon? Why did Calvin connect offerings for the poor with the worship service?

5. Describe Calvin's high regard for the diaconal office. Why is it important that we keep a high view of the office of deacon today?

6. How has the heritage of the Reformation with respect to the office of deacon been transmitted to churches on the European Continent and in England? How is that heritage evident today in your church?

Chapter 8: Women and the Diaconate

1. Why did the early church eventually have women deacons? How widespread was the practice? How long did it last?

2. In general, how did churches of the Reformation view women in the office of deacon? What were the exceptions?

3. What were the motivations for ordaining women into the office of deacon in the twentieth and twenty-first centuries? What do you think of these motives?

4. How can women be used in diaconal work without ordaining them officially? How much freedom should deacons have in

making use of the talents of women in their work of ministering to the needy?

5. Could more use be made of widows (see 1 Tim. 5:9–10)? What are some of the benefits and possible disadvantages?

6. How much influence should culture have with respect to the diaconal work of women and whether they should be ordained?

Chapter 9: The Official Position of the Deacon Today

1. Should deacons be ordained with the laying on of hands? Why or why not?

2. What are the advantages and disadvantages of a deacon being ordained for lifetime service?

3. Is it necessary for church trustees to be ordained deacons? Why or why not?

4. How should deacons and elders work together in combined meetings? How can each office's distinctive be safeguarded?

5. When should a deacon approach an elder with respect to a need in the congregation, and vice versa? What are some of the pitfalls to watch out for?

6. Should someone serve as a deacon before being nominated for the office of elder? Could it serve the well-being of the church to ordain a former elder to become a deacon? Discuss.

Chapter 10: Enabling and Prioritizing

1. What is the best way to equip current and future deacons for their office?

2. What are some of the blessings of giving for the needy, both within a local congregation and in the larger ecclesiastical

community? Why is tithing an inadequate guideline for the New Testament church?

3. What are some of the potential challenges facing a family giving material assistance to its needy members? How can they be overcome? Discuss different scenarios, including those involving sickness, unemployment, and family members who have moved far away. How soon should the church community get involved?

4. What is the most effective way for the communion of saints to reflect the love of Christ (see Phil. 2:4–7)?

5. What obligations does the state have with respect to its needy citizens? How do the state's obligations intersect with those of the church?

6. What are some ways that deacons can make use of government resources and programs without affecting the integrity of their work as administering the love of Christ?

Chapter 11: The Diaconal Ministry within the Congregation

1. What is the best way for deacons to visit the members of the congregation? In your discussion, keep in mind issues like prioritizing, frequency of visits, items to discuss during a visit, and the use of Scripture and prayer in such visits.

2. What are some ways to encourage using the gifts of the elderly and the youth for the benefit of the congregation? How can help be given within the communion of saints without being perceived as intrusive?

3. Should deacons be involved in premarital counseling, or is this the sole responsibility of the parents or family? Discuss whether the deacons should be involved and, if so, how?

4. What does it mean to help the poor wisely and with discernment? Should deacons, for example, in certain cases ask for proof of the family's income? How strict should deacons be in dispensing funds and asking for accountability? What sort of policies should be in place?

5. Make a list of how deacons can help in nonmonetary ways. How can the congregation be responsible for meeting some or all the needs on the list?

6. How can deacons best be of service to those institutionalized in, for example, care facilities for the aged or homes for those with mental disabilities?

Chapter 12: The Diaconal Ministry outside the Congregation

1. What can we learn from the parable of the good Samaritan? Read through it and try to imagine the narrative in the context of our current society.

2. What objections have been brought against diaconal work outside the local congregation? Evaluate and comment on them.

3. How can help best be given to local people in need who are outside the church? What are the respective responsibilities of the members of the church and the deacons? How can we ensure that help is given in such a way that the love of Christ is shown? How much should the deacons be involved in the local community?

4. How can diaconal help best be given to support foreign mission endeavors?

5. What are the advantages and disadvantages of short-term mission trips? Should deacons be involved in them? If so, how and why?

6. What are the opportunities and limitations of diaconal help going to disaster zones? How can such help best be given to ensure that it gives a Christian witness?

Chapter 13: The Blessing of the Poor

1. Describe three blessings of helping the poor and, where possible, relate it to your life experience.

2. Besides the material help that they receive, what other blessings can the poor experience in receiving diaconal assistance? What obligations does such assistance bring?

3. The task of a deacon is not easy, but the apostle Paul encourages deacons: "Those who have served well as deacons obtain for themselves a good standing and great boldness in the faith which is in Christ Jesus" (1 Tim. 3:13). What does this mean, and how has this impacted your life as a deacon?

Select Resources on Deacons

Berghoef, Gerard, and Lester DeKoster. *The Deacons Handbook: A Manual of Stewardship*. Grand Rapids: Christian's Library Press, 1980.

Brown, Mark, ed. *Called to Serve: Essays for Elders and Deacons*. Grandville, Mich.: Reformed Fellowship, 2006.

Croft, Brian, and Austin Walker. *Caring for Widows*. Wheaton, Ill.: Crossway, 2015.

De Jong, Peter Y. *The Ministry of Mercy for Today*. Grand Rapids: Baker, 1961.

Huizinga, W. *Deacons Go Visiting!: Studies on the Work of the Deacons*. Armadale, Australia: The Reformed Guardian, 2003.

Keller, Timothy J. *Ministries of Mercy: The Call of the Jericho Road*. 2nd ed. Phillipsburg, N.J.: P&R, 1997.

————. *Resources for Deacons: Love Expressed through Mercy Ministries*. Lawrenceville, Ga.: PCA Christian Education and Publications, 1985.

Kuyper, Abraham. *The Problem of Poverty*. Edited by James W. Skillen. Washington, D.C. / Grand Rapids: The Center for Public Justice / Baker, 1991.

Shishko, William. "Reforming the Diaconate, Part 1." *Ordained Servant* 1, no. 2 (April 1992): 43–45. http://www.opc.org/OS /html/V1/2f.html.

———. "Reforming the Diaconate, Part 2." *Ordained Servant* 1, no. 3 (September 1992): 63–66. http://www.opc.org/OS/html /V1/3c.html.

———. "Reforming the Diaconate, Part 3." *Ordained Servant* 2, no. 1 (January 1993): 16–18. http://www.opc.org/OS/html /V2/1b.html.

———. "A Training Program for Deacons." *Ordained Servant* 9, no. 3 (July 2000): 62–70. http://www.opc.org/OS/html/V9/3c .html.

Strauch, Alexander. *Minister of Mercy: The New Testament Deacon.* Littleton, Colo.: Lewis & Roth, 1992.

Van Dam, Cornelis. "The Diaconal Task: Some Old Testament Roots and Their Continuing Significance." *Ordained Servant* 1, no. 1 (January 1992): 14–21. http://opc.org/OS/pdf /OSV1N1.pdf

———. "Where Is the Old Testament Deacon? Taking Care of the Poor Then and Now." In *Perspectives on Worship, Law and Faith: The Old Testament Speaks Today,* 61–92. Kelmscott, Australia: Pro Ecclesia Publishers, 2000.

Willborn, C. N. "The Deacon: A Divine Right Office with Divine Uses." *The Confessional Presbyterian* 5 (2009): 185–98.

———. "The Gospel Work of the Diaconate: A Ministry 'Proportioned in Number.'" *The Confessional Presbyterian* 10 (2014): 23–32.

Additional Specialized Resources
for Further Study

Those wishing further study into particular aspects of poverty and the diaconal task may consult these additional resources. They are organized according to the main divisions of this book.

Part 1: The Old Testament Background

For a comprehensive study that sets the Old Testament material in the context of the ancient world, see David L. Baker, *Tight Fists or Open Hands? Wealth and Poverty in Old Testament Law* (Grand Rapids: Eerdmans, 2011). A helpful general book on Old Testament ethics, with a perceptive chapter on poverty, is Christopher J. H. Wright, *Old Testament Ethics for the People of God* (Downers Grove, Ill.: InterVarsity, 2004). There are several useful chapters connecting Old Testament principles regarding poverty, welfare, and social concerns to contemporary issues in Michael Schluter and John Ashcroft, eds., *Jubilee Manifesto: A Framework, Agenda, and Strategy for Christian Social Reform* (Leicester, U.K.: Inter-Varsity, 2005).

Part 2: New Testament Times

A clear, detailed explanation of the relevant passages in Acts 6, Philippians 1, and 1 Timothy 3 can be found in Alexander Strauch, *Minister of Mercy: The New Testament Deacon* (Littleton, Colo.: Lewis & Roth, 1992). A study on the biblical requirements is Archibald A. Allison, *Biblical Qualifications for Elders and Deacons:*

An Exegesis of 1 Timothy 3:2–13 (Willow Grove, Pa.: Committee on Christian Education of the Orthodox Presbyterian Church, 1998).

An insightful book showing that God expects us to share our wealth is Craig L. Blomberg, *Neither Poverty nor Riches: A Biblical Theology of Material Possessions* (Grand Rapids: Eerdmans, 1999). Although Blomberg discusses the Old Testament, his emphasis is on the New. Bruce W. Longenecker, *Remember the Poor: Paul, Poverty, and the Greco-Roman World* (Grand Rapids: Eerdmans, 2010) is a detailed study that aims to show that caring for the poor was an essential part of the gospel as proclaimed by the apostle Paul.

Part 3: The Office of Deacon in the History of the Church

Jeannine E. Olson provides a lucid historical survey in her *Deacons and Deaconesses through the Centuries*, rev. ed. (Saint Louis, Mo.: Concordia, 2005).

For a well-informed study of early Christian attitudes to wealth and poverty, see Helen Rhee, *Loving the Poor, Saving the Rich: Wealth, Poverty, and the Early Christian Formation* (Grand Rapids: Baker Academic, 2012). For a magisterial look at how Christians struggled to deal properly with wealth, see Peter Brown, *Through the Eye of a Needle: Wealth, the Fall of Rome, and the Making of Christianity in the West, 350–550 AD* (Princeton, N.J.: Princeton University Press, 2012).

The standard work for Calvin and the diaconal office is Elsie Anne McKee, *John Calvin on the Diaconate and Liturgical Almsgiving*, Travaux d'Humanisme et Renaissance 197 (Geneva: Librairie Droz, 1984). A popular version of some of the highlights of this research is found in her *Diakonia in the Classical Reformed Tradition and Today* (Grand Rapids: Eerdmans, 1989). For a fascinating account of how the French Reformed churches transformed the diaconate from Roman Catholic to Protestant, see chapter 5 in Glenn S. Sunshine, *Reforming French Protestantism: The Development of Huguenot Ecclesiastical Institutions, 1557–1572*, Sixteenth Century Essays and Studies 66 (Kirksville, Mo.: Truman State

University Press, 2003). An interesting study of how Reformed consistories struggled to provide for the poor in the face of municipalities that considered it their prerogative to care for the needy is found in Charles H. Parker, *The Reformation of Community: Social Welfare and Calvinist Charity in Holland, 1572–1620*, Cambridge Studies in Early Modern History (Cambridge, U.K.: Cambridge University Press, 1998).

Two important works on women and the diaconal office in the early church are Aimé Georges Martimort, *Deaconesses: An Historical Study*, trans. K. D. Whitehead (San Francisco: Ignatius Press, 1986); and Kevin Madigan and Carolyn Osiek, eds. and trans., *Ordained Women in the Early Church: A Documentary History* (Baltimore, Md.: Johns Hopkins University Press, 2005). Presbyterian history on women in the diaconate is surveyed in Brian M. Schwertley, *A Historical and Biblical Examination of Women Deacons*, ed. Stephen Pribble (Southfield, Mich.: Reformed Witness, 1998).

Part 4: The Current Functioning of the Office

Beneficial for many aspects of the work of the deacon is Timothy J. Keller, *Resources for Deacons: Love Expressed through Mercy Ministries* (Lawrenceville, Ga.: PCA Christian Education and Publications, 1985).

Two other useful books are Gerard Berghoef and Lester DeKoster, *The Deacons Handbook: A Manual of Stewardship* (1980; repr., Grand Rapids: Christian's Library Press, 2013); and an older, somewhat dated work which has served well: Peter Y. De Jong, *The Ministry of Mercy for Today* (1952; repr., Grand Rapids: Baker, 1961). Although both of these books have been written for Christian Reformed readers, they contain much useful information.

Excellent practical books on extending support to those outside the church include Timothy J. Keller, *Ministries of Mercy: The Call of the Jericho Road*, 2nd ed. (Phillipsburg, N.J.: P&R, 1997); and Steve Corbett and Brian Fikkert, *When Helping Hurts: How to Alleviate Poverty Without Hurting the Poor…and Yourself*

(Chicago: Moody, 2009). Helpful in introducing some of the issues of our global village and offering both analyses and solutions is Wayne Grudem and Barry Asmus, *The Poverty of Nations: A Sustainable Solution* (Wheaton, Ill.: Crossway, 2013).

A valuable collection of essays highlighting current problems with state welfare and suggesting ways forward is David W. Hall, ed., *Welfare Reformed: A Compassionate Approach* (Phillipsburg, N.J. / Franklin, Tenn.: P&R / Legacy Communications, 1994. Abraham Kuyper's address espousing the differences between a liberal or socialist approach to poverty and a Christian one is *The Problem of Poverty*, ed. James W. Skillen (Washington, D.C. / Grand Rapids: Center for Public Justice / Baker, 1991). Although Kuyper delivered this speech in 1891, the principles he espoused are as timely as ever.

A stimulating book discussing Hispanic immigration issues is M. Daniel Carroll R., *Christians at the Border: Immigration, the Church, and the Bible* (Grand Rapids: Baker, 2008).

Scripture Index

Subject Index